# TO SPEAK OR BE SILENT

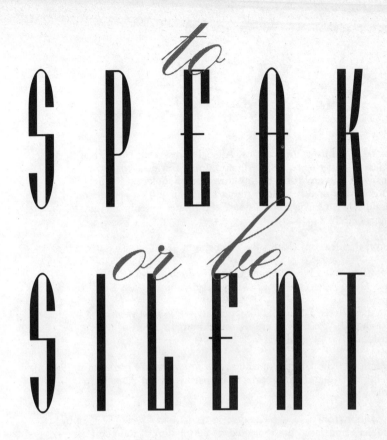

# to SPEAK or be SILENT

## THE PARADOX OF DISOBEDIENCE
## IN THE LIVES OF WOMEN

EDITED AND WITH AN INTRODUCTION BY
LENA B. ROSS

CHIRON PUBLICATIONS
WILMETTE, ILLINOIS

Chiron Publications thanks the following:

Quotations from Paula Gunn Allen, *Skin and Bones* (© 1988 by Paula Gunn Allen) are reprinted by permission of West End Press.

Quotations from Dahlia Ravikovitch, *The Window*, translated by Chanah and Ariel Bloch, are reprinted by permission of the translators.

Quotations from Gloria Anzaldua, *Borderlands/La Frontera* (© 1987 by Gloria Anzaldua) are reprinted by permission of Aunt Lute Books.

Quotations from Cordelia Candelaria, *Ojo de la Cueva* (© 1984 by Cordelia Candelaria) are reprinted by permission of the poet.

Quotations from Pat Mora, *Chants* (© 1984 by Arte Publico Press) are reprinted by permission of the publisher.

Library of Congress Catalog Card Number: 92–45106

Printed in the United States of America.
Book design by Siobhan Drummond.
Cover design by Mercedes Santos.

**Library of Congress Cataloging-in-Publication Data:**

To speak or be silent : the paradox of disobedience in the lives of
    women / edited and with an introduction by Lena B. Ross.
        p. cm.
    Includes bibliographical references and index.
    ISBN 0-933029-68-3 : $17.95
    1. Women in literature. 2. Women—Mythology. I. Ross,
Lena B., 1951-        .
PN56.W6T6     1993
809′.93352042—dc20
                                                    92–45106
                                                    CIP

ISBN 0-933029-68-3

In memory of my beloved mother,
Hannah Ross, 1911–1991.
She endured, but could never disobey.

*Dat poena laudata fides.*

# CONTENTS

## RAGE AND DISOBEDIENCE: LIKE A RAISIN IN THE SUN

## WOMEN OF POWER: WHOSE HERO IS SHE, ANYWAY?

# ACKNOWLEDGMENTS

I would like to thank Nathan Schwartz-Salant for his interest in and support of this project from its inception. Thanks also to doctoral candidate Janet Ng, researcher extraordinaire from Columbia University; Doris Albrecht, librarian at the Kristin Mann Library of the C. G. Jung Foundation of New York, whose invaluable assistance saved much time and energy; and Siobhan Drummond, managing editor at Chiron, who among other things indexed this book.

Most of all, I would like to thank the contributors to this book, who embraced with enthusiasm the theme of disobedience — and many of whom were completely disobedient when requested to work on a specific topic of *my* choosing! I soon realized that each author had her own literature and ideas, and that my suggestions for material were usually irrelevant. I am so glad this was the case.

# INTRODUCTION

Lena B. Ross

I began this book because of my faulty memory of a line from Shakespeare's *King Lear*. Near the beginning of that great play, Cordelia, Lear's youngest daughter, is faced with her father's requirement that each of his three daughters tell him how much they love him before he gives up his throne and divides his kingdom between them. In an aside, Cordelia, appalled by the thought of being false to herself, as her older sisters obviously have been, thinks, "Shall Cordelia love or be silent?" All of my life I had remembered this line as "Shall Cordelia speak or be silent?" despite the fact that I had both read and seen the play many times. Apparently, my unconscious was wiser than I, because that is the real dilemma. Neither speaking nor being silent would have helped Cordelia: if she spoke, she either had to lie to please Lear (betrayal of self) or speak her truth aloud, thus incurring his wrath. Trying silence was, under the circumstances, impossible and would also have incurred wrath. She chose to speak her truth; the end is known.

To speak or be silent — always a dilemma for women, as history and literature tend to reflect. As a Jungian analyst, I am most captured by the universality of disobedience in tales by and about women. Except for "Patient Griselda," I can think of no enduring tales in Western culture about women whose claim to fame is their unquestioning obedience. Speech for women *is* disobedience. Women were to be silent, though they rarely were or are. Political columnist Molly Ivins cites an interesting study. When researchers asked a group of college women what they feared in men, the women answered rape, violence, murder. When a similar group of college men were asked the same question regarding women, they answered that they were afraid the women would laugh at them. Silence prevents both laughter and speech that confronts us with our own failings; this is why the notion of a free press was so radical two hundred years ago in the new United States and remains so precious now. The first amendment to the United States Constitution guarantees freedom of speech; it tries to forestall the silence that oppresses, by implication endorsing the notion of disobedience to authority — and it is constantly under attack.

But what of other countries, where freedom of speech or movement has at times been, and in some cases remains, a fantasy? I chose to listen for the sound of women's voices in literature, both oral and written, because universally the figures of women in literature, whether written by women or men, were almost always disobedient to the culture of the times. Viewed one way, this seemed an artifact of the position that women have traditionally held in patrifocal culture. That position was never central but always peripheral, never an object but always a subject as related to the man. But I found that even in the mythology of cultures which were most likely not patriarchal, such as certain Native American tribes in North America, women were often associated with disobedience (although that disobedience was viewed very differently). So it seemed to me that another way of viewing disobedience was as having a special and specific value in connection with the feminine archetypes, possibly playing some vital and necessary role in the drama of human life and relations.

C. G. Jung presents us with the notion that "the self seeks consciousness," a drive which sets up a conflict in humans, as it opposes what Jung characterizes as "a primordial instinct for obedience," which also exists within us (1958, par. 1630). If indeed there is a kind of pull toward an inertial state of being which can be characterized as obedience, then actions taken against this "primordial instinct" by an individual would have a teleological basis, a prospective function. Anthropologist Lila Abu-Lughod's paper, "Analyzing Resistance: Bedouin Women's Discourses," which appears in the section entitled "Creating a World," supports such an idea. She sketches out the various ways in which women in a Bedouin community circumvent the rules of the men, although the women also support these rules in other ways, such as veiling. In effect, her paper suggests that the methods of resistance of the women subvert the authority of the men, so that the life of the community is not paralyzed by the rigid rules of "honor" by which the men have bound themselves and the women. An Arabic scholar has remarked to me that Bedouin society may reflect pre-Islamic traditions; if so, this would make sense in terms of societies not yet rigidly patriarchal, with an almost hydraulic function for power/resistance developing in the relationships between the sexes.

Abu-Lughod also suggests a shift in a position of Foucault's: he asserts that where there is power there is resistance, while she suggests that where there is resistance there is power. This can be understood in two ways: that the fact of resistance gives us a means by which we can view and analyze the power structure (Abu-Lughod's point), and also, that there is power *in* resistance itself. The kind of power that may be seen in resistance — or, as I would maintain, disobedience — is the power of creativity to which Erich Fromm refers when he writes of the potency which creates as opposed to the power which destroys.

I would argue that from the earliest myths and legends, the feminine has embodied a particular kind of creativity, which I call world building or world transformation. In Judith Hubback's article, we see reflections on Eve as a kind of first scientist, "calmly going forward into danger"; her disobedience involves her desire to know through touch, smell, and taste of what good and evil consist. This is a slow exploration, which takes nothing for granted but seeks knowledge that, as Hubback notes, was at one point in Genesis freely offered to Adam. Although Eve is excoriated in the Judeo-

Christian tradition as the cause of our expulsion from paradise, her disob dience results in the creation of our world, and looked at from a different perspective, her act of disobedience can be seen as brave and risk-taking. If Adam had taken the bold step of defying Yahweh on his own, rather than simply following Eve, my guess is that he would have been celebrated as a hero. We have a modern-day example of this in the Anita Hill/Clarence Thomas investigation. Both were disobedient: Hill, by speaking up about hitherto unspeakable events in a woman's life, with unimpeachable poise and dignity; Thomas, with an angry attack on his questioners, as though they were guilty of lèse-majesté. The result: the woman was pilloried (but only outside of her presence), the man lauded and confirmed to sit on the Supreme Court.

Sojourner Truth, the great nineteenth-century hero, said, "the first woman God ever made was strong enough to turn the world upside down all alone," and it is true that mythologically speaking, our (Western and Middle Eastern) world was born out of a woman's disobedience. That a non-European culture like the Iroquois Mohawk, for instance, would have a creation myth where the world is born out of a woman's endurance, determination, and curiousity (Allen 1989, p. 65), or that a savior myth, part of which is recounted in Patricia Clark Smith's passionate and painfilled article, "Before the Fall(s): Native American Women and the Concept of Disobedience," where a people is rescued because of a woman's brave trick, is, I think, what Jung would have called a synchronicity, not a coincidence. In these myths, the disobedience is celebrated rather than condemned, and it is viewed thankfully, as an act of creativity. Smith notes that the story of Ahweyoh, or Water Lily, bears superficial similarity to European tales such as that of Psyche or Cinderella. Ahweyoh's path, after she says no to oppression, is indeed quite different from Cinderella's; Ahweyoh comes out of a tradition that clearly reflects what Paula Gunn Allen calls a fundamental identity of "women at war" (1989, p. 20). This tradition of warrior women is not unique in world history (as other articles in this book demonstrate) — but in nonpatriarchal civilizations, we find that it is not entirely repressed by later developing patriarchy, so the tradition may flourish in story form at least.

From the early stages of civilization, when patrifocal culture was not yet fully consolidated, there are many tales of extremely brave women who take charge for their people — the story of Judith, who slew Holofernes in order to save her people, the Hebrews, is exemplary. In that tale, the Hebrews are beset by the Assyrians, who threaten their existence as a separate people. The old men, or elders, of the tribe have no idea what to do and are facing imminent disaster, when Judith speaks up and says, "Listen to me, and I will do something that will go down to the sons of our nations for endless generations . . . *But you must not inquire about my act for I will not tell you what I am going to do until it is done*" (my emphasis). The elders and rulers say to her: "Farewell, and the Lord God go before you, to take vengeance upon our enemies" (Goodspeed 1959, p. 20).

What is interesting here precedes the main action of the tale, wherein Judith first seduces, then beheads the commander of the enemy, Holofernes. In this early scene, she announces to the ruling men of the tribe, who do not know what to do, that she *does* know, and they are not to question her, and they accept this! The tale of Judith is, not surprisingly, left out of the accepted text of the Hebrew scriptures; Hadas notes that it may be based on a Hellenistic tale, ca. second century B.C. (Goodspeed 1959, p. xxii). One can speculate that such early warrior women, saviors of their people, predate solid patriarchy. Since Native American life appears never to have become solidly patriarchal, there is a better chance for the tradition of strong warrior women to persist. What did become masked, however, were historical facts, some of which are related by Smith, about women who were the leaders of their people, such as Weetamoo and Awashonks, left out of the history books of Euro-Western culture.

One can begin to speculate about the nature of disobedience: the aspect of it epitomized, for example, by Psyche, in Apuleius's story of Cupid and Psyche, versus the way it appears in other cultures worldwide. Psyche's disobedience (and I am referring here specifically to the Psyche of Lucius Apuleius) arises out of a culture where patriarchy was already consolidating (as exemplified in the West by the Romans); therefore, her quest becomes one that moves more toward redefinition of self and culture, toward union. In a way, this begins the basis for the tradition in the West. Symbolic of the developing ego, Psyche's painful journey makes it plain that disobeying is central for her to learn to be herself, and the thrust of much literature in the European West has been a quest in search of the individual self. For women, this poses a double problem, because while the male journey to selfhood has most often been seen as heroic, a woman's has most often been seen as deviant and unfeminine, and therefore both the collective *and* the individual man disapprove. However, as history indicates, despite the disapproval, some (maybe many) women have always "disobeyed" the rules of the collective.

Falling well within this tradition are the articles in the section entitled, "Creating a Self," although the approaches reflect the differing traditions of each culture. In Judith Grossman's "Strategies of Defiance: The Quest of the Wife of Bath," it becomes apparent that the wife seeks the right of self-definition as well as the right to choose her path. Grossman is mainly concerned with the strategies Alison employs in her quest, which, simply put, is to live her own life without the constant criticism of the male clergy. Grossman defines Alison's dual agenda in succinct fashion as "martial opposition to the male authorities by whom she has been stigmatized" and "efforts to secure places out of reach of their voices, their judgments, where her authentic desires can be expressed."

Her way is the body's way, and she gives credit for her splendid genitalia to astrology, particularly the sign of Venus, rather than God. Her celebration of her sexual prowess and of her vulva signals a clear although unconscious link back to the early Sumerian queen and goddess, Inanna, who in a particularly delightful passage in that most ancient of stories, celebrates her own vulva. Grossman also expresses a facet of disobedience which will appear often in these chapters: the meaning of writing for women, both theirs and other's. While Chaucer makes use of early anti-woman Church writings to sketch Alison, her own voice comes through loud and clear, and she is remembered now as a vital, living, unruly presence.

In "Stepping Off the Path: Disobedience and Story-Making in 'Little Red-Cap,' " a Red Riding Hood variant from the Brothers Grimm, Jeanie Watson leads us further into the making of the self by varying from the wellworn path, where "making one's own story necessitates a move from what *is* to what *might be*." Analyzing the tale in a literary and psychological light, Watson underscores how anyone may identify with the female protagonists of this and other fairy tales, as they take their stories into their own hands. In Euro-Western life, it is this quality of singularity which distinguishes the disobedience of women: making one's own self through risky steps, as Psyche did, as Alison did.

No one's story embodies a culminant singularity more than Jane Eyre—one which leads to union, as did Psyche's. In my essay, " 'Speak I must': *Jane Eyre* and the Discourse of Disobedience," I seek to demonstrate that there is a shift taking place on the archetypal level in energies which finally begin to incarnate through a true discourse of disobedience. In her extraordinary novel, Charlotte Brontë limns a character whose every act is disobedient to the prevailing culture, but true to her inner voice. Jane is in harmony with herself, one might even say in Tao; thus, no matter what befalls her, she remains whole and wholly Jane. One interesting aspect of Jane Eyre only touched upon in my article is her affinity for nature and landscape over any Christian creed. Her oneness with the natural world is one of the elements that she shares with Sogolon, a protagonist described in Marjolijn de Jager's paper, "To Speak or Be Spoken: Some Women in African Literature." Sogolon is depicted as close to the life of the animals, interacting with them as equals in her world. Another similarity between these two seemingly divergent heroes is the question of beauty. Jane is described as plain, drab, and poor in a society where women must have beauty or money to have worth; Sogolon, who begins as a beauty, chooses to become ugly in order to avoid being used for commerce. Thus, both stories raise, in different ways, the question of the worth of beauty to women in patrifocal culture as well as challenge that culture's equation of woman = beauty = value.

A further link to the world of Jane Eyre is the point that de Jager makes, through her discussion of literature from Senegal and the Ivory Coast, that in the falsification of one's own voice, women risk the danger of "being said" by the culture rather than "speaking" who they are. From Werewere Liking's portrait of the grandmother Madjo and all of the female voices which "sing" this "roman-chant" (novel-song), as well as the story of the pseudonymous "Ken Bugul," what resonates is Liking's point that the "original sound of creation was probably a voice"; finding one's own voice remains essential or women (and men) will certainly be spoken by the culture around them.

The question of voice remains central in Miriam Cooke's essay, "Apple, Nabila, and Ramza: Arab Women's Narratives of Resistance," as she guides us, using three contemporary tales, from survival that is dependent on inarticulateness through survival and change dependent on the development of a voice and a stance. The ancestry of Arabs is partially shared with the West, since we have the same creation stories. But the line of descent can be seen to split, and the shift becomes apparent in the folk literature with the appearance, for example, in the ninth century (Christian era) of a well-known folk heroine, Scheherazade. In this early manuscript, one can see how the development of future feminism in the Arab world may take on a more culturally oriented rather than individually oriented tone. As opposed to Psyche, who single-mindedly sets out to regain lost love and in the process of achieving union develops a self, Scheherazade's great task is to find a way to change the course of a king's madness and rescue her people from destruction. Scheherazade begins with a fully formed self and her orientation is of necessity different from Psyche's, although the ultimate goal of a healing union may be the same.

Cooke, a professor at Duke University, includes the reactions of her students to previously unknown (to them) and unthought-of Arab feminist writings. Her students learn, as we do, that Arab women have been writing feminist literature since the nineteenth century and that Western stereotypes may have prevented the recognition of what one student describes as "a worldwide community of women," struggling with similar issues although often with a culturally different orientation toward those issues. While women of each culture tend to handle the problem differently, there is a general recognition in many of the essays in this book that *both* men and women are trapped by the rigid rules of a patriarchal society. Robert Moore has theorized that patriarchy is "boy psychology" and that boy psychology robs both men and women of their full maturity (Moore and Gillette 1990, p. xvii), but as Cooke points out, women, who have less invested in the maintenance of the status quo, are the ones to break its constricting hold.

The stories that Cooke analyzes have as one element the daughter's ambivalent connection to the father. In Cooke's essay, all three fathers can be seen to abandon their daughters: Apple's, through lack of understanding (although he does tolerate her disobedience without understanding it), Nabila's, through both lack of understanding and the attempt to assert control, and Ramza's, through opening the world of thought to her and then closing the door, betraying her by putting class issues above her welfare. Similarly, Nili Gold's essay, "Staying in the Place of Danger: The Disobedient, Poetic "I" of Dahlia Ravikovitch," suggests that the work of this fine Israeli poet was much influenced by the early trauma of losing her father. In Gold's introspective and analytical piece, the poet is seen to suffer from the suspicion that her father abandoned her by unconsciously courting death when he is killed by a drunken driver while walking on the highway. Gold enables us to see, by blending the cultures of West and East, the "webs of gold" and "magical incantations" of Ravikovitch's poetry as well as the links to tales such as Medea's. The garment that Ravikovitch seems to be weaving through her early work is the disobedience of the child who refuses to grow up and listen to the admonitions of the adult world, a stance that Gold theorizes Ravikovitch may have absorbed unconsciously in reaction to her father's carelessness. Gold demonstrates, through the poetry, that the writing itself may belong to an internalized, masculine other, one who is "luring, seductive, and dangerous." (Such a view might help illuminate the larger issue of why writing has often been a dangerous rather than a healing place for women.)

In the next section, "Transforming a World," the three papers are concerned with a *collective* response to oppression that culminates in a transformation of the culture. In the first piece, "Women Who Disobey: Examples from India," Manisha Roy chronicles, through the literature of Bengali women, the type of oppression in existence then and now in India. Her paper deals largely with the efforts of these women to escape the ingrained and horrific depredations of a rigidly patrifocal society, where a girl could be married at age two and a half and widowed by five, never to marry again. I have included it in this section because of the transformative nature of the efforts these women and men brought, as a result of their disobedience, to a culture and a society that emphasized conformity. Looking at disobedience from the vantage point of analytical psychology, Roy notes its archetypal nature and views it as exemplary of a "compensatory opposite" emerging "when we obey one idea or authority or even one god." The ossified Hindu system prevented growth and acted to maintain a stagnant status quo which, as Roy notes, not only women but, uniquely, men joined to shatter. One of the points Roy makes as well is that the effect of foreign contact with Indian society seems to have "created the grounds for both oppression and the consciousness to change it." Like Ramza in Miriam Cooke's paper, the Bengali women, whom we come to know through their letters, diaries, and autobiographical writings, seize knowledge of a different way of life to help free them from the claws of the old.

Collective disobedience is more clearly the theme in Teresa Anderson's paper. Here, the specter of a terrorist state, in which rulers turn on their own people in a frenzy of cultural autoimmune destructiveness, provides the framework for Anderson's analysis, "The Whirlwind and the Spiral: State-Sponsored Terror and Psychic Resistance in Marta Traba's *Mothers and Shadows*." Anderson demonstrates how, for Traba, reacting to the events in Latin America, the ultimate and unforgettable symbol became the long protest of the Mothers of the Plaza de Mayo, who refused to submit to silence when their children became the *desparaciedos*, or disappeared ones, taken, tortured, often killed and buried in unmarked graves by the totalitarian regime then in power in Argentina. The reaction of the these women was to march for years until their silent presence, at first ridiculed and rejected, was acknowledged. Due largely to their lengthy protest, the conscience of both a world and a nation was aroused, the regime of terror ended, and a world was transformed. Anderson recounts Traba's statement in 1982 that "she had found herself incapable of writing about anything else." Traba's novel details the experience of two women in countries beset by these terrorist regimes, as they come to terms with themselves and each other. The changes are internal and psychic in nature but result in participation in collective forms of disobedience, differentiated perhaps in this way: as potential or actual mothers, these women acted out of a deep sense of loss of the children of their futures, what Anderson describes with more particularity as "the ache in the womb every mother feels when her child goes out one morning never to return." Archetypally, this may be connected to the roots of compassion, encapsulated in the Bedouin tale recounted in Lila Abu-Lughod's paper, where a word meaning pity, compassion, or mercy is linked etymologically to the word for womb.

In the third paper in this section, "At Home with War in South Africa: A Discussion of Ellen Kuzwayo and Lauretta Ngcobo," Jane Foress Bennett presents a society split by the economic and racist characteristics of apartheid. Bennett acquaints us with racism used as a tool by the state to enforce a rigid system of separation geared to production for whites. Separation of people by color lines into white South Africa and black bantustans worked as well if not better than the rigid class lines of Hinduism. The women in these novels demonstrate an intrinsic ability, in the face of what Bennett shows to be the dehumanizing destruction of the idea of home, to redefine and keep very much alive an idea of what home means for them. But, as the stories amply demonstrate, this is a constantly evolving process. For instance, when Kuzwayo sought to assuage her sense of homelessness by finding herself a life partner, "she went through both physical and mental sufferings [in her relationship with her husband] . . . an experience I have in recent years come to realize is suffered by many women the world over, within different races, cultures, and religions." In Bennett's discussion of both Kuzwayo and Ngcobo, she emphasizes her view that transformation of this society, which is and has been in process, needs a re-definition of reproduction as *humanity* rather than as units of labor. Bennett also highlights the importance of the authorial "I" and demonstrates how, whether in autobiography or fiction, the assertion of the "I" acts against the notion of "erasure" of presence. In a culture where one's "dispersal" is attempted by the ruling group, coherence of identity, the statement made by autobiography, becomes not naïve but rather a forceful declaration of absolute presence. The Bengali women with whom we become familiar in Roy's paper present another such example.

In these three essays, the authors demonstrate collectively transformative situations where anger is certainly warranted and was surely felt. Nevertheless, the anger of the women, while informing their struggles in a powerful way, never took precedence over the goal of a better life for themselves and those they loved. But what about rage so powerful that it overwhelms any other thought, any other prospect? This kind of rage can be a result of living in a culture where the likelihood of change, of forging a different world, is not yet a possibility. As an analyst, I know that rage diverts the ego from its own creative sources and feeds complexes that lead a person to loop back continuously to the very real harm that was done in the past. On the other hand, anger that can be channeled and used productively leads to growth.

The next section, "Rage and Disobedience: Like a Raisin in the Sun," takes its subtitle from the poem "Harlem" by Langston Hughes, which begins, "What happens to a dream deferred / Does it dry up / like a raisin in the sun?" (Bain et al. 1977, p. 619). Although the result of rage may be outward explosion, the inward effect is corrosive and can lead to a drying up. On the larger, archetypal level, the result can be desiccation of the collective body, an effect which only appears fully as millennia pass. In the first essay in this section, "Medea's Fiery Chariot," Carol Savitz presents Medea's chariot, in which she escapes the devastation she has left behind, as an archetypal sanctuary that while leaving the realm of human suffering and passion also relinquishes any possibility of change in the human condition. Medea's disobedience, born out of the rage of betrayal, causes psychic splitting within Medea which "helps us to understand how she can murder her own children and why, refusing to sacrifice her rage and archetypal illusions, her disobedience cannot become a transformative act."

One of Savitz's central points is that there is a necessary link between disobedience and sacrifice. The creative disobediences in preceding essays were accompanied by a willingness to sacrifice, even one's life. Eve, after all, sacrificed immortality; Ahweyoh resigns herself to death rather than submit to a horrible marriage; Sogolon sacrificed her beauty; Jane Eyre risked destitution and death—the list goes on. Certainly the women in the previous section, "Transforming a World," risked their lives. Using the story of Medea symbolically, Savitz demonstrates the falseness of Medea's sacrifice, equating the "escalating chaos of *The Medea*" to Jung's "unmitigated catastrophe" of "unwilling sacrifice," where "the daemon throws us down, makes us traitors to . . . the selves we thought we were." In Medea's world, there seemed no place yet for the rage of betrayal to become anything but splitting; Medea and Jason represented two parts which, brought together in a false union, self-destructed when that union split apart.

Was there, in each culure, a time when repression of the feminine archetype began? Mythic accounts of a "rape" can represent the tearing of power from the feminine realm by the rising masculine. Sylvia Brinton Perera's essay, "Some Archetypal Foundations of Self-Spite," chronicles such a temporal dislocation through the tale of the Celtic Aranrhod, from the Welsh *Mabinogion*, which begins with a rape. Perera acquaints us with the earth-goddess nature of Aranrhod, demonstrating how she was deprived, through trickery and magic, of her rightful place in the culture. Her response was to refuse to participate in a meaningful way. Viewed symbolically, we are also shown how, in Perera's words, the tale "presents one mythic paradigm for the psychological pattern underlying . . . inner disobedience to one's own gifts and nature." This often appears in clinical practice as spite toward the self; that is, when natural powers are usurped, as they so often are in our culture for both women and men, the pattern of response may be akin to Aranrhod's example. This means that, in the unconscious, the initiatory and transformative powers belonging to the feminine archetype will be disavowed in favor of a spiteful refusal to draw on creative energies.

Notice that in the fourth section, three of the four papers are by Jungian analysts. When therapy is working, it can act to heal and reverse trends such those described by Savitz and Perera, through the analytic encounter. As analysts, we perhaps see more of the damage that is done to individuals in our culture; but we also have the privilege of participating in the change in that direction. Both authors offer paths to healing, correctives which are not readily visible in the texts which they study here. In retrospect, female characters who were notable in their own time as objects of cultural condemnation, can be interpreted in later eras as carrying a meaning unintended by the authors of the texts. Such a figure is found in "Suchieh: The Untamed Shrew of *Hsing-shih Yin-yuan*." In her article, Fan Pen Chen introduces us to Suchieh, whose sorry tale is well known throughout China. The title, which contains a Confucian-style warning, *Marriage Destinies to Admonish the World,* is given through Suchieh's tale, which depicts her as a "willful beauty" whose actions in defiance of her society are so harsh and cruel as to appear mad.

As in *The Medea,* the central character of Suchieh is so strong that, in the eyes of her patriarchal Confucian society, she was viewed as despicable as well as dangerous. After all, she inflicts unbelievable pain on her husband, among others. Chen demonstrates how, in hindsight, this eighteenth-century text speaks rather differently to the modern world.

Leaving out none of the horror which Suchieh perpetrates, Chen nevertheless is able to look at her through the perspective allowed by time and finds
ways of understanding Suchieh's situation which derive from her condition
as a woman in the repressive society of the day, one which attempted to
erase any vestige of the power that inheres to the archetypal feminine. The
author of the text could find nothing but karma to explain Suchieh's repre-
hensible behavior. Unlike Medea, of whom Sarah Pomeroy has remarked
that at least she succeeded (1975, p. 109), it is difficult to admire Suchieh.
However, to Chen, "the reasons for her behavior are readily visible without
having to resort to a karmic explanation." Chen describes the novel as
"mimetically faithful," which is another way of saying that, as with the Wife
of Bath, the voice of Suchieh resonates despite the conscious intentions of
the author to denigrate his character in the eyes of the reader. As Chen
notes, through twentieth-century eyes, all of the horrible behavior exhibited
by Suchieh may be attributed to her "personal history [and] the influence of
her mother in particular." What is highlighted here is her development in a
rigid class society, where her acts may be seen as those of " 'an avenging
angel' for her oppressed mother."

There is no way out for Suchieh, and her story and her end are
frightening. Between the extremes of complete obedience and complete
shrewishness, no margin for movement was possible in the society of her
day. In the final piece in this section, Jane White-Lewis demonstrates that
one of the saddest facets of the life of Virginia Woolf may be that she lived
in a transitional time, just barely too soon to benefit from the changes in
society's recognition of anger and the fact of incest. In "Virginia Woolf:
The Tragedy of Unconscious Disobedience," White-Lewis makes a case for
the tragedy which she sees at the root of Virginia Woolf's life: that it was
Woolf's inability to live her anger fully which eventually defeated her,
despite her enormous accomplishments as a writer. White-Lewis takes an
analytic approach to Woolf, using her diaries, life events, fiction, and
nonfiction. Here, too, the mother is seen as central to the later development
of the daughter, this time as "the angel in the house" which Woolf could
never quite banish from her psyche. White-Lewis implies that there is an
inner voice for each individual, which we ignore at our peril. In a way not
completely dissimilar to the model of Aranrhod, Woolf's "decision" was to
spite her inner voice by disobeying *it*. Since she was a writer, she could not
be silent; because of her inability to know her anger consciously, however,
she could not speak. As this article demonstrates, the conflict could not be
contained, and Woolf eventually took her own life at the age of forty-nine.

In the fifth section, "Women of Power: Whose Hero Is She, Anyway?" the subtitle is a variation on the play, *Whose Life Is It, Anyway?* by
Brian Clar. The play concerns the question of reclaiming one's life from the
hands of others, in this case, a technological society which has the capacity
to prolong the life of the individual even when the individual doesn't want

life prolonged. This section of the book also has as its aim reclamation. Being redeemed here, however, are the definitions of *heroic*, *powerful*, and *feminine*, words which, in a patrifocal society, are often mutually exclusive. From first to last, all of the women in these texts provide a re-definition of the heroic. The papers in this section reveal the existence of powerful feminine archetypes, integral to the viability of the race, which, though repressed or distorted in the conscious discourse of patrifocal society, not only survived but thrived through the stories that were written.

In Wen-chin Ouyang's paper, "The Princess of Resolution: The Emergence of Al-Amira Dhat al-Himma, a Medieval Arab Woman Warrior," the protagonist is a commanding presence who is both devout and womanly, warlike and feminine, intelligent, unyielding, and certainly never servile. Like her better-known compatriot, Scheherazade from *The Arabian Nights*, Dhat al-Himma's story appeared in the ninth century (C.E.). Unlike Scheherazade, Dhat al-Himma is a fighter and a warrior who Ouyang compares, in part, to the Greek goddess Athena. Her story is told in an epic cycle of more than seven thousand pages, the only woman so celebrated out of the ten extant epic cycles of Arabic folk literature. Ouyang's paper covers both the personal history of Dhat al-Himma, including forebears such as Qattalet al-Shuj'an, or "The Slayer of Courageous Men," and the rough transition of Arabic society itself into a unified whole. While the epic cycles generally are folk literature about heroes whose stories represent in different ways the transition to Islam, what makes Dhat al-Himma different in Ouyang's eyes is her symbolic embodiment of the healing power of the archetype of the Great Mother, which could survive constant violation yet still retain a strength and energy capable of guiding warring factions to unity under the banner of Islam. Unlike Aranrhod, the Welsh goddess and queen who turned her energies against herself, Dhat al-Himma is able to provide both a unifying force and a healing energy, the latter component deriving from an aspect embodied in the feminine.

Tey Diana Rebelledo's article, "From Coatlicue to Doña Luz: *Mitotes* in Chicana Literature," also concerns powerful energies that are embodied by the feminine. From the ancient Aztec goddesses and legendary or historical figures like La Malinche and La Llorona through contemporary fiction and poetry of Chicana writers, Rebelledo shows us how female images of power, although distorted by the dominant patrifocal culture, remain very much alive through the use and creation of mythology by Chicana writers to "subvert traditional literary discourse . . . of traditional or patriarchal hegemony." While patrifocal society can offer only one interpretation of the women and goddesses who flout its rules, what Chicana writers have done is invent anew the lives, powers, and most specifically, the meanings of these ancient archetypes of the feminine. Rebelledo explains how these early, extremely complex symbols of power, comprised of multifaceted elements, have been rewoven into a new tapestry of empowerment by Chicana writers such as Margarita Cota-Cárdenas, Sandra Cisneros, Pat Mora, and others.

Rebelledo demonstrates how these images persist through time and have then been picked up and revivified by today's writers. In "Lye-Throwers and Lovely Renegades: The Road from Bitch to Hero for Black Women in Fiction and Poetry," Jewelle Gomez wonders where the women heroes, especially black women, are in the literature of today and tomorrow. Scanning history provides considerable material, from the Queen of Sheba, Makeda, through more recent black historical figures like Sojourner Truth and Anita Hill. But as Gomez shows, until recently, the tapestry of characters reflecting the authentic nature of the black woman's struggle never became popular. She analyzes several reasons for this, one of which is that, under oppression, "the same words used to describe a male hero — aggressive, fearless, unyielding — mean bitch when applied to a woman." By taking the word *bitch* as a positive description of some very dynamic characters in the fiction and poetry she discusses, Gomez seizes the heroic by subverting meaning. Fantasy fiction, as she demonstrates, is a particularly supple medium within which to develop female characters of great strength and tenacity. Gomez evokes the sense of a burgeoning literature of future-oriented heroism, literature which can remind us of our dreams.

*To Speak or Be Silent* opens with Eve, creator of her world, and closes with Delilah, whom Elaine Hoffman Baruch sees, in the Saint-Saëns opera, as representing "the forbidden mother . . . insofar as [she is] sexually desiring." As Baruch notes in her essay, "Forbidden Words/Enchanting Song: The Treatment of Delilah in Literature and Music," Milton's Dalila "ceases to be a woman for Samson but becomes a hero for the Philistines." Delila is a particularly ambiguous figure, and this may account somewhat for the appeal she has held for writers and composers over the centuries. Baruch covers considerable territory in her discussion of the manifestations of Delilah, from the Bible to Milton, Voltaire, Handel, and Saint-Saëns. Opera is a place where women *cannot* be silent, so her voice is heard loud and clear, and remains complex and fascinating. Did she love Samson? Did she seek influence, self-gratification, money? Particularly in Saint-Saëns's opera, we can see the power that her words afford her to sway Samson, and, as Baruch demonstrates, throughout her literary history, it is her words which empower her. She remains a complicated and enigmatic figure, who, "possess[ing] language and a voice . . . is all that culture condemns and at the same time is fascinated by in woman." Depending on who is looking (and listening), early, strong female figures can represent heroes or villains. For the Philistines, Delilah represents a savior figure; for the Hebrews, she is an example of why a woman's words are dangerous. In opera, she represents simply a powerful voice that must be heard.

Many of the texts and figures discussed herein are well known from mythology and literature; many, however, are not. With *To Speak or Be*

*Silent,* we seek to fill gaps in understanding the centrality of women's words. Narrative, mythology, and history have traditionally been interpreted from the viewpoint of the masculine. These essays offer a necessary compensation from a perspective that allows the voice of the feminine to be heard, with a sound that resonates as disobedience in the dominant patrifocal culture.

## References

Allen, P. G., ed. 1989. *Spider Woman's Granddaughters: Traditional Tales and Contemporary Writing by Native American Women.* New York: Fawcett Columbine.

Bain, C. E., Beatty, J., and Hunter, J. P., eds. 1977. *The Norton Introduction to Literature.* New York: W. W. Norton and Co.

Goodspeed, E. J. 1959. *The Apocrypha: An American Translation.* New York: Random House.

Ivins, M. 1991. *Molly Ivins Can't Say That, Can She?* New York: Random House.

Jung, C. G. 1958. Jung and religious belief. In *CW* 18:702–744. Princeton, N.J.: Princeton University Press, 1976.

Moore, R., and Gillette, D. 1990. *King Warrior Magician Lover.* San Francisco: Harper Collins.

Pomeroy, S. B. 1975. *Goddesses, Whores, Wives, and Slaves.* New York: Schocken Books.

# CREATING

## a

## WORLD

# EVE

## REFLECTIONS ON THE PSYCHOLOGY OF THE FIRST DISOBEDIENT WOMAN

### Judith Hubback

*There is no subject so old that something new cannot be said about it.*

F. Dostoevsky, *A Diary of a Writer*, 1876

The first woman known in Judaism and Christianity, Eve, is shown at the beginning of the book of Genesis as disobeying the creator God. According to the ancient myth, that disobedience was the first sin; man (meaning mankind) fell from grace when the two earliest male and female partners, having been tempted by the serpent, ate the forbidden fruit of the tree of knowledge of good and evil. The woman was the first to fall for the temptation, and she persuaded the man to do the same. Dire punishment followed: both were expelled from Paradise. She features as the more sinful of the two. Disobedience thereby became, in Hebraic and later in Christian teaching, the prototypical sin. Is is now, thanks to Eve, better seen as an assumption which can be challenged.

In the book of Genesis, two versions are given of the creation of Eve. One reads: "And God said, Let us make man in our image, after our likeness . . . So God created man in his own image, in the image of God created he him; male and female created he them. And God blessed them and God said unto them, Be fruitful and multiply, and replenish the earth and subdue it" (Genesis 1:26–28). Modern views of the equality of men and women can be traced back to that account. The creativity of men and women ever since Adam and Eve is the manifestation in us of God's gift of creativity. We are not gods, but we have a bit of God in us. And "we" is woman just as much as man.

The second version of the creation of Eve is the one which, on the whole, has had more influence than the first on the Jewish and Christian theologies relating to the two sexes. "And the Lord God said, it is not good that the man should be alone; I will make him an help meet for him"

(Genesis 2:18). It goes on: "And the Lord God caused a deep sleep to fall upon Adam, and he slept: and he took one of his ribs . . . And the rib, which the Lord God had taken from the man, made he a woman, and brought her unto the man" (Genesis 2:21–22). It is worth noting that (at least in the translation used here) by the time of the second version the creator has become more of an authority figure than in the first: he is called "The Lord God." The forces of authority and power call into action an opposite, a confrontation, in the form of the questioning of them; the shared creativity of the first version had suggested that there would be partnership, rather than hierarchy. Disobedience was a greater risk once one of the three characters in the drama was named Lord, combining Adam and Eve into "man." Erich Fromm writes: "Man challenges the supreme power of God, and he is able to challenge it because he is potentially God. Man's first act is *rebellion*, and God punishes him because he has rebelled and because God wants to preserve his supremacy" (1966, p. 23). But Eve, as offered to us in the early chapters of Genesis, exemplifies one major part of total human psychology, and Adam shows the other part.

When partnership has been discarded and differentiation has been set going, the male and the female emerge as slightly different from each other. Adam's attitude to law is more compliant than Eve's. They had come out of the original matrix and there could be two responses to God's commands and prohibitions, which later became the Law. Some Talmudic commentators considered that *binah*, "the intelligence of woman, matures more quickly than the intelligence of man" (Ginzberg 1913, p. 67). Another writer, referring also to the Talmud, gives understanding as another meaning of *binah* (Steinsaltz 1977, p. 138). According to choice, that characteristic can be seen as either more frequent in women or as potentially capable of being developed in men as well. The third possibility is that the two original people are not yet fully differentiated.

The text of Genesis is explicit that God, speaking to Adam, set limits on what he was allowed to eat: "Of every tree of the garden thou mayest freely eat: but of the tree of the knowledge of good and evil, thou shalt not eat of it: for in the day that thou eatest thereof thou shalt surely die" (Genesis 2:16–17). It is worth noting, in passing, that in the earlier version of the creation, God had said, "Behold, I have given you every herb bearing seed . . . and every tree . . . to you it shall be for meat." Forbidding Adam to eat from the tree of knowledge of good and evil is a major change from the earlier, more permissive state of affairs.

In the creation myth, God features as a kind of person: he has ideas, concepts, thoughts, and performs actions; he needs to rest after six days of hard work. He also has emotions; he saw it was good, he felt pleased with himself. So when Eve disobeyed him, she is shown as opposing a person rather than an abstract power, such as fate. Yet, at the same time, the story exemplifies the need humans have to try to find out what fate is.

Hebrews must have noticed, I think, while the myth was gradually growing, that everybody was fated to die. So that the ancient creator God was not simply believed to be a kind of person as shown in Genesis; he was more than a person by virtue of being a god, he was a puzzling, impersonal power. The connection between different kinds of facts — individuals as people and collective or abstract ideas such as fate — was something about which Eve implicitly wanted to know more.

At that stage in the early history of man, it was easier to personify the central powers of nature than to see them as impersonal forces. That was part of the effort to understand them, which is the basis of many myths (Hubback 1990, pp. 11-12). If God was portrayed in some ways like a person, he was not quite so distant, so different, so frightening. Also in the Genesis creation myth, God was not-man, he was exterior to man, and he was not yet internal spirituality. The God outside could be related to, as the infant relates to the mother who gives both body-made milk and emotional love. Before God was goodness, let alone goodness inside, he was the maker of good things. So when Eve disobeyed the command which had been given to Adam — by eating from that one specified tree — she was going against the God outside, not in any sense against her inner conscience. Conscience did not yet exist, but God did. The powerful parent/God precedes its internalized version. By disobeying parent/God/Law, Eve was laying the foundation for developing her own inner law, her truthfulness to herself, to the Self.*

Until Eve had performed the action of eating the forbidden fruit she had been passive, created, and given to Adam as a companion. She had exercised no active choices. According to the tragedy on offer in the myth, her first action was a disobedient one. If she had merely complied with God's orders, she would only have been fitting in with what was required and depriving herself of her potential as an active researcher. But since disobedience is so much stressed, the message emerges that when she made a decision, even though under the influence of the serpent's skillful arguments (of which more later), she was reacting against God's decree and that emerges as value-laden: it was a *bad* thing to do. To a modern mind, it is regrettable that disobedience colored Eve's desire to respond to her inner need to ask questions and thereby to begin to find out facts about the world. She wanted to study science: that was her response to finding she could no longer tolerate being passive.

Eve's place in myth is a secure one, since what the book of Genesis tells about her fits well with what any natural person, unshackled insofar as

---

*Editor's note: For definitions of Jung's concept of the Self, see Perera (p. 160), Ross (p. 64), and Savitz (p. 157) in this book.

is possible by prohibitions, inhibitions, or conscience, would be likely to want: to find out about the world in which he or she lives. In spite of accretions of culturally loaded observations, assumptions, and ideas about the differences between males and females in much of the world since early mythological times, it seems to me—a late-twentieth-century person—unlikely that a desire for knowledge is inherently sex-linked and stronger in males than in females. Eve can be seen as the carrier of one half of the human psyche. I do not think that she can be understood on her own, in isolation from Adam. She shows up, when we focus on her, as needing the serpent to tempt her to do what she had not dared to do without his instigation, but the other part of her psyche, the cautious part, is lived out by Adam. Either he was less inquisitive than she was or more alarmed by the idea of disobeying God. But the Creator's command was a negative one, a prohibition. So the reactions and responses of these two archetypal humans are only to be fully understood by searching into how they differed, without saying that one was necessarily "better" than the other. A good scientist, like a good mountaineer, takes some risks but draws the line at the ones judged to be excessive. And in such a judgment, the balance of intuition and thinking may be very difficult to achieve. Although Adam, which is the "Adam" in each of us, is thought of as a flake, a wimp, or a nebbish by many modern people, this is an aggressive view of a necessary part of each person's psyche.

If Eve was a scientist, acting on her need to listen to some internal voice rather than to comply with God's voice from the outside, then Adam was representative of the part of her that she temporarily disregarded. The serpent—the inner tempter of each of us—realized intuitively that he would have more success with Eve than with Adam: she was more likely to have faith in the Self, although she was, in action, the more foolhardy of the two. It does not seem to be stretching a point too far to see her as the carrier of the human need to take risks, if the alternative is denying the inner truth. "Adam" was anxious that the search for knowledge would lead to almost unimaginable dangers about which he had been warned in a general way. "Eve," without giving the matter enough reflection, went forward into the unknown. They were each differentiating themselves from what post-Darwinians know to be the facts: that our animal nature mainly keeps us in a patterned rut, but our humanness pulls and pushes us out of it.

The myth of Eve is useful psychologically because it offers itself as being about the natural woman, what she is and what she does with how she is. In the late eighteenth century, Jean-Jacques Rousseau tried to find out what natural man is. In his treatise on education (1762), he depicted the child as enjoying the tutor's practical lesson in geography—not in the classroom but out in the open air, learning the points of the compass by experience, not through books. In *The Social Contract*—an essay on power—he opens boldly with the statement, "Man is born free; and everywhere he is in chains" (1762). The modern sociologist sees woman in relation to social states and forces, while the depth psychologist sees her as influenced by internal as well as external pressures. Eve was subjective in the sense that she had been created, as compared with the uncreated God. But unlike all later people, she had no infancy, so that she had never been subjected to any kind of nurture. What prefigured nurture were the gifts of life and the paradisal environment. In the same way as the growing child wants to know all sorts of things about its family and surroundings, so Eve wanted knowledge of the basics. But the trouble was that the most fundamental questions about the world were not meant to be asked: What is good? If there is goodness, does it taste nice? How do we know what is good? What is evil? Why does goodness have a bad opposite? What is the connection between the two trees at the center of the Garden, the tree of knowledge of good and evil and the tree of life? Why do we have to be held back by God?

In modern thought, it is, I think, safe to assume that learning about good and evil is the basis for all ethical and interpersonal applications of those famous opposites. Developing the capacity to study how good and evil interact is one of the central preoccupations of philosophers, of most modern psychotherapists, and of spiritually religious people, each in their own way. I am presenting a view of Eve according to which she was compelled to try to find out more about her world than she could on her own or from Adam. Eve in Genesis is the basic natural woman and must have been motivated by the drive of instincts. Controversial though the theory of instincts has been for many years (the physiological ones and the psychological ones), the instinctual angle on Genesis merits exploration, via both analytical science and intuitive ideas. Jung, writing about the psychological factors determining human behavior, might have been elaborating on the story of how Eve responded to the suggestions of the serpent when he wrote that, in addition to the well-known instincts of hunger and sexuality, there are two others:

> the drive to activity and the reflective instinct . . . the richness of the human psyche and its essential character are probably determined by this reflective instinct. . . . Reflection is the cultural instinct *par excellence*, and its strength is shown in the power of culture to maintain itself in the face of untamed nature. . . . man has the distinctive power of creating something new in the real sense of the word. (1937, par. 240–245)

And Jung added to that statement, "Creation is as much destruction as construction" (ibid., par. 245) – a doom-laden comment to the Eve in each of us.

It is worth linking reflections on Eve with mention of certain early goddesses who held sway before Hebraic days and who were associated with wisdom. While knowledge may be taken to be acquired by means of mental processes, increasing with the use of intellect, wisdom manifests as a quality or a capacity of the whole person. It might be argued that Adam was effectively wiser than Eve insofar as he at least tried to refrain from disobeying the all-powerful God, yet a counter-argument would be that Eve represents the forces of human development as compared with animal acceptance of things as they are. Since Adam and Eve in the Genesis myth are the prototypes of all later men and women, they had to emerge from primitive nonknowledge, innocence, and naiveté. An innocent is primarily someone who has not done anything wrong, also someone who does not yet know much about the ways of the world. In the Garden of Eden, the first man and woman were innocent — but not for long. As compared with the pre-Hebraic goddesses during the matriarchal centuries in the Middle and Near East, Eve can be seen neither as a goddess nor as an incarnation of wisdom. Indeed, in one particular way she was the opposite: I have referred to her as foolhardy, and foolishness is the most obvious opposite to wisdom. On the other hand, it is possibly to surmise that at both the physical instinctual level and at the psychologically unconscious level she was being pushed toward painful emergence from primitive bliss. Of course, to consider Eve, who is a mythological person, using the concept of unconsciousness, is very risky — but that is what I decided to do. If Eve could take risks, so can a modern woman. The theme of Eve and wisdom arises also in connection to comments on the part the serpent plays in the story.

Many writers, interested in the emergence of women from various cultural and psychological states of submission to males, have studied the vicissitudes along the way toward real partnership with men. To deduce from the text of Genesis that Eve was, in the history of the Hebrews, the earliest wise woman is speculation. But she is mythological, not historical, which justifies using modern eyes and modern concepts to examine the fascination that she still engenders. She and Adam have throughout the ages been depicted in sculpture, in painting, and in embroidery. They belong to us today as well as to earlier times when the literal quality of the Genesis myth was not questioned.

Nearly a century ago, a group of American feminists published a commentary on selected passages in the Bible. It contains such gems as:

> In this prolonged interview [between the serpent and
> Eve] the unprejudiced reader must be impressed by
> the courage, the dignity, and the lofty ambition of
> the woman. The tempter evidently had a profound
> knowledge of human nature, and saw at a glance the
> high character of the person he met by chance in his

> walks in the Garden. He [tempted her] with the
> promise of knowledge, with the wisdom of the Gods
> . . . he roused in the woman that intense thirst for
> knowledge that the simple pleasures of picking
> flowers and talking to Adam did not satisfy. (Stan-
> ton, Blake et al. 1895, pp. 24–25)

Although it shows a dated ignorance that "man" means mankind, another
passage worth rescuing from oblivion reads:

> Note the significant fact that we always hear of the
> "fall of man," not the fall of woman . . . it is amazing
> that any set of men ever claimed that the dogma of
> the inferiority of woman is here set forth. The con-
> duct of Eve from the beginning to the end is so supe-
> rior to that of Adam . . . when the Jehovah God
> appears to demand why his command has been dis-
> obeyed, Adam endeavours to shield himself behind
> the gentler being he has declared to be so dear, "The
> woman thou gavest to be with me, she gave me and I
> did eat," he whines — trying to shield himself at his
> wife's expense! (Stanton, Blake et al. 1895, pp.
> 26–27)

But if we take these archetypal people as two parts of a whole person, it is
possible to say that Eve was carrying and acting on the forward-going
possibilities that all our psyches contain. In cultural history, males are
usually shown as the thrusting or active ones, and women as the receiving or
passive ones. Such characteristics are easily projected onto, and introjected
from, two distinct but interrelating people. A contemporary reading of the
text of Genesis has to take this into account. Blake offers the interesting
view that the serpent told Eve, "that if the mortal body does perish, the
immortal part shall live for ever and [offered] as the reward of her act the
attainment of knowledge" (Stanton, Blake et al. 1895, p. 26). Eve has been
"immortal" in the sense that her story is still a gripping one, and archetypal.
She still lives in each of us.

A link between the simple, or even simplistic, view of the myth and
the current interest in how the early matriarchies were succeeded by Hebraic
patriarchy is amusingly provided by an extract, quoted by Seltman, from
the Vatican newspaper of 1955. "Adam was to blame . . . [he] should have
given Eve a smart slap in the face when he was aware he was gradually being
seduced." This was a statement on which the editor of the *Osservatore della
Domenica* commented that he deplored "the fact that Eve has always had to
bear the brunt of the blame for introducing sin into the world as intermedi-

ary between the Devil and Adam" (Seltman 1956, p. 170). That was generous on his part, but since he was interested in sin rather than in the history
of ancient religions, the editor was taking no account of the view according
to which the Hebrew doctrine of the creation by a patriarchal God super-
seded the earlier matriarchal religious one. If Eve is seen—as she is by
several modern writers, men as well as women—as representing earlier
female deities, slapping her on the face would have been a considerable
insult, but in keeping with the view of Merlin Stone who showed that in
ancient Sumeria man was regarded as having been created from clay by the
Great Mother Goddess. "Perhaps one thousand years later," she writes, "the
worshippers of Yahweh asserted that it was a male who initially created the
world" (1976, p. 236). She also writes that the *asherim*, the sacred groves of
the sycamore fig, or black mulberry tree in ancient Egypt and other Near
Eastern countries, were anathema to the Hebrew Levite priests, who
"destroyed the shrines of the female deity wherever they could, murdering
when they could not convert" (1976, p. 234). Certainly a slap in the face of
the goddesses.

Up to this point Eve has been referred to as "the first woman." And
in the text of Genesis, she is that. Yet there has been a revival of interest in
an earlier mythical female, Lilith, coinciding with recent years when feminists played a more combative role than they did in previous centuries.
Research has traced her in Hebrew legends and in pre-Hebraic texts, Baby-
lonian and Assyrian as well as later Cabbalistic and alchemical ones, unfortunately too numerous to expand on here (for example, Patai 1967, Colonna 1980, Koltuv 1983, Vogelsang 1985). Put simply, Lilith, Adam's first
wife, features in all the legends as (in Jungian terms) the shadow of Eve. I
think the serpent can validly be regarded as the shadow of Adam.

It seems to me very clear that Lilith is the prototype of the woman
that both the man and the second wife are afraid of, and they are also
envious of her. She was an amazingly energetic creature, but unfortunately
vital in a negative way. It could even be thought that Jehovah himself was
envious of her creativity. Lilith was a nocturnal creature who made children
at a phenomenal rate—far more than God in those early days. She was also
unfortunately the one through whose agency "countless demons and spooks
arose from [Adam's] nocturnal emissions" (Jung 1955–1956, par. 589).
There are passages in the Jewish Encyclopaedia which suggest that Adam's
duality was understood early on: the contrast between his physical and his
spiritual nature, his "two faces," his fascination with Lilith and his very
different relations with Eve. Yet Eve also knew of her duality, which is
expressed in the conflict between her loyalty to God's decree and to Adam
and her need to listen to her inner voice urging her forward. The Lilith of
the legends was so dynamic that she, as well as the serpent, could easily be
envied. Both these females demonstrate the desire for freedom, although
this includes the freedom to make mistakes.

Coming more particularly to the part played in Eve's psychology by the serpent, the notorious tempter, certain interesting aspects of him emerge in some of the legends of the Jews collected by Louis Ginzberg. "The serpent, like man, stood upright upon two feet" (1913, p. 71). He was thought to be endowed with "superior mental gifts." This explained "his envy of man, especially of man's conjugal relations. Envy made him mediate ways and means of bringing about the death of Adam" (ibid.). The serpent, according to another legend, told Eve she could touch the fruit. But "she could not bring herself to disobey the command of God utterly . . . [so] first she ate only the outside skin of the fruit, and then, seeing that it did not fell her, she ate the fruit itself" (ibid., pp. 73–4). Following that, the legend holds that if Adam and Eve had both confessed their transgression, they would have been pardoned. The serpent did not try to defend himself, so he was cursed. "The serpent is a villain, and the wicked are good debaters. If God had questioned him, the serpent would have answered: 'Thou didst give them a command, and I did contradict it. Why did they obey me, and not Thee?' " (ibid., p. 77). Why, indeed? And he was too proud to ask for forgiveness. In the text of Genesis, there is no mention of Eve or Adam asking to be forgiven. It is possible to speculate that since they had, in the words of Jehovah, "become as one of us [Gods] to know good and evil," Eve for her part felt sad and anxious, but not apologetic. She did not ask for pardon. The idea of the Godhead did not yet include mercy.

There are many more angles than there is space for here, from which to consider Eve, speculating on her through modern analytical eyes. Yet what we see is, of course, influenced both by personal experience and by an inevitable slipping into projective identification with her as "the first woman." We cannot think about Eve in isolation from either Adam or the serpent, who is the earliest incarnated example of the archetypal shadow and "the third" in that part of the drama. He was the shadow in both Eve and Adam inasmuch as what he succeeded in doing had not previously been seen by either of them as part of themselves. He was also the shadow of God, or perhaps it should be said, of God as he was believed to be at that early stage of human history. The role played by the serpent is a factor that must have represented part of God, since he created everything. Yet the serpent and indeed also the tree—both nature symbols—took part in the challenge to God's unitary character and his supremacy. Eve took into herself some of God's decisiveness, which modern analysts see as an integral part of ego functioning. Adam introjected a possibly more female tendency to draw back from decisions which fear sees as probably calamitous. While Eve may perhaps have dimly perceived that if she used, in as positive a way as possible, the valuable animus that she had received from the male God, she was pointing the way ahead, for males as well as for females.

Integrating contrasexual factors and bringing to consciousness previously damaging shadow features of our personalities are essential steps toward self-knowledge, as well as knowledge of the world in "the garden" around us. So I bring these reflections on Eve's psychology to a close with the observation that her disobedience to the Jehovah-God can be seen as the first crucial step forward for mankind, the first manifestation of the urge toward science and individuation. Fear of the consequences of a disobedient action began to be faced with the paradoxical help of what was thought of as evil. The internal serpent, the symbolic fruit, the necessary disillusion about the Garden, they all have to be integrated. Knowledge of good and evil, and of life and death, still have to be brought into relation with difficult everyday existence. As God insisted, we are not to "be as gods," so we have to accept limitations on our potential for wisdom, as well as thanking Eve for calmly going forward into danger.

# References

Colonna, M. T. 1980. Lilith or the black moon. *Journal of Analytical Psychology* 25:325–350.

Fromm, E. 1966. *You shall Be as Gods: A Radical Interpretation of the Old Testament and Its Traditions*. New York: Holt, Rinehart and Winston.

Ginzberg, L. 1913. *The Legends of the Jews*, vol. 1. Philadelphia: The Jewish Publication Society of America.

Hubback, J. 1990. Tearing to pieces: Pentheus, the Bacchae and analytical psychology. *Journal of Analytical Psychology* 35:3–17.

Jung, C. G. 1937. Psychological factors determining human behaviour. In *CW* 8:114–125. Princeton, N.J.: Princeton University Press, 1960.

———. 1955–1956. *Mysterium coniunctionis. CW*, vol. 14. Princeton, N.J.: Princeton University Press, 1963.

Koltuv, B. B. 1983. Lilith. *Quadrant* 16(1):63–87.

Patai, R. 1967. *The Hebrew Goddess*. New York: KTAV Publishing House.

Rousseau, J-J. 1762. *Emile, ou de l'education*. London: Dent.

Rousseau, J-J. 1762. *Le contrat social, ou principes du droit politique*. London: Dent, 1916.

Seltman, C. 1956. *Women in Antiquity*. London: Pan Books.

Stanton, E. C., Blake, L. D. et al. 1895. *The Woman's Bible: The Original Feminist Attack on the Bible*. Abridged edition. Edinburgh: Polygon Books, 1985.

Steinsaltz, A. 1977. *The Essential Talmud*. New York: Bantam.

Stone, M. 1976. *The Paradise Papers: The Suppression of Women's Rites*. London: Virago.

Vogelsang, E. 1985. The confrontation between Lilith and Adam: the fifth round. *Journal of Analytical Psychology* 30:149–163.

# BEFORE THE FALL(S):

## NATIVE AMERICAN WOMEN
## AND THE CONCEPT OF
## DISOBEDIENCE

### Patricia Clark Smith

*(for my mother, Rita Mary Clark)*

Sometimes I dream I'm back at Turner's Falls. The real name of this waterfall is Peskeompskut, an Algonquin word that signifies fish and water spilling over rocks. But you won't find that name on a map. To locate the falls, you have to look for Montague, Massachusetts, where in my dream I stand at the end of Main Street, also known as State Route 2A, a street lined with the ordinary, shabby, red brick and wood frame buildings common to New England mill towns along the Connecticut River. Often, like Montague, these towns came to be because of a natural cascade that became a dam site, a place for a mill, a huddle of raw houses and stores built along an old trail. As it happens, many old trails once converged here near Montague. But unlike some of its more charming neighbors—Deerfield, say, or Amherst, towns that are enshrined in Anglo-American colonial and cultural history—Montague gets passed over in the tour books, the bed-and-breakfast listings, even in the southern New England edition of the *Smithsonian Guide to Historic America*. And yet something happened here.

The town stops where 2A crosses the Connecticut River, heading north over a WPA bridge with a full view of the big falls, and this is where my dream really begins, when I set foot on the bridge. Always, it is spring. There are new leaves, and the air is pale green, all washed in soft, fresh light. The opposite bank of the river is white in patches along the high wooded ledges where the Juneberry is in bloom, that shrub whose flowering has always signaled the time of the migratory fish runs. My family called it shadblow.

Two others join me on this dream walk, a tall shadowy person on either side of me. They link their arms with mine; they accompany me. Although I cannot see their faces, I have a strong sense of older women presences about me. Did I ever walk across this bridge as a child in the

company of both my grandmothers? It's just possible. I am certain that I
came here with my mother and *one* grandmother, but these women of my
dream, the two of them, they don't feel like mothers exactly. More like
grandmothers. Or great-grandmothers. Elders. But I do not turn to look at
them, nor do we speak in the presence of the falls, where the force of the
water in its fifty-foot drop thunders up through the bridge struts, straight
up through the soles of my feet and into my body, my heart. For a few miles
above the falls, the river has careened around sharp bends and been pent in
by rocky narrows; now comes its terrific burst into air and freedom. Moreover, it is high-water time, the runoff still coming down from the mountains
to the north.

Whoever we are, we three, we pause at the midpoint of the span
and look upstream toward the great dam, where water booms and boils
beneath the spillway and nearly obscures the long islands of granite outcrop
far beneath our feet. This dream water, I see, is alive, not merely with its
own energy but with fish. Shad, of course, and alewives, and the big, native
Atlantic salmon that in truth abandoned this river before my birth, in part
because of such power dams as the one before us. (*Power dam*: indeed,
doubly well named, for the power such a structure squeezes off, as well as
for what power it generates.) But here below us now are the fish, a welling
profusion of silver backs and fins, rolling and leaping and writhing splen-
didly beneath us.

And then. And then. In one instant the whole scene is frozen. The
cascade simply stops, and white rapids cease bucking. The fish are arrested
in mid-jump. The river below lies glassy, inert, dead. Silence. And then,
filling the air as vastly as the dam did, there is only the sound of human
weeping. Heartbroken, heartbreaking.

Once, Peskeompskut was one of the major fishing-meeting-trading
sites for the Algonquin peoples of New England. From the time I was little,
and our gas-rationed Sunday drives often ended here, I knew this was a
place where a terrible thing had happened. A massacre. A massacre, not of
white settlers, but of Algonquins, and not of "braves," but of women like
my mother, children like me, elders like my grandparents, the people who
drove us here during World War Two Sundays in my father's absence.

*"Imagine, Patsy, as if the Nazis sneaked over here and killed us
while your Daddy and all the other fathers were away being soldiers."*

Imagine, indeed.

I did not know the whole story of Peskeompskut until many years
later. Certainly I never heard any details from anyone in my family. Now I
think that my family knew about Peskeompskut and other things hazily, in
the way that mixed-blood, assimilated people far removed from their tribal
centers of population and consciousness often do seem to intuit the trace of
things by some combination of oral history and genetic memory. No one in
my family, I am sure, was ever taught anything about Peskeompskut in the

schools of the Commonwealth of Massachusetts, except that it is the site of the first hydroelectric dam in New England.

Down the road a few miles west and south, at Old Deerfield, visitors are overwhelmed by saltbox houses turned into museums, confronted at all turns by signs describing everyday life in the seventeenth-century village, and the events leading up to King Philip's War, and, above all, by signs marking each terrible moment of the Deerfield Massacre, the Battle of Bloody Brook. No sign marks Peskeompskut, where at dawn on May 19, 1676, Captain William Turner led one hundred and fifty men from those shadblow ledges in a surprise attack upon the great encampment below of Algonquin women, children, and elderly people, mostly Wampanoags, who were gathered here for the annual salmon run. No one knows how many Algonquin people died; contemporary accounts speak of Turner's men gazing down upon "hundreds of wigwams," and between two and three hundred dead is the usual estimate.

We know, of course, the precise toll in English blood: thirty-one dead, including Turner, whose name the falls now officially bear, instead of the sounds that mean rock, fish, water. And William Holyoke, Turner's second-in-command, wounded in the sudden English "retreat" undertaken when some of the Wampanoag "brutes" unexpectedly returned to defend the encampment—Holyoke got a city named for him, the same city where the grandmother who used to bring me to these falls was born.

More than any single action, this slaughter broke the native resistance movement that came to be called King Philip's War. The dead were the children, the promise; the elders, the memory; and the women, who in this particular society were the curers and, sometimes, the war chiefs. For not all the fighters who were absent at the moment of Turner's attack were, after all, "soldiers like my father." Two of the sachems who figured importantly in the war were women like my mother, like my grandmothers. Like me.[1]

One of these women sachems was Weetamoo, leader of the Rhode Island Pokassets, born into a heritage of native resistance; her father had challenged the presence of the Plymouth colonists in the earliest years of their settlement. Weetamoo's first marriage was to Alexander, son of Massasoit, the Pokasset sachem who figures in all the "First Thanksgiving" pageants as the noble leader of the quintessential Friendly Indians. While not as conciliatory as his father, Alexander continued Massasoit's practice of selling land to the English. One of the few things we know about the marriage of Alexander and Weetamoo is that she successfully brought suit

---

[1] For a readable account of King Philip's War, see Russell Bourne, *The Red King's Rebellion: Racial Politics in New England 1675–1678* (1990).

against him in the Plymouth courts to stop him selling off land belonging to her people. More than he, she seems to have comprehended the terrible implications of bargaining away the source of her people's life and identity.

Alexander died suddenly in the summer of 1664, after he had been force-marched into Plymouth for questioning about his attempts to sell land to rival colonies. The Plymouth authorities shrugged off his death as a result of his "choleric" temper, but most Algonquins, including Weetamoo and Philip, Alexander's younger brother and heir, believed the English had poisoned him, a conviction that helped Philip's efforts over the next decade to forge the Algonquin tribal groups into an American Indian resistance.

In 1675, after some hesitation, Weetamoo left her neutralist second husband and committed herself and her Pokassets wholly to Philip's cause. With Quinnapin, the young Narragansett sachem she married in this final year of her life, she attended Philip's councils of war, where she danced for power, helped to plan attacks and, increasingly, to direct retreats, as internal divisions among the Algonquin forces and the ravages of disease and hunger upon a population-on-the-run weakened Philip's allied forces. Weetamoo seems to have been especially brilliant at evasive actions, slipping hundreds of her people quietly past enemy lines, then dispersing them safely in the recesses of swamps and forests. And brilliant, above all, at sustaining them in hope, for she was clearly a spiritual as well as a tactical leader.

The end came for Weetamoo on August 6, 1676, when she was swept from a raft and drowned during a last-ditch escape attempt. The English impaled her severed head upon a pole at Taunton, Massachusetts, a sight that caused Algonquin people imprisoned there to send up "a most horrid and diabolical lamentation" for this woman whom the colonial strategists called "next unto Philip" in making the war.

In Mary Rowlandson's famous narrative, *A True History of the Captivity and Restoration of Mrs. Mary Rowlandson* (1682), we get an invaluable glimpse through English eyes of twelve weeks of daily wartime life in the band led by Weetamoo and Quinnapin, whose prisoner Mrs. Rowlandson became. Initially, Rowlandson of course sees all her captors as "hellhounds." In time, she grows to think of Quinnapin as a real friend; she marvels that no "savage" makes a move to rape her and that no one in this company starves, despite the scarcity of food; she notes with real respect the endurance and survival skills of Algonquin women. But when she speaks of Weetamoo, Rowlandson has not a good word to say. It isn't that she perceives Weetamoo as a leader who is complicit in the deaths of her loved ones; indeed, she seems to have no idea of Weetamoo's status except as one of Quinnapin's wives. It is Weetamoo's "vanity" that provokes Rowlandson to sound like a maid in a Restoration comedy, making sly remarks behind her pompous mistress's back. In Rowlandson's judgment, Weetamoo is "insolent," "haughty," "severe," a "proud gossip" who "bestow[s] every day, in dressing herself neat, as much time as any gentry of the land." It would seem above all to be Weetamoo's sure sense of her own self-worth and her commanding physical presence that most drive Mrs. Rowlandson up the wigwam wall. As well she might be driven: reading Rowlandson's narrative, one is struck by the rhetorical tensions between her obvious pride in her own feisty survival and her efforts to strike the proper notes of humility and gratitude to God expected in Puritan narrative. Weetamoo must truly have galled her.[2]

Mrs. Rowlandson was not alone. The unsubmissive behavior of American Indian women, the sexual freedom they enjoyed, and the political and economic authority they exercised in many tribes from widely scattered areas often confounded English, French, and Spanish colonists alike. During King Philip's War, a Massachusetts Bay colonist wrote despairingly back to England:

> . . . vain it is to expect anything but the most barbarous usage from such a people amongst whom the most mild and gentle sex delight in cruelties, and have utterly abandoned at once the two proper virtues of mankind, Pity and Modesty. (Bonfonti 1984, p. 38)[3]

The word *abandoned* here implies, of course, a falling away on the part of these tribal women from some natural and universal standard, one that must needs be biblical and patriarchal. Indeed, as Paula Gunn Allen (1986) and others have argued, there is much evidence to suggest that most New World societies were originally either gynocentric or organized on a "partnership model" that accorded authority to both sexes. But as colonization deepened, and tribes began to adopt the patriarchal system of the invaders, American Indian males often perceived their own women as harsh and unreasonable in their defiance of European Christian ethics and custom. In Quebec, the males of a Montagnais band joined with French Jesuits in a jeremiad against the Montagnais wives:

---

[2]For important insights on Rowlandson's narrative, see Annette Kolodny's chapter "Captives in Paradise" in *The Land Before Her: Fantasy and Experience of the American Frontiers, 1630–1860* (1984).

[3]To be fair, the writer was reacting to an incident, never verified, in which a number of Indian women were alleged to have attacked two colonists outside Sudbury, Massachusetts, beaten them to death with clubs, and then "cut off their privy members, which they carried away in triumph."

> It is you women . . . who are the cause of all
> misfortunes—it is you who keep the demons among
> us. You do not urge to be baptised . . . you are lazy
> about going to prayers; when you pass before the
> cross, you never salute it; you wish to be indepen-
> dent. Now know that you will obey your husbands.
> (Thwaites 1896–1901, vol. 18, pp. 105–107)[4]

Disobedience is a slippery concept, implying as it does an authority that claims some right to exact certain behaviors, generally a Father Who Knows Best. Disobedience is a doubly tricky concept for a woman in most societies. To obey external authority may mean she is disobeying the promptings of her truest self; her choice of whether to be obedient or disobedient is often really a choice between being good and being powerful, between being someone's good girl and being herself. And disobedience can only be a trebly complex issue for the women of a colonized people, where *two* outside authorities lay claim to her, when she is called, as Paiute-Shoshone poet nila northSun would put it, by both the way and the way things are (1977, p. 13).

For the few who know about their stories, it's probably easy enough to see those Montagnais wives as spunky rebels engaged in a war of nerves with the Jesuit "blackrobes" and Christianized husbands; it is easy enough for us to understand that Weetamoo was a hero of the resistance. "*Of course*," we say, from the distance of three centuries, "*rebels with abundant cause*." But when I think about history's treatment of the women who figured in King Philip's War, it is Awashonks who troubles me; Awashonks, the *other* woman sachem; Awashonks, leader of the Sakon-nets, whose ancestral lands abutted on those of Weetamoo and the Pokassets.

The glimpses we have of Awashonks through colonial documents and memoirs are scattered and contradictory, but she seems to have valued peace and survival above all else. Apparently, she felt bullied by both Philip and the English and tried to steer a neutral course. She was sufficiently assimilated to send her son to the Indian Charity School at Cambridge, but those who proposed to educate him did not themselves seem overly bright to her. In 1671, obeying orders from Plymouth, Awashonks confiscated forty-two rifles from her own warriors, but despite the repeated letters and mes-

---

[4]See also the wonderful article by Carol Devens, "Separate Confrontations: Gender as a Factor in Indian Adaptation to European Colonization
in New France" (1986).

sages she sent, the colonial authorities never came to collect them, and the weapons lay stacked for months in her wigwam.

Awashonks finally joined Philip, succumbing to pressure from her own young warriors, but broke with him sometime in the spring of 1676 and made her way back to Rhode Island, where she at last agreed to sign a treaty with Plymouth in return for a blanket pardon. For her pains, she and her Sakonnets were made prisoners of war for weeks. When at last Plymouth decided she was trustworthy, Awashonks staged a great celebration, with the Sakonnets ranging themselves in concentric dance circles about a bonfire and snatching from the fire different burning brands, each of which they named for enemies of the English they would now help to vanquish. With that ceremony, Awashonks vanishes from the attention of history, dancing, as Benjamin Church once described her, "in a foaming sweat," trusting that her people may yet be safe and free (Church 1854, p. 22).[5]

Awashonks, to be sure, is not a name familiar to most people. But La Malinche, who conducted her lover Cortés into Mexico; Pocahontas, who rescued John Smith and wed John Rolfe; Sacagawea, who guided Lewis and Clark clear to the Pacific—these are the better-known native women whose fame rests upon being good Indians. They are the "Indian princesses," the "forest flowers," the "dusky virgins" of American iconography, who so charmingly acquiesce to European desires. But no matter how "good" an American Indian woman's conduct in European eyes, there remains the white chronicler's tendency to mistrust her, even to snicker at her. Despite her obedient capitulation to the conqueror and her willingness to satisfy his needs, she is tainted to some degree by her "betrayal" of her own people, by her very compliance, even if it is abetting the dominant culture, even if her compliance is a strategy of survival for her, for her people. In most societies, any woman who takes definitive action of some sort is bound to come in for criticism; for a woman trying to negotiate between two cultures, like Awashonks, or Pocahontas, or Sacagawea, it is a no-win situation. The white critic Charles Larson's remarks about Pocahontas are typical of this phenomenon: "In a way," he writes, "Pocahontas was a kind of traitor to her own people. Again and again she let them down. All the things she has been admired for over the years . . . must have increased [their] rancor" (1978, p. 27).

Laguna Pueblo/Sioux writer Paula Gunn Allen has undertaken the project of a series of brilliant poetic monologues in which these native women accused of selling out tell their own stories. Allen lifts these stories beyond the reach of simplistic judgment, conveying the true moral and

---

[5]Benjamin Church's son based his account of King Philip's War on his father's reminiscences. It first appeared in 1716.

historical complexity of their situations. Allen's Sacagawea, for example, muses in "The One Who Skins Cats":

> Oh, I probably betrayed some Indians.
> But I took care of my own Shoshonis.
> That's what a Chief Woman does, anyway.
> And the things my Indian people call me now
> they got from the whiteman, or, I should say,
> the white women. Because it's them who said
> I led the whitemen into the wilderness and back,
> and they survived the journey with my care.
> It's true they came like barbarian hordes
> after then, and that the Indian lost our place.
> We was losing it anyway.
>
> I didn't lead the whitemen, you know. I just
> went along for the ride. And along the way
> I learned what a chief should know,
> and because I did, my own Snake people survived . . .
>
> Maybe there was a better way to skin that cat,
> but I used the blade that was put in my hand — . . .
> (Allen 1988, p. 18)

Allen sees her Sacagawea as operating and making choices in a most complex world. It is, precisely, a world of such moral and historical complexity that is projected in traditional American Indian oral tales. Understandably, non-Indian translators have often tried to twist and pinch and edit American Indian material into a shape that accords with Euro-American understandings of how the world works. But, in fact, almost every body of traditional tribal literature suggests that its creators understand and tolerate a very wide range of possible human actions. The coyote tales told by the Navajo and Pueblo peoples of the Southwest, for example, are often presented as teaching stories that convey simple lessons in the manner of Aesop's fables: *Don't be like Old Lady Coyote and be disrespectful to your elders, or Grandmother Spider will see to it that you fall off a cliff.* The stories *can*, of course, suggest proper behaviors; Coyote does things that are recognizably foolish or forbidden. But as one of Barre Toelken's Navajo informants attempted to explain to him, that is not all they do. Yellowman told Toelken, "If [Coyote] did not do all those things, then those things would not be possible in the world" (Toelken 1969).[6] The stories, in other words, partly serve to model the astonishing range of human behavior possible in the variegated and dynamic world we inhabit.

Traditional stories are often especially interesting in what they have to say about women's roles. There is a particular sort of story found all over the Americas that suggests that women's primary relationship and responsibility is not exactly toward human beings, but rather toward the natural world of which all beings are part. Such stories usually begin in a human setting that is somehow depleted—the young woman's people may be suffering from sickness, or famine, or war, or from an overbearing human leader. The woman asserts herself by some act; she may simply wander carelessly away from the village or she may deliberately flout an order. In any case, this act somehow serves to put her in contact with a spirit being who embodies some aspect of the natural world. Often, she and this being become lovers. Sooner or later, she returns to the human village, usually with some gift of power or knowledge that helps restore her community to its proper balance. The spirit being she encounters may be a bird or an animal, like Great Horned Owl Husband; it may be a plant, or a weather being like Whirlwind Man. It can even be the essence of a great waterfall.[7]

> In the old days, a young Iroquois woman lives in a village near Neahga, the great waterfall. Her name is Ahweyoh, Water Lily. Every year in her village many people suddenly fall ill and die, and now Ahweyoh has no family left except for her father's sister, who mistreats her. This aunt assigns Ahweyoh the hardest chores, feeds her scraps, dresses her in tatters, and allows no man to come courting her, though many would like to because of her beauty and her good nature.
>
> One day, the Aunt announces that she has at last found a husband for Ahweyoh, who is excited until she learns that the prospective bridegroom is Sweaty Hands, the meanest, ugliest wife beater in the village, who is rumored to practice evil medicine on the side. When Ahweyoh realizes she cannot persuade her aunt to undo the match, she defies her. By night, she steals a canoe and paddles off down the Niagra River, where she is swept toward the great falls. As she hears the voice of the Thunder

[6]See also my essay "Coyote Ortiz" in Paula Gunn Allen's *Studies in American Indian Literature: Critical Essays and Course Designs* (1983).

[7]For a much more leisurely discussion of this sort of story, see my chapter, written with Paula Gunn Allen, "Earthy Relations, Carnal Knowledge: Southwestern American Indian Writers and Landscape" (1987).

Beings who live in the cataract, she closes her eyes and resigns herself to death, but just when her boat spills over the lip of the falls, she feels herself being caught up and then gently set down on some soft surface. She opens her eyes upon a curtain of plunging water and mist; she is behind the waterfall, and three handsome men are smiling down on her. They are the Thunder Beings, who have caught her in a blanket and brought her to their place behind the falls, where they take pleasure in the way the falls echo the noise of their own thunderstorms. For some years, she makes her home happily with them. In time, she falls in love with the head Thunder Being and bears him a little son, which necessitates her return to her village, for, as her Thunder-husband points out, the child must know what it is to live as a human being. But she must conceal both her identity and her son's, and she must listen very carefully to the next thing he tells her. The cause of the sickness that ravages her village is a great snake who hides beneath their graveyard and feeds on their buried dead. In secret, this snake poisons the village water sources every year in order to ensure a good supply of corpses. Now, while the snake is still sleeping, she is to convince the villagers to move to a new site.

There is not space here to tell all of Ahweyoh's story, but suffice it to say that she does defeat serpent, aunt, and Sweaty Hands all three. In its writhing death struggle, the serpent knocks off a sizeable chunk of ledge, at once creating Horseshoe Falls and destroying the Thunder Beings' watery house, but they take up permanent residence in the sky, where Ahweyoh eventually joins them. By the end of the story, she has redeemed her village from the rigid, life-denying tyranny of her aunt and Sweaty Hands and realigned her people more closely with the spirits of the natural world with whom it is vital to be in touch. And she has become a being of power in her own right, and all because she did not do as she was told.[8]

The story of Ahweyoh may sound superficially at points like certain European stories — "Cinderella" and the myth of Psyche come to mind. But how different is this tale's emphasis, from the point when Ahweyoh just says no to oppression and makes off in her canoe. How different, too, from the legions of white-manufactured "Indian tales" of Indian lover-martyrs throwing themselves off precipices and into rivers; Ahweyoh and her Thun-

[8]For Ahweyoh's story, I am mainly following Joe Bruchac's version in his *Iroquois Stories: Heroes and Heroines, Monsters and Magic* (1985, pp. 146–154). Thanks, Joe.

der Being are a far cry from Running Bear and Little White Dove, who can only be together in the Happy Hunting Ground of American popular music and imagination.

Here, at the end, I am lost in waking thoughts about my dream of those other falls, Peskeompskut, whose images have possessed me all during the time I have been writing this essay. Images of the falls themselves, of course, but images of my family as well, distantly Algonquin on both sides—Micmac on my mother's, most likely Micmac on my father's as well, but just possibly Montagnais. And I think of all those Frenettes and Gignacs on his side, who I never met, but who I am said to resemble—one pair of sisters, especially, who my elderly second cousin will only describe, through tight lips, as having been "wild." I think of those seventeenth-century Montagnais women defying husbands and priests, and of my father's favorite damning epithet, one that did not strike me as odd until I was well into my thirties. *This is a house of matriarchs*! he would scream at my mother and her mother and me, slamming the door of our small crowded apartment. At his own mother he did not dare to scream, but behind her back that was what he called her, too, at his angriest: *matriarch*.

And I wonder, still, who those two women may be who accompany me on my dream walk over the falls. Images of my relatives, probably; grandmothers, or mother and grandmother. Or maybe those two wild Gignac sisters on my father's side. Or maybe, in some way, it's those two sachems who chose such different paths of disobedience, Weetamoo and Awashonks, who visit my dream. Yes, it might be them. Or some women like them.

# References

*In this welter of wild women, special thanks to John
Crawford for some cunning whitewater navigation.*

Allen, P. G. 1986. *The Sacred Hoop: Recovering the Feminine in American Indian Traditions.* Boston: Beacon Press.

_____. 1988. *Skins and Bones.* Albuquerque: West End Press.

Bonfanti, L. 1984. *Biographies and Legends of the New England Indians,* vol. 4. Wakefield, Mass.: Pride Publications.

Bourne, R. 1990. *The Red King's Rebellion: Racial Political New England 1675-1678.* New York: Atheneum.

Bruchac, J. 1985. *Iroquois Stories: Heroes and Heroines, Monsters and Magic.* Freedom, Calif.: The Crossing Press.

Church, Thomas. 1854. *The History of the Great Indian War of 1675 and 1676, Commonly Called King Philip's War.* Hartford: Silas Andros and Sons.

Devens, C. 1986. Separate confrontations: Gender as a factor in Indian adaptation to European colonization in New France. *American Quarterly* 38:461–480.

Kolodny, A. 1984. *The Land Before Her: Fantasy and Experience of the American Frontiers, 1630–1860.* Chapel Hill, N.C.: University of North Carolina Press.

Larson, C. 1978. *American Indian Fiction.* Albuquerque: University of New Mexico Press.

northSun, n. 1977. The way and the way things are. *Diet Pepsi and Nacho Cheese.* Fallon, Nev.: Duck Down Press.

Rowlandson, M. W. 1682. *A True History of the Captivity and Restoration of Mrs. Mary Rowlandson, a Minister's Wife in New England.* London: Joseph Pool.

Smith, P. C. 1983. Coyote Ortiz. In *Studies in American Indian Literature: Critical Essays and Course Designs*, P. G. Allen, ed. New York: The Modern Language Association, pp. 192–210.

Smith, P. C., and Allen, P. G. 1987. Earthy relations, carnal knowledge: Southwestern American Indian writers and landscape. In *The Desert Is No Lady: Southwestern Landscapes in Women's Writing and Art*, Norwood and Monk, eds. New Haven, Conn.: Yale University Press, pp. 174–196.

Thwaites, R. G., ed. 1896–1901. *The Jesuit Relations and Allied Documents: Travels and Explorations of the Jesuit Missionaries in New France, 110–1791,* 73 vols. Cleveland: The Burrow Brothers Co. Reprinted New York: Pageant Book Co., 1959.

Toelken, B. 1969. The "pretty languages" of Yellowman: Genre, mode, and texture in Navajo Coyote narratives. *Genre* 2:211–235.

# ANALYZING RESISTANCE

## BEDOUIN WOMEN'S DISCOURSES

### Lila Abu-Lughod

**R**esistance has become in recent years a popular focus of work in anthropology, feminist studies, and a range of other fields. Despite the theoretical sophistication of many such studies and their contribution to the widening of our definition of the political, it seems to me that because they are more concerned with finding resistors and explaining resistance than with examining power, they do not explore as fully as they might the implications of the forms of resistance they locate. There is perhaps a tendency to romanticize resistance, to read all forms of resistance as signs of the ineffectiveness of systems of power and of the resilience and creativity of the human spirit in its refusal to be dominated. By reading resistance only in this way, we collapse distinctions between forms of resistance and foreclose certain questions about the workings of power.

I want to argue here for a small shift in perspective in the way we look at resistance—a small shift that will have serious analytical consequences. I want to suggest that resistance may be used as a *diagnostic* of power. In this, I am taking my cue from Foucault, whose theories, or, as he prefers to put it, analytics of power and resistance, although complex and not always consistant, are at least worth exploring. One of his central propositions, advanced in his most explicit discussion of power, in the first volume of *The History of Sexuality*, is the controversial assertion that "where there is power, there is resistance" (1978, pp. 95–96). Whatever else this assertion implies, certainly Foucault is using this hyperbole to force us to question our understanding of power as always and essentially repressive. As part of his project of deromanticizing the liberatory discourse of our twentieth-century so-called sexual revolution, he is interested in showing how power is something that works not just negatively, by denying, restricting, prohibiting, or repressing, but also by producing forms of pleasure,

This article has been adapted from "The Romance of Resistance: Tracing Transformations of Power Through Bedouin Women." Published in *American Ethnologist* (1990) 17:41–55. One folktale also previously appeared in *Veiled Sentiments: Honor and Poetry in a Bedouin Society* (Berkeley: University of California Press, 1986).

systems of knowledge, goods, and discourses.[1] He adds what some have viewed as a pessimistic point about resistance by completing the sentence just quoted as follows: "where there is power, there is resistance, and yet, or rather consequently, this resistance is never in a position of exteriority in relation to power" (1978, pp. 95–6). This latter insight about resistance is especially provocative, but to appreciate its significance one must invert the first part of the proposition. This gives us the intuitively sensible "where there is resistance there is power," which is both less problematic and potentially more fruitful because it enables us to move away from abstract theories of power toward methodological strategies for the study of power in particular situations. As Foucault puts it, when he himself advocates this inversion, we can then use resistance "as a chemical catalyst so as to bring to light power relations, locate their position, find out their points of application and the methods used" (1982, pp. 209, 211). We could continue to look for and consider nontrivial all sorts of resistance, but instead of taking these as signs of human freedom, we will use them strategically to tell us more about forms of power and how people are caught up in them.

To illustrate the usefulness of this idea, I will be discussing some forms of resistance I found among the women of the Awlad 'Ali Bedouin with whom I lived for several periods in the late 1970s and mid-1980s. The Awlad 'Ali are former sheepherders along the Egyptian coast from west of Alexandria to the Libyan border. The first arena of resistance, one I have described elsewhere (Abu-Lughod 1985), is the sexually segregated women's world where women daily enact all sorts of minor defiances of the restrictions enforced by elder men in the community.

Women use secrets and silences to their advantage. They often collude to hide knowledge from the men; they cover for each other in minor matters, like secret trips to healers or visits to their friends and relatives; they smoke in secret and quickly put out their cigarettes when children come running to warn them that men are approaching. These forms of resistance indicate that one way power is exercised in relation to women is through a range of prohibitions and restrictions, which they both embrace in their

---

[1]A particularly clear statement of his view of power as productive is the following: "What makes power hold good, what makes it accepted, is simply the fact that it doesn't only weigh on us as a force that says no, but that it traverses and produces things, it induces pleasure, forms of knowledge, produces discourse. It needs to be considered as a productive network that runs through the whole social body, much more than as a negative instance whose function is repression" (Foucault 1980, p. 225). His position on resistance is more ambiguous. Despite his insistence that resistance is always tied to power, he occasionally implies the persistence of some residual freedom (Foucault 1982, p. 225).

support for a system of sexual segration and resist as suggested by the fact that they fiercely protect the inviolability of their separate sphere, that sphere where the defiances take place.

A second and widespread form of resistance is Bedouin girls' and women's resistance to marriages. Indeed, one of the major powers that families, and especially elder male relatives like fathers and paternal uncles, wield is control over the arrangement of marriages. Despite their apparent power, actual marriage arrangements are always complicated and involve many people, especially mothers and female relatives. Mothers sometimes successfully block marriages their daughters do not want, even though fathers or other male guardians are supposed to have control. For example, on my last visit to the Bedouin community, I found out that my host's eldest unmarried daughter had just narrowly avoided being married off. Her father had run into some friends in the market and they had asked if their sons could marry his daughter and niece. Marriages are normally arranged between allies, friends, and kin, and to refuse someone without a good excuse is difficult. He had agreed to it and then returned home to inform his wife.

She reported to me that she had been furious and told him she refused to let her daughter marry into that family. They lived in tents in the desert and her daughter, who had grown up in a house and did not have many of the old Bedouin skills such as taking care of tents or milking sheep, would find it a hard life for which she was not prepared. Moreover, the family that had asked for her was in trouble. The reason they lived in tents was that two of their members had gotten into a fight with someone and accidently killed him. According to Bedouin customary law, they had to seek refuge with another family, leaving behind their homes and land. They lived in fear, knowing that the kinsmen of the man they had killed would want revenge. My host's wife did not want her daughter to be a widow. So she refused. Her husband got angry, she told me, and he said, "What am I suppose to tell them? I already agreed." He then marched off to his niece's mother, to enlist her support. But she refused to let her only daughter marry into that family. The women suggested that he inform the men to whom he had promised the girls that the girls' male cousins had decided to claim them. This is a cousin's right, so he was able to save face and, indeed, the marriages never went through.

When men are stubborn, however, or so caught up in strategies and relations of obligations with other men that they will not or cannot reverse a decision, the women may not succeed. Even then, they are not necessarily silent. One woman, whose daughter was forced to marry a cousin, sang a song as the groom's relatives came to pick up her daughter for the wedding:

> You're not of the same stature as these
> your true match is the man with the golden insignia . . .

The song taunted them with the suggestion that her daughter was more worthy of an officer than of the poor man who was getting her.

Neither are unmarried girls always silent about their feelings about marriages. Girls sing songs as they get water from the wells and publicly at weddings. Among the songs I heard about the men they did not want to marry were the following:

> I won't take an old man, not I
> I'll give him a shove and he'll fall in a ditch
>
> I don't want the old fez on the hill
> what I want is a new Peugeot
>
> God damn the uncle's son
> Lord don't lead me near no blood relative

Significantly, the young women singing these songs were objecting in particular to older men and their paternal cousins, two categories of men who tend to have binding ties on their fathers that would make their marriage requests hard to refuse.

The most interesting cases are those where women themselves actually resist marriages that have been arranged for them. Their retrospective narratives of resistance were among the most popular storytelling events I heard. The following one was told to me and a group of her daughters-in-law by the old matriarch of the community in which I lived. The events must have taken place at least sixty years ago. She began by explaining that the first person to whom she was to have been married was a first cousin. His relatives had come to her household and conducted the negotiations and had even gone so far as to slaughter some sheep, the practice that seals the marriage agreement. She went on:

> He was a first cousin, and I didn't want him. He was an old man and we were living near each other, eating out of one bowl [sharing meals or living in one household]. They came and slaughtered a sheep and I started screaming, I started crying. And my father had bought a new gun, a cartridge gun. He said, "If you don't shut up, I'll send you flying with this gun."
> Well, there was a ravine and I went over and sat there all day. I sat next to it, saying, "Possess me, spirits, possess me." I wanted the spirits to possess me; I wanted to go crazy. Half the night would pass and I'd be sitting there. I'd be sitting there, until Braika [a relative] came. And she'd cry with me and

then drag me home by force and I'd go sleep in her tent. After twelve days, my cousin's female relatives were dying the black strip for the top of the tent. They were about to finish sewing the tent I'd live in. And they had brought my trousseau. I said, "I'll go get the dye for you." I went and found they had ground the black powder, and it was soaking in the pot, the last of the dye, and I flipped it over— Pow!—on my face, on my hair, on my hands until I was completely black.

My father came back and said, "What's happened here? What's the matter with this girl? Hey, you, what's the matter?" The women explained. He went and got a pot of water and a piece of soap and said, "If you don't wash your hands and face I'll . . ." So I wash my hands, but only the palms, and I wipe my face, but I only get a little off from here and there. And I'm crying the whole time. All I did was cry. Then they went and put some supper in front of me. He said, "Come here and eat dinner." I'd eat and my tears were salting each mouthful. I had spent twelve days, and nothing had entered my mouth.

The next afternoon my brother came by and said to me, "I'm hungry, can you make me a snack?" I went to make it for him, some fresh flatbread, and I was hungry. I had taken a loaf and I put a bit of honey and a bit of winter oil in a bowl. I wanted to eat, I who hadn't eaten a thing in twelve days. But then he said, "What do you think of this? On Friday they're doing the wedding and today is Thursday and there aren't even two days between now and then." I found that the loaf I was going to eat I'd dropped. He asked, "Well, do you want to go to so-and-so's or do you want to go to your mother's brother's?" There was an eclipse; the sun went out and nothing was showing. I said, "I'll go to my maternal uncle's." I put my shawl on my head and started running. I ran on foot until I got to my uncle's. I was in bad shape, a mess.

She then went on to describe how her uncle had sent her back, with instructions to his son to send greetings to her father and ask him to delay a bit, perhaps she would come around. She continued,

>So I went home. After that I didn't hear another
>word. The trousseau just sat there in the chest, and
>the tent, they sewed it and got it all ready and then
>put it away in their tent. And autumn came and we
>migrated west, and we came back again. When we
>came back, they said, "We want to have the wed-
>ding." I began screaming. They stopped. No one
>spoke about it again.

This old woman's narrative, which included two more episodes of resisted marriages before she agreed to one, follows the pattern of many I heard — of women who had resisted the decisions of their fathers, uncles, or older brothers and eventually won. Her story, like theirs, let others know that resistance to marriage was possible.

A third form of Bedouin women's resistance is what could be called sexually irreverent discourse. What I am referring to are instances when women make fun of men and manhood, even though official ideology glorifies them and women respect, veil for, and sometimes fear them. In this irreverence one can trace the ways the code of sexual morality and the ideology of sexual difference are forms of men's power. Women seem only too glad when men fail to live up to the ideals of autonomy and manhood, the ideals on which their alleged moral superiority and social precedence are based, especially if they fail as a result of sexual desire. Women joke about certain men behind their backs and they also make fun of men in general ways. For example, in a folktale I recorded in 1987, a man with two wives is cuckolded by the younger one but foolishly rewards her and punishes his obedient and faithful senior wife.

It began as the story of a young man who, with his brothers, had kicked out their mother. They were poor, and he began to wander around looking for work. A rich family took him in, gave him animals to raise, found a wife for him, built him a house, and gave him a slave to herd for him. He became rich and proud and suddenly announced that he wanted to leave them, to live on his own. They were disturbed and didn't understand why, but he insisted and took his wife and slave somewhere else. Not satisfied with the wife they had chosen for him, he then married a second wife he chose himself.

Then one day he announced that he wanted to go on the pilgrimage to Mecca. He told his wives and the slave to stay camped in the same place until he returned. He had his two wives sewn up as a precaution to preserve their chastity.

The woman who was telling me this tale paused because this was as unusual a detail for her as it is for us. She then proceeded dramatically with the telling.

Every day the slave went off to herd the camels and then came home to the camp where the two wives were. Now the older wife, I guess she was pathetic, modest. And the wife that he took second, she was one of those who . . . Well, shortly after he left, the young wife said to the slave, "Let's move camp." The older wife said, "No, we shouldn't move. He told us to stay till he returned." The young wife said, "No, I want to set up my tent in a new place. Let's go to another area." So they moved.

The young wife had undone the stitches. Right away this woman had said "come here" to the slave. The other one remained sewn up. The old one. So they moved and set up camp in an empty area. There was nothing to eat or drink there and the camels and the sheep started going hungry and dying. The carcasses of the dead beasts lay there and crows came to eat them. Then each day the crows would circle around the camp. As the slave was putting medicine on the camels, he'd say:

> Crows make people happy but I'm afraid of crows
> they bring us the shadow of the one who's longing
> and blinded from missing us

The slave was afraid because he and the old wife knew what the crows meant — they herald the arrival of people who've been away. The young one didn't know. Then one day, the man arrived home. He said to them, "You moved camp. I wouldn't have found you if the crows hadn't brought me. I started walking in their trail, every night in a place, every night in a different place. I moved with the crows until I found you."

That one had met him, the young one. She had come running out to greet him saying,

> In my joy for you
> I undid it just for you
> but Ahmad's mother is still all sealed up

"See what women are like!" the woman telling the story commented. Then she continued, "So he went to the old one and found her disgusting, bound and putrid." She laughed as she ended the tale, "He said to her, go away. I divorce you. And he took back only the young wife and they moved camp."

The folktale has many messages, but one of them is certainly that men are fools whose desires override their supposed piety and undermine their overt demands that women be proper and chaste. The kind of power this tale attempts to subvert, and thus diagnoses, is the power of control over women's sexuality that the Bedouin moral system entails.

Bedouin women's resistance also takes the form of an irreverence toward the mark of masculinity and the privileges this automatically grants. For example, Bedouin men and women avow a preference for sons, saying people are happier at the birth of a boy. And yet, in one discussion, when I asked what they did when the baby turned out to be a boy, one old woman said, "If it's a boy, they slaughter a sheep for him. The boy's name is exalted. He has a little pisser that dangles." And all the women present laughed. Another woman told the following folktale, illustrative of the difference in moral nature between a compassionate and loving daughter and an abusive and heartless son.

There was once a woman with nine daughters. When she became pregnant again, she prayed for a boy and made an oath to give up one of her daughters as an offering if she were granted a son. She did give birth to a boy. When they moved camp, she left behind one daughter. Soon a man came by on a horse and found the girl tied up. He asked her story, untied her, and took her with him and cared for her. Meanwhile, the boy grew up and took a wife. His wife demanded that he make his mother a servant. He did this, and the old mother was forced to do all the housework for the daughter-in-law [a reversal of proper relations between mother-in-law and daughter-in-law].

One day they decided to move camp. They loaded up the camels and traveled and traveled. The old mother had to walk, driving the sheep. She got tired and was eventually left behind. Lost, she wandered and wandered until she came upon a camp. The people in the camp called to her and invited her in. They asked her story. She told them she had not always been a servant and recounted her tale. When the people in the camp heard this story, they went running to tell one of the women. It turned out she was the old woman's daughter who had been abandoned as a child. She came, questioned the old woman, and, once convinced, embraced and kissed her, took her into her tent, washed her clothes for her, fed her, and cared well for her.

By and by, the son came looking for his mother. He rode up to the camp and asked people, "Have you seen an old servant wandering around?" The woman who (unknown to him) was his sister invited him into her tent. She demanded that a ram be brought and slaughtered in his honor. She then asked him, "Where is the *rihm* [womb] of the ram?" The brother looked at her in surprise, answering, "A ram has no *rihm*, didn't you know?"

She then revealed her identity and told him her story. She refused to let him take his mother back and scolded him for having so mistreated her.

The moral of the story turns on the double meaning of the Arabic trilateral root *rahama*, from which the word *rihm* (womb), as well as a word meaning pity, compassion, or mercy, is derived. Thus the story links wombs (femaleness) with compassion and caring. The woman who told me the story added this commentary:

> You see, the male has no womb. He has nothing but a
> little penis [laughingly wiggling her finger in a con-
> temptuous gesture].

Here the usual terms are reversed and the male genitals are made the sign of a lack — the lack of a womb.

An even clearer example of women's irreverence is a folktale I heard women and girls tell to children, which went as follows.

> There were an old woman and old man who traveled into the desert and set up camp in a lonely area where there were wolves. They had brought with them seven goats, a cow, a donkey, and a puppy. The first night, a wolf came to the tent. He called out to them "Ho!" and then demanded, "Give me someone to eat for dinner tonight!" So the old man and woman gave him a goat. He came the next night and called out the same thing, asking, "Who will you give me to eat for dinner tonight?" They gave him another goat. This went on night after night until the old couple had given the wolf all seven goats, the donkey, the cow, and the puppy. Then they realized that they had no more animals to give him and that he would eat them. The old man said to his wife, "Hide me in a basket we'll hang from the tentpole. And you, hide in the big urn." So she hung up the basket with the old man in it and she hid inside the pottery urn.
>
> When the wolf came that night, no one answered his call. He came into the tent and sniffed around. Then he looked up. Now, the basket had a tear in it and the old man's genitals were showing — they were dangling out of the hole in the basket. The wolf kept jumping up, trying to bite them. The old woman watching this started laughing so hard she farted. This split open the urn she was hiding in, and the wolf ate her. Then he nipped at the old man's genitals until he brought down the basket and

ate the old man whole, too. And then he went to sleep in their little tent.

The last time I heard this story, the group of women and girls with whom I was sitting laughed hard. The storyteller teased me for having asked to hear this story, and her final comment was, "The old woman was laughing at the wolf biting her husband's genitals." There is rich material for a Freudian analysis here, and there is no doubt that male fears of castration and of being cuckolded could be read in this folktale and the one about the man and his two wives discussed above. The messages in both are complex. Yet it is important to remember that it is women who are telling the stories, women who are listening to them, and women who are responding with glee to the things men dread.

Folktales, songs, and jokes are not the only subversive discourses among women in Bedouin society, although they indicate the significance of the ideology of sexual difference itself as a form of power. In my book (Abu-Lughod 1986) I analyzed what I consider to be the most important of the subversive discourses of resistance in Bedouin society—a kind of oral lyric poetry. These poem/songs, known as *ghinnāwas* (little songs), are recited mostly by women and young men, usually in the midst of ordinary conversations between intimates. What is most striking about them is that people express through them sentiments that differ radically from those they express in their ordinary-language conversations, sentiments of vulnerability and love. Many of these songs concern relationships with members of the opposite sex toward whom they respond, outside of poetry, with anger or denial of concern.

I argued that most people's ordinary public responses are framed in terms of the code of honor or modesty. Through these responses, they live and show themselves to be living up to the moral code. Poetry carries the sentiments that violate this code, the vulnerability to others that is ordinarily a sign of dishonorable lack of autonomy and the romantic love that is considered immoral and immodest. Since the moral code is one of the most important means of perpetuating the unequal structures of power, the violations of the code must be understood as ways of resisting the system and challenging the authority of those who represent and benefit from it. When examined for what it can tell us about power, however, this subversive discourse of poetry suggests that social domination also works at the level of constructing, delimiting, and giving meaning to personal emotions.

The Bedouin attitude toward this type of poetry and toward those who recite it returns us to some of the central issues of power and resistance. Poems are recited mostly in situations of social closeness and equality. The only exception to this in the past were wedding festivities, which, not surprisingly, dignified older men avoided. This avoidance, along with people's opinions that this type of poetry was risqué and un-Islamic, suggested their uneasy recognition of the subversiveness of the genre. On the other hand, among the Bedouins with whom I lived, poetry was cherished.

This ambivalence about poetry suggested to me that certain forms of resistance by the less powerful in Bedouin society could be admired, even by those whose interests the system supported. I argued that this attitude was connected to the Bedouin valuation of resistance itself, a valuation associated with the larger political sphere and men's activities, whether traditional and tribal or current and government-directed. It is a value in contradiction with the structures of inequality within the family, where gender comes into play. Women take advantage of these contradictions in their society to assert themselves and to resist. But they do so, most clearly in the case of poetry, through locally given traditional forms, a fact which suggests that, in some sense at least, these forms have been produced by power relations and cannot be seen as independent of them. I take this as a good example of what Foucault (1978, pp. 95–96) was trying to get at in suggesting we not necessarily see resistance as a reactive force somehow independent of or outside of the system of power.

The everyday forms of Bedouin women's resistance described above pose a number of analytical dilemmas. First, how might we develop theories that give these women credit for resisting in a variety of creative ways the power of those who control so much of their lives, without either misattributing to them forms of consciousness or politics — something like feminist consciousness or feminist politics — or devaluing their practices as prepolitical, primitive, or even misguided? Second, how might we account for the fact that Bedouin women both resist and support the existing system of power (they support it through practices like veiling, for example) without resorting to analytical concepts like false consciousness, which dismisses their own understanding of their situation, or impression management, which makes of them cynical manipulators? Third, how might we acknowledge that their forms of resistance, such as folktales and poetry, may be culturally provided without immediately assuming that even though we cannot therefore call them cathartic personal expressions, they must somehow be safety valves. I struggled with some of these dilemmas in my earlier work and I find them in the work of others.

With the shift in perspective I am advocating, asking not about the status of resistance but about what the forms of resistance indicate about the forms of power that they are up against, we are onto new ground. In addition to questions such as whether official ideology is really ever hegemonic or whether cultural or verbal resistance counts as much as other kinds, we can begin to ask what can be learned about power if we take for granted that resistances, of whatever form, signal sites of struggle. The forms I have described for Bedouin women suggest that some of the kinds of power relations in which they are caught up work through restrictions on movement and everyday activities, through elder kinsmen's control over marriage, through patrilineal parallel cousin marriage, through a moral system that defines superiority in terms of particular characteristics (like autonomy) that men are structurally more capable of achieving, through a set of practices that imply that maleness is sufficient justification for privilege, and through the linking of sets of sentiments to respectability and moral worth. These are not the only things at work — there are also such things as elder kinsmen's or husbands' control over productive resources, things which may or may not be resisted directly. But to discount the former as merely ideological is to fall into the familiar dichotomies that have kept people from looking at the most significant aspect of this situation: that power relations take many forms, have many aspects, and interweave. And by presupposing some sort of hierarchy of significant and insignificant forms of power, we may be blocking ourselves from exploring the ways in which these forms may actually be working simultaneously, in concert or at cross-purposes.

## References

Abu-Lughod, L. 1986. *Veiled Sentiments*: *Honor and Poetry in a Bedouin Society*. Berkeley, Calif.: University of California Press.

_____. 1985. A community of secrets. *Signs: Journal of Women in Culture and Society* 10:637–657.

Foucault, M. 1978. *The History of Sexuality. Vol. 1: An Introduction*. New York: Random House.

_____. 1980. *Power/Knowledge*. Colin Gordon, ed. New York: Pantheon.

_____. 1982. Afterword: the subject and power. In *Beyond Structuralism and Hermeneutics*, Hubert Dreyfuss and Paul Rabinow. Chicago: University of Chicago Press, pp. 208–226.

# CREATING

*a*

# SELF

# STRATEGIES OF DEFIANCE

## THE QUEST OF THE WIFE OF BATH

## Judith Grossman

**W**hen the Wife of Bath, in Chaucer's *Canterbury Tales*, rips three pages out of her husband's book of treatises against women, it is an act of vengeance for her oppression by the written word. The authority of the text, wielded by a male clerical elite, she correctly sees as her enemy. And this presses a question on any woman writer who takes her in hand: Which side are you on? For we know with what adroitness, across generations, the cultural high ground and privileges of interpretation continue to be held by advantaged inner circles, inclusive though these may be of select cadres of women. Consequently, even as we participate in the making of meaning through written texts, it's proper to imagine the presence of a woman standing now in the place of Alison of Bath, slighted for living the body's life more than the mind's, whether for reasons of temperament or of cultural or economic coercion.

In this matter the example of Chaucer's mature writing, which effectively undermines coherence of judgment, has always seemed instructive to me, and nowhere more than in the Wife of Bath's Prologue and Tale. To be sure, he begins in the General Prologue with a satirical design, offering his aristocratic audience the comic spectacle of a shamelessly vulgar *bourgeoise*, flaunting her too-big hat, gaudy red stockings, and aggressively sharp spurs. But once he turns to impersonating her own voice, it is as if suppressed energies rise up through that original intention. One may speculate that Chaucer's own history as an upwardly mobile *bourgeois* dependent on royal patronage made its mark here. But my concern is rather with the dual agenda that emerges in the discourse as ascribed to Alison herself: first, her belligerent opposition to the male authorities by whom she has been stigmatized; and second, her efforts to secure places out of reach of their voices, their judgments, where her authentic desires can be expressed. Feminist literary scholars in the past decade and more have developed thorough interpretations of the Wife as a transgressive figure, but one who both confesses her fault and complains of the *a priori* definition of all women as evil. Certainly she is an admitted sinner, chiefly through sexual promiscuity beyond the bounds of her five marriages:

> For God so wys be my savacioun,[1]
>  ⸳ I ne loved nevere by no discrecioun,
> But evere folwede myn appetit,
> Al were he short, or long, or blak, or whit;
> I took no kep,[2] so that he liked me . . . (3.621–625)[3]

She admits also to pride, anger, acquisitiveness, lying, drunkenness, and systematic violation of the wife's duty of obedience to her husband. Since all is known to God, why deny it? She can only cast herself before him and hope for compassion.

However, the language she uses in making her confession is not precisely hers, since Chaucer is known to have drawn freely here on the extensive body of anti-woman literature — typically composed by churchmen to persuade young men to embrace ordination and celibacy (Martin 1990, p. 6). The issue of authenticity this raises has been explored by Carolyn Dinshaw, among others; she argues that Alison through her self-accusations enacts a primary stage in the awakening of women's independent consciousness that has been defined by Luce Irigaray in terms of a kind of aggressive mimicry. In Irigaray's words, "to play with mimesis is thus, for a woman, to try to recover the place of her exploitation by discourse, without allowing herself to be simply reduced to it" (quoted in Dinshaw 1989, p. 115). The Wife, Dinshaw states, "not only uncovers what is hidden in the workings of patriarchal ideology but simultaneously appropriates the place of the Other that ideology openly creates; she assumes the place of the feminine (the stereotype) to which patriarchy explicitly relegates her" (1989, p. 119).

This Alison clearly does, and more, since she attacks the incoherence of this ideology, and the bind in which multiple authorities and a multiplicity of texts have placed women like herself. First, the Church commanded her to follow the spiritual course of purity and virtue as exemplified by Christ; so that was added the Pauline injunctions regarding women's silence and subjection to their husbands "as unto the Lord" (Eph. 22); and third, the Church endorsed the authority over girls and women of the secular family, headed by its *paterfamilias*, binding them to serve its inter-

---

[1]salvation

[2]care

[3]All quotations from Chaucer are from *The Riverside Chaucer*, Larry D. Benson, ed.

ests and demands (Knapp 1990, pp. 100–102). Thus, when Alison was first married at the age of twelve to a rich old man, she was doing her filial and economic duty — blessed, of course, by the Church which, while exalting the ideal of virginity, excluded from its fulfillment any girl usable in the prevailing trade of daughters for wealth and advantageous alliances.

Committed by those who had charge of her youth to the inferior, contaminated path, and aware of the fact that her success in it receives no validation or spiritual rewards, Alison defiantly asserts her worth and standing another way:

> Experience, though noon auctoritee
> Were in this world, is right ynogh for me
> To speke of wo that is in mariage. (3.1–3)

That there is a world operating independently of text and doctrine she would know by virtue of her membership (as a weaver) in the urban community of skilled artisans, whose expertise was gained through appreticeship, not book learning. In that context, experience constituted significant value: the Wife, accordingly, wants her own history of marital *praxis* recognized. This, too, is learning:

> Diverse scoles maken parfyt clerkes,
> And diverse practyk in many sondry werkes
> Maketh the werkman parfyt sekirly;[4]
> Of fyve husbondes scoleiyng[5] and I. (3. 44c–f)

The difficulty with this project is that whereas commercial activity was for the most part benignly neglected by Church authorities, not so sexual activity, which came under close supervision. Virginity was a woman's state of perfection, chaste marriage to one man was still honorable, and the widow was permitted to remarry (among the propertied classes, she was often compelled to) — however, with each additional chapter in her sexual history a woman departed farther from the ideal. The text of sexual experience is not simply uncanonical and unprivileged but a threat to salvation. And Alison's declaration that she finds herself adequately instructed by experience carries far-reaching implications. Only a few decades after her time, the burning of women for heresy and for extracanonical modes of knowledge under the rubric of witchcraft would have made her boldness unwise. It even resonates with Galileo's claim of the sufficiency of ocular

[4]certainly

[5]studying

evidence to disallow the Ptolemaic planetary model approved by the Church; for him, too, the world was constituted by experience.

The *locus* of experience, as Alison receives it, is the body, and in marital relations it is above all the genitals which she interprets in artisan's terms. Like a good craftsman, she says: "In wyfhode I wol use myn instrument/As trely as my Makere hath it sent" (3.149-150) – although "frely" is not quite accurate given the entrepreneurial considerations that sometimes enter in (Martin 1990, pp. 92-102). And experience has taught her the worth of her own equipment, which has the power to produce bliss as well as the "wo" of marriage:

> As help me God! I was a lusty oon,[6]
> And faire, and riche, and yong, and wel bigon;[7]
> And trewely, as myne housbondes tolde me,
> I hadde the beste *quoniam*[8] myghte be. (3.605-608)

This, what she elsewhere fondly calls her *bele chose*, her beautiful thing, is the source of a value forever unavailable to a celibate Church.

Moreover, while she recognizes God as her maker, she does not credit him with the specific gift of her splendid genital endowment. That, like the characterizing temperament and constitution of the whole bodily self, is by Alison's account a product of astrological configurations. She carries the birthmarks of planetary influence, and more:

> Venus, me yaf[9] my lust, my likerousnesse;[10]
> And Mars yaf me my sturdy hardynesse;
> Myn ascendent was Taur, and Mars therinne.
> Allas! allas! that evere love was synne!
> I folwede ay myn inclinacioun
> By vertu of my constellacioun. (3.611-616)

Before the Church baptizes the child into its spiritual community, she has received her physical sponsorship and definition from forces derived through astrology from an older order rooted in paganism and indifferent to the claims of orthodox Christian morality. Alison's outcry

[6]one

[7]arrayed

[8]vulva

[9]gave

[10]licentiousness

over the criminalization of sexual love implies the intuition—though she has not the historical vision—that it is not a necessary state of affairs: it comes late, too late for the child born under the sign of Venus.

This passage exemplifies, incidentally, the very real usefulness of astrology to women, which the ubiquity of star columns in women's magazines continues to indicate. It is not only the diverse array of influential planets and constellations, from Luna to Saturn and from Virgo to Leo, that rules temperaments and lives cuts across gender lines—though this in itself can serve to validate those preferences and ambitions of women which go against conventional restrictions. But simply the existence of an alternative order of power, no matter how doubtfully derived or how crudely deterministic in nature, has provided a way of escaping the tyrannical single vision of the prevailing patriarchal orthodoxy. And the more culturally suspect or despised—as astrology is—the better, confirming paradoxically its status as denied truth. So astrology here supports the claims of Alison's lived experience; and Venus, who along with the sinful Eve supplied in medieval visual art the representative instance of a woman's naked figure, validates her sexual power.

Less recognized by commentators than the Wife's claiming of the territory of her body's nature and history is her need of access to the world beyond the household, which I believe to be equally important. As the priest rules in the church, so the husband has authority in the home, but in the streets between and the fields and commons outside town and beyond lies the freedom of the margins. Her first statement on this point is a general claim: "We love no man that taketh kep or charge / Wher that we goon; we wol ben at oure large" (3.321–322). Sovereignty of her person is never enough; the body must have scope to roam. But this was a strongly contested matter in medieval doctrine and custom. The most constantly repeated charges against woman were that she was "garrula et vaga" (Knapp 1990, p. 97): women talked when they should be silent and wandered when they should stay home. Significantly, the portrait of Alison in the General Prologue focuses most on her credentials as a world-class wanderer:

And thries[11] hadde she been at Jerusalem;
She hadde passed many a straunge strem;
At Rome she hadde been, and at Boloigne,
In Galice at Seint-Jame, and at Coloigne.
She koude[12] muchel of wandrynge by the weye. (1.463–467)

[11]thrice

[12]knew

What her strenuous pilgrimages indicate is not, of course, exceptional piety but, as the last line indicates, going astray from the strict path of duty and virtue. This, like love, is sin, and both came together later in Alison's lyrical memory of the last occasion when she fell in love:

> And so bifel that ones in a Lente—
> So often tymes I to my gossyb wente,
> For evere yet I loved to be gay,
> And for to walke in March, Averill and May,
> Fro hous to hous, to heere sondry talys[13]—
> That Jankin clerk, and my gossyb Dame Alys,
> And I myself, into the feeldes wente.
> Myn housbonde was at Londoun al that Lente;
> I hadde the bettre leyser[14] for to pleye,
> And for to se, and eek[15] for to be seye
> Of lusty folk. . . . (3.543–552)

Still married to her fourth husband at this point, she has become disaffected because of his infidelity. After a winter of discontent, spring has come, and the customs of northern Europe endorsed the human need to escape houses rank and stifling from the months of human and animal confinement, and to seek health and renewal of spirits outdoors. This is also the season of Alison's birth sign, ruled by Venus, in which she can expect good fortune. "What wiste[16] I wher my grace[17] / Was shapen[18] for to be, or in what place?" (3.553–55) she asks and does not wait for it to come to her. In the fields, with the complicity of her friend, she and Jankin, who will become her fifth and best-loved husband, begin their romance.

But it's to be noted that even when married to the man she truly loves and sexually satisfied, she still requires the freedom to talk and to walk independently:

[13]tales

[14]leisure

[15]also

[16]knew

[17]good fortune

[18]destined

> Stibourn[19] I was as is a leonesse,
> And of my tonge a verray jangleresse,[20]
> And walke I wolde, as I had doon biforn,
> Fro hous to hous, although he had it sworn.[21] (3.637–640)

Jankin as a husband forbids her this right; she will have to fight for it, and she does. He beats her repeatedly and harasses her with those learned indictments of women that bring the final confrontation in which, after tearing his book, she knocks him into the fireplace, and he retaliates with a blow to the head that puts her life in danger—and, in fact, leaves her permanently deaf on that side. Although in the aftermath he concedes her full freedom— "Do as thee lust[22] the terme of al thy lif; / Keep thyn honour, and keep eek[23] myn estaat" (3.820–821)—she has paid heavily for it. The importance of the right to freedom of movement has been taken for granted so long in Western discussions, no doubt because restriction of it in modern times is found chiefly among segments of the population farthest removed from the centers of political and economic power: in ghettos and other isolated communities. But this passage reminds us that it is the physical equivalent to the basic rights of free thought and expression and no less crucial.

There remains one other refuge from judgment available to the Wife of Bath, which is the imagination of a prior state of affairs more benign than that currently in force. This, of course, is what the Arthurian setting of her tale represents. Here, the transcendental powers are feminine and pleasure loving, sharing her taste for the outdoors: "The elf-queene, with hir joly compaignye / Daunced ful ofte in many a grene mede" (3.860–861). Yet it is not a place without risks; for when a young girl goes walking alone (something that the sociable Alison does not do), she is surprised by a young knight—

> a lusty bacheler,
> That on a day cam ridynge fro ryver;
> And happed that, allone as he was born,
> He saugh[24] a mayde walkynge hym biforn,

[19]stubborn

[20]gossip

[21]forbidden

[22]please

[23]also

[24]saw

Of which mayde anon, maugree hir heed,[25]
By verray force he rafte[26] hire maydenhede. (3.883–888)

Since the riverbank was commonly the hawking ground, he had presumably been practicing that form of hunting; it might be said that, in raping the girl, he continues his predatory vocation in another, unacceptable mode. But since courtly reverence for women rules this world of romance fantasy, he is condemned to death for his crime. In an original twist of the traditional plot, the queen and her ladies claim disposition of the case; as Priscilla Martin puts it in her discerning account, the queen "proposes re-education as a possible alternative to the death sentence. The knight is given a year to find the answer to the question which Freud was later to ask: 'What thyng is it that wommen moost desiren?' " (1990, p. 55). The aim here is not to destroy male sexuality, whose eagerness they value, but to bring it into harmony with women's desire.

Such a process is not easy to achieve, and in this tale (fittingly, given its teller), it is the man who must take on the greater burden of the work. He spends a year in fruitless research, until riding by the edge of a forest—

he saugh upon a daunce go
Of ladyes foure and twenty, and yet mo;[27]
Towards the whiche daunce he drow[28] ful yerne,[29]
In hope that som wysdom sholde he lerne. (3.989–994)

The ladies vanish magically at his approach, but in their place appears an old crone who will deliver the truth, that what women want is the sovereignty they have been denied in their relations with men. But this is not yet all. The knight must be taken experientially through the traditional woman's ordeal of sexual humiliation in a coerced marriage, and ultimately to the recognition that his own fulfillment can only come through surrender— a solution that is also in accord with the deepest Christian wisdom. In this concluding sequence, the wife in the guise of "the Wise Woman of the Forest is her ideal self; calm, reasonable, right, supported by authorities, a force for reconciliation in the confusing world" (Martin 1990 p. 62).

[25]against her will

[26]robbed

[27]more

[28]drew

[29]eagerly

Full harmony among competing desires remains a fantasy, as the tale's ending concedes, for that depends on the crone's power to transform herself at will into a radiant young beauty, completing her husband's bliss and her own. In the contentious world where the Wife of Bath's wisdom has been hard earned, she must ride on in the guise of an Amazon, armed with a sharp wit and spurs. Like some contemporary fictional heroines—the wandering Sylvie of Marilynne Robinson's novel *Housekeeping*, or Thelma and Louise from the 1991 movie of that name, she continues to seek the reliable freedom of the road.

## References

Geoffrey Chaucer. 1987. *The Canterbury Tales*. In *The Riverside Chaucer*, L. D. Benson, ed. Boston: Houghton Mifflin.

Dinshaw, C. 1989. *Chaucer's Sexual Politics*. Madison, Wisc.: University of Wisconsin Press.

Knapp, P. 1990. *Chaucer and the Social Contest*. New York: Routledge.

Martin, P. 1990. *Chaucer's Women: Nuns, Wives and Amazons*. London: Macmillan.

# STEPPING OFF THE PATH

## DISOBEDIENCE AND STORY-MAKING IN "LITTLE RED-CAP"

### Jeanie Watson

In the fairy tale, as in our ordinary existence, that which is forbidden has great power and allure. Further, most often, beauty and power themselves form the forbidden: the princess asleep in the tower, the kingdom yet to be won. The core of both beauty and power resides in their manifestation of a life energy, a force which generates each new creation and propels growth. This energy—occurring within nature, within us, and within the heroines and heroes of the fairy tales—is unbounded, potential, dynamic, and dangerous. It is also beautiful and seductive and rich with possibility: mysterious. The world of the family, the palace, and the cottage protects, places limits, makes safe—and waits for the power and beauty of the forbidden to intrude.

Fairy tales show the process of human growth. The central characters, safe in one stage of development, reach out for the power and beauty of the next. Making one's own story necessitates a move from what *is* to what *might be*, that is, a move from the known into the unknown. Without movement, without the ongoing creative process of "making," without an act of the imagination, the individual self stagnates and dies. Moving beyond the limits of the known, moving into an imagined space, constitutes an act of disobedience. Therefore, disobedience must be at the core of any "making." "Fairy tales take us into a world where taboos may still be in force but where transgression is the motor of the plot" (Tatar 1987, pp. 55–56). The forbidden lives in Faery, and the disobedient one seizes the birthrights of life and creation and story.

In the main, the fairy tales that hold the most imaginative power are ones whose central characters are female: "Cinderella," "Snow White," "Sleeping Beauty," "Rapunzel," "Beauty and the Beast," "Little Red Riding

Hood"—even "The Three Bears."[1] One can posit a number of reasons why this is the case. First, the girls and young women at the center of each story are, contrary to received opinion, active initiators of their own stories. They are not simply acted upon; rather, they take their stories into their own hands. And in each case, this action is one of disobedience, a disobedience that places the heroine in great danger. Cinderella disobeys the midnight curfew placed on her by her fairy godmother, as well as the king's son's command not to run away. She is, in fact, quite good at evading him and others—whether it be by climbing into a dove cote or simply managing to get home before her stepmother and stepsisters—until she is ready to be "discovered." Snow White repeatedly disobeys the dwarves' warnings. Sleeping Beauty, climbing the tower steps and reaching out to touch the spindle, aligns herself with the disobedience of the old woman who—despite the king's orders to the entire kingdom—sits spinning. Rapunzel's mother craves the forbidden rampion and sets in motion the events which lead to Rapunzel letting down her hair, in secret, to the prince.

There are other reasons for the hold that Cinderella, Rapunzel, and their fairy-tale sisters have on the listener's imagination. Girls and women are typically thought to be more vulnerable and powerless than boys and men; therefore, their move outside the safety of the known seems especially dangerous. This additional danger, in turn, intensifies the identification and vicarious experience of the audience. As a result, when the journey into Faery and the capture of the heroine's own life and story is successful—as it inevitably must be in fairy tales—the imaginative satisfaction for the audience is likewise strengthened. Moreover, the imaginative identification between fairy-tale heroine and the hearer of the tale is augmented by the fact that the female embodies symbolically the inspiriting, creative principle, the *anima* of the imagination. Thus, a female character at the center of a narrative concerned with the "making" process of human development functions symbolically as the creative principle of imagination by the very act of making her own story. Her success is emblematic of the potential success of the listener in making her or his own life story progress creatively. And, one might add, her success, initiated by her necessary act of disobedience, is especially encouraging to little girls.

The power of the fairy-tale genre itself, then—and particularly as it employs a female protagonist—is imaginative and psychological. Originally

---

[1] As Maria Tatar summarizes: "It is . . . no secret that the most celebrated characters in fairy tales are female. Cinderella, Snow White, Little Red Riding Hood, and Sleeping Beauty: these are the names that have left so vivid an imprint on childhood memories"(1987, p. 85).

oral in nature, the literary versions of the tales have, in the last two centuries, exerted their own compelling attraction, so much so that the literary versions are now the source of our oral recounting to each new childhood generation. This essay, then, will use the Grimm Brothers' story of "Little Red-Cap" as an example of female disobedience and story-making in the fairy tale. Further, the analysis will be literary and psychological rather than historical, since these analyses are most congenial to the land of Faery itself.

> Fairy-tale heroes may begin their folkloric careers at home in a commonplace setting and they may end them in a castle in a naturalistic milieu, but the world that lies in-between is less natural than supernatural, less ordinary than extraordinary, and less real than surreal. The magic and enchantment of that world have some bearing on everyday reality, but it is generally pointless to turn the historian's beacon on that particular world in search of signs of the times. Once a fairy-tale hero leaves the realistically portrayed world designated as home to enter a realm that admits the supernatural, he moves into an arena that lends itself more readily to literary and psychological analysis than to historical inquiry. The magical spells cast by witches, ogres, and fairies have a habit of transforming, not just a single character, but an entire universe. An enchanted prince lives in a charmed world; a talking animal inhabits a marvelous realm; and a princess who cannot laugh lives in a quaintly exotic kingdom. The spheres are more likely to harbor inner than outer realities, to incarnate psychic truths rather than social facts, and to represent figurative expressions rather than literal meanings. (Tatar 1987, p. 57)

"Little Red Riding Hood" stands as one of the most popular of all the well-known fairy tales. Charles Dickens's declaration that Little Red Riding Hood was his first love with whom, if only he could have married her, he "should have known perfect bliss" (Opie and Opie 1974, p. 119) may sound excessive, but it does describe the passionate attachment of centuries of children to the story's central character. Little Red Riding Hood, as Jack Zipes (1984) has catalogued in detail, has, in the multiple versions of her story, undergone numerous "trials and tribulations," most of which have moved the story at least as thoroughly into the realm of cautionary tale as that of fairy tale. Charles Perrault's version—part of his 1697 *Histories ou*

*Contes du temps passé)* and the first known written version—ends with the wolf eating Little Red Riding Hood and with a moral poem attached to the tale which warns that nice girls should not listen to all sorts of people. If they do, it is not surprising that a wolf would eat them up. Further, wolves come in all varieties, but the most dangerous wolves are the gentle ones who will follow young girls into the streets and even into their homes. The Grimm Brothers' "Little Red-Cap," however, tells a significantly different tale, one in which Little Red-Cap steps off the path and, by her act of disobedience, succeeds in making her own story. She moves from the village to the wood, from the safely known to the dangerous unknown. She moves into Faery, risks what "is," and creates for herself the ability to grow into maturity.

Zipes also emphasizes Red-Cap's disobedience as central to the story, but for the purpose of arguing that "when the Grimms revised *Little Red Riding Hood* to *Little Red Cap* for their collection of 1812 (Tale 6), they were consciously working with a bourgeois literary tradition, and the significant changes they made reflect the social transformations in how children were viewed and reared. . . . What is most significant is that Little Red Riding Hood as Little Red Cap is transformed even more into the naive, helpless, pretty little girl who must be punished for her transgression, which is spelled out more clearly as disobedience and indulgence in sensual pleasure" (1984, pp. 14, 16). Before the Grimms and before Perrault, however, there were multiple oral folktale versions of the Red Riding Hood story, in none of which, according to Zipes, is the child killed by the wolf. Instead, "she shrewdly outwits the wolf and saves herself. No help from granny, hunter, or father! Clearly, the folk tale was not just a warning tale, but also a celebration of a young girl's coming of age. . . . Whether the story is about initiation, warning, or both, one thing is clear: the folk tale celebrates the self-reliance of a young peasant girl" (1984, pp. 7–8). My argument is that despite the trials of revision Little Red Riding Hood is made to undergo by the time the Grimms tell her story, the details of the story and her character are subversive enough to outwit them and that her very disobedience shows her faith in herself and allows for her ultimate triumph. In short, Little Red-Cap refuses to obey the revisers of her story. She, like her folktale ancestress, insists on telling her own.

Much of the appeal of "Little Red-Cap," for children and adults alike, becomes understandable if the story is read as the successful attempt of a young girl to tell her own story, in the face of attempts by others to tell her story for her. There are, in fact, three would-be storytellers in the tale of "Little Red-Cap": the mother, the grandmother, and the wolf. In the course of the tale, the differing stories that each of these wants to tell are shown to be inadequate; each, if played out by Little Red-Cap, would leave her without beauty and without power. Only by making her own story, by disobeying the story lines drawn for her by others, can she become her own person. At the same time, taken together, the other storytellers provide a framework for the self-formation and self-integration that is Red-Cap's task. The narrator validates Little Red-Cap's success by the coda to the tale proper, ending with: "But Red-Cap went joyously home, and no one ever did anything to harm her again."

The stories of the mother, grandmother, and wolf are anticipated by the structural elements of "Little Red-Cap," that is, the relationships between the various characters, the setting within which the actions of the tale occur, and the details of description. Despite the deliciously menacing quality of the wolf, the central relationships in the tale are those of Red-Cap to mother, Red-Cap to grandmother, and mother to grandmother. These relationships and the stories told in these relationships provide the key to Red-Cap's self-development and her ability to deal with the wolf.[2] The mother and grandmother are both mothers; both have daughters. What, then, is the meaning of these reiterated, generational mother/daughter relationships for Red-Cap's own storytelling?

The mother/daughter relationship is hardly unusual in fairy tales. Nor is a "two mothers"/daughter relationship, in which the mother figure splits into a usually dead "good" mother and a present "evil" stepmother or witch whom the young girl must overcome on her way to a happy ending. Of course, as the young girl marries and has her own daughter, she inevitably must become the evil witch-stepmother as well as the good mother. Further, the identity between mother and daughter is such that the "good mother"/"bad mother" split simply externalizes forces and possibilities within the daughter herself. Daughters "mirror" their mothers.[3] "Little Red-Cap" provides a variation on the "splitting" of the mother as the daughter reaches out for the beauty and power promised by the making of her own independent female self, a variation that is supportive rather than inevitably adversarial.

Dorothy Dinnerstein describes the role of the mother in the child's formation of the self in a way relevant to the mother/daughter relationship

[2]Similarly, Madonna Kolbenschlag notes: "Both Snow White fairy tales — and there are numerous others — focus on the fundamental connection between women that is the precondition of their development into full personhood" (1979, p. 38).

[3]For example, Bettelheim notes: "The readiness with which Snow White repeatedly permits herself to be tempted by the stepmother, despite the warnings of the dwarfs, suggests how close the stepmother's temptations are to Snow White's inner desires" (1976, p. 211). Gilbert and Gubar extend the observation as they discuss the relationship between the passive Snow White and the active Queen: "Indeed, it suggests that . . . the Queen and Snow White are in some sense one" (1979, p. 41).

in "Little Red-Cap," saying, "each subjective self starts forming itself in a world which is both a stimulus and an obstacle to the self-forming venture. In this world, the mother is the most vivid and the most active presence. . . . Even while she provides [the] vital support for the early growth of the self, the mother is inevitably felt as a menace to that self." Additionally:

> There is also the fact that when the active project of selfhood feels too strenuous or too dangerously lonely, the temptation is strong in all of us to melt back into that from which we have carved ourselves out. The mother supports the active project, but she is also on hand to be melted into when it is abandoned. She may, indeed, encourage the child's lapses from selfhood, for she, as well as the child, has mixed feelings about its increasing separateness from her. There is, of course, no such thing as a wholly benevolent mother, with no antagonism whatsoever to the child as an autonomous being. But even if there were, she would be experienced by the child, in its struggle to become such a being, both as an interfering influence and as a lure back into non-being. (1976, pp. 110–111)

The mother, then, actively encourages the development of the daughter's autonomous self, while providing the limits and boundaries and safe place also necessary for the safety of the child—necessary for societal as well as psychological reasons.

In "Little Red-Cap," Red-Cap's mother represents the safety, familiarity, and limitations of "non-being." She lives in the village, a societally, interdependent world which can function only because individuals agree to obey rules and stay within boundaries. This is also the world in which cakes are baked and wine is made. The cake and wine symbolize and celebrate communion, the interrelation of one person with another. Communion and relationships are healthy, productive, and good. At the same time, if the rules of the "village" become rigid, if they stifle imagination and creativity, they will also stifle the possibility for individual selfhood. If Red-Cap sees herself only as an extension of the village world, as personified by the mother, she will never achieve the independence necessary for mature relationships. The mother's admonitions before Red-Cap sets out are instructions in good manners: "When you go into her room, don't forget to say 'good morning,' and don't peep into every corner before you do it." In other words, follow the rules of polite, conventional conduct; don't act without restraint or thought for the other person.

Restraint and limit are also apparent in the mother's instruction to "set out before it gets hot, and when you are going, walk nicely and quietly and do not run off the path, or you may fall and break the bottle, and then your grandmother will get nothing." The mother tells Red-Cap the story of the stereotypical female "good girl" who is nice, polite, and quiet and who takes no risk, for fear of falling and breaking the wine of communion and sustenance. Stepping off the proper path, as the mother tells the story, forebodes harm to self and others. Curiosity—"peeping into every corner" and wanting to explore beyond the edge of the path—is dangerous and selfish. As expected, Little Red-Cap gives her promise and "her hand on it" to her mother: "I will take great care," thereby aligning herself with rather than differentiating herself from her mother. But the breaking of the promise—Red-Cap's disobedience—is inherent in the statements and conditions surrounding the promising. First, Red-Cap's promise is itself ambiguous. She promises to "take great care." A child can easily promise to be careful without, in her own mind, promising to abide by the specifics of the mother's admonitions. One could, for example, carefully set the cake and wine down by the path before running off the path for a few moments. In addition, the longer the list of admonitions and restraints, the more likely that one or more will be broken, especially when they run counter to the natural curiosity that is the requisite to growth and development. Thus, the "promising scene" itself sets up the expectation of disobedience.

Red-Cap's grandmother, unlike the mother, lives "out in the wood, half a league from the village." The wood is the wood of Faery, the realm in which wolves converse with humans and persons eaten by wolves are not really dead, the realm of imagination in which the self can initiate its action of psychological growth. The grandmother, in the splitting of the mother figure in "Little Red-Cap," represents the female impulse toward individuation and selfhood and the mother role of encourager of self-formation in the daughter. The story she would tell for Little Red-Cap is embodied in the very "cap of red velvet" she gives to her "grand" daughter. Whether the red cap encourages associations with "sin, sensuality, or the devil"; a sign "to stigmatize social nonconformists or outcasts"; or witches,[4] it is clear that all the associations fall outside the boundaries legitimized by society for little girls. Unlike the element of restraint embodied by the mother, then, the relationship between Red-Cap and the grandmother lacks boundaries. Red-Cap is described as "a dear little girl who was loved by everyone who looked at her, but most of all by her grandmother, and there was nothing she would not have given to the child." No one loves the daughter as much as the

[4]Zipes cites the observation that in parts of England witches were "dressed exactly like fairies. They wear a red mantle and hood, which covers the whole body . . . called 'little red riding hoods' " (1984, pp. 9, 60).

mother who gives—in unlimited fashion and most inevitably—the red cap of passionate love which, because it suits her so well, intensifies the beauty of the child. The cap may represent existence outside the narrow limits of society, but it obviously also "belongs" to the little girl. Knowing this and claiming the power inherent in the "wayward" beauty it represents, Red-Cap "would never wear anything else." Thus, "she was always called 'Little Red-Cap,' " named, in effect, by grandmother/mother/self, all three. The gift of the cap names the child and sets in motion the story in which the grandmother is the teller. This story, while essential for the vital imaginative growth necessary for Red-Cap's development, has—like the mother's story—inadequacies that will ultimately be dangerous and destructive if allowed to run to its completion.

In fact, however, the story the mother tries to impose on her daughter is shown by the narrative itself to be false. And the destruction which could be the end of the grandmother's story for Red-Cap is not allowed. Although the mother warns that if Red-Cap runs off the path, she will fall and break the bottle of wine, that consequence does not occur. Instead, having run from the path to pick flowers for her grandmother, Red-Cap returns to the path, with the wine still safe and able to serve its original function: "The grandmother ate the cake and drank the wine which Red-Cap had brought, and revived." In addition, the advice the mother gives to say "good morning" first and "not to peep into every corner" before doing so—advice which Red-Cap follows—turns out to be exactly wrong:

> She was surprised to find the cottage door standing open, and when she went into the room, she had such a strange feeling that she said to herself: "Oh dear! how uneasy I feel to-day, and at other times I like being with grandmother so much." She called out: "Good morning," but received no answer; so she went to the bed and drew back the curtains.

Red-Cap's instincts and feelings—not the advice she has been given—are right. She is very observant, of both her external surroundings and her own emotional response. "Surprised" by the open cottage door, she is filled with a "strange feeling" of extreme uneasiness when she steps into the cottage. One might argue that had she peeped quietly into the corners before calling out her "good morning," she might have avoided the wolf entirely. But, if the admonitions of the mother are not entirely to be trusted, an existence in which no boundaries or limits are imposed evolves into no existence at all: the wolf eats Red-Cap as he has eaten Grandmother—clearly, an unsatisfactory ending in every aspect. Self-discovery and exploration are necessary for growth, but the wolf cannot be allowed to tell the story, or there will be no story to tell.

The inadequacies of the stories called forth by the mother/ grandmother split emerge within the initial paragraphs of the tale. Cut off from the village — and, more specifically, from her daughter — the grandmother is "ill and weak." The mother knows that cake and wine "will do her good." And who better to convey those symbols of connection than Red-Cap? On the other hand, for all her warnings not to be curious and not to "run off the path," it is the mother who deliberately initiates Red-Cap's journey, sending her into the woods of imaginative self-discovery.

The identification of mother/grandmother, Red-Cap's movement between the two worlds — or psychological impulses — represented by the mother and grandmother, and the allure and danger of self-discovery, are all neatly compressed into the one sentence that takes Red-Cap into Faery: "The grandmother lived out in the wood, half a league from the village, and just as Little Red-Cap entered the wood, a wolf met her." The wolf always waits at the edge of exploration. In a story of female self-discovery and maturation, the wolf is inevitable. Because he is male, he is unknown, not-female, not-mother; he is the differentiated one and, therefore, both tempting and dangerous. What mother — faced with the allure of life energy represented by the joining of masculine and feminine, along with the accompanying potential for destruction — has not sought to keep her daughter safe in the house, while giving her, in the same breath and out of her love, the red cap of beauty and love which will attract the wolf?

Thus, the wolf functions simultaneously as the "wicked creature" bent on eating both grandmother and Red-Cap and a creature of Faery aligned with the grandmother/mother as they send Red-Cap to her encounter in the woods. It is necessary in this encounter that Red-Cap experience the unfamiliar pleasures of the imagination allowed by her disobedience, without which she can never imagine or create her own story. At the same time, she must be able to return to the village. She must disobey the rules of the mother, but her selfhood cannot isolate or destroy her. She must be able to imagine new roles for herself, while learning to place her *own* boundaries on her self. Red-Cap must progressively imagine and actively create the next chapters of her own story, mature, and become independent, while participating in communion and relationship. The goal, in other words, is a mature, integrated self.

True "selfhood" calls for an integration of both active and passive, initiative and responsive principles, the "masculine" with the "feminine." That the formation of an androgynous selfhood should be the task of a fairy-tale heroine comes as no surprise, since the Land of Faery itself often symbolizes the working of the creative imagination, characterized as androgynous.[5] In her discussion of the story of Snow White, Kolbenschlag argues that a woman must "seek spiritual maturity and wholeness through androgyny":

> Androgyny is not a certain type of sexuality, it is the result of a dynamic interchange of energies in a continuous system. Not to progress in it would be like trying to prevent one cerebrum of the brain from interacting with the other. Nor does androgyny mean "masculinizing" women. Rather, it means abandoning a stereotypical constellation of qualities for a dialectical sexuality, a creative selfhood. Androgyny, then, can be the link, the bridge, the turning point between heteronomy and autonomy — a step toward full personhood. (1979, p. 61)

The androgynous existence is one of an ongoing creative reconciliation of opposites which, rather than denying or annihilating either the masculine or the feminine, provides for the simultaneous integration and manifestation of both which is necessary for life itself. As Marie-Louise von Franz explains: "Though it is a great thing for a woman not to be masculine, she can be too one-sidedly feminine, and then she is out of life and will not be able to cope with it. . . . So it is a question of integrating the masculine side into the feminine world without going a step too far" (1972, pp. 56–57). What is wanted is a dialectical interchange between the masculine and the feminine.

If Red-Cap identifies only with the feminine mother, she identifies — to the detriment of her selfhood's ability to mature and create its own, separate existence — with the societal "feminine," characterized by passivity, dependency, and emotion. The wolf takes the societal "masculine," characterized by activity, independence, and rationality, to its distorted extreme: violent action and clever cunning. Grandmother and the wolf encourage Red-Cap to look beyond the village and to the sides of the path; they encourage and represent the play of imaginative possibilities outside the strict and straight. Both are inhabitants of the Faery woods. Red-Cap, in fact, is sure that the wolf "must know" her grandmother's house. The wolf is entirely isolated, however, without relationship, without caring; and, while the grandmother is "weak," she is still linked to daughter and

---

[5]See *Risking Enchantment: Coleridge's Symbolic World of Faery* (Watson 1990), for further discussion of the relationship of androgyny, Faery, and imagination.

granddaughter. Red-Cap must somehow find the androgynous bridge that will allow her to integrate the masculine into the feminine so that she will escape the non-self of the totally feminine without going "a step too far" and being endangered by the totally masculine. As von Franz notes, "no one hits the bull's eye the first time; it takes practice" (1972, p. 57). Thus it is that, although the wolf eats Grandmother (who represents not only the encourager side of the mother but also, because of the daughter's identification with the whole mother, the impulse toward selfhood and "wholeness" of personhood residing in Red-Cap herself) and then eats Red-Cap, Red-Cap and the grandmother get a second chance. And Red-Cap succeeds in telling her own story.

Before Red-Cap can tell her own story, however, she must disobey the admonitions of her mother in the village. She must break her promise and step off the path. And for that to happen, she must encounter the wolf in the wood. The exchange between Red-Cap and the wolf, as Red-Cap enters the wood, exactly counter-balances their later exchange in the Grandmother's house. Thus, in the first, the wolf initiates the conversation with a polite, "Good-day, Little Red-Cap," to which she responds in kind, "Thank you kindly, wolf." No introductions are necessary, and the wolf—in contrast to their second exchange—proceeds to ask a series of questions which Red-Cap answers and to put into play his story for the little girl: she is to become merely "a nice plump mouthful." At this stage, for his story to be told and for her story to begin, she must experience the natural freedom, beauty, and song of the wood. So the wolf makes clear the attraction of the wood over the village:

> See, Little Red-Cap, how pretty the flowers are about here—why do you not look around? I believe, too, that you do not hear how sweetly the little birds are singing; you walk gravely along as if you were going to school, while everything else out here in the wood is merry. '

The wolf invites Red-Cap to become part of the world of nature. Her world is closed in: she cannot see the flowers or hear the birds' songs; she gravely walks the path as though toward the school of rules which will end in her grave if she refuses to be merry and participate in life.

When Red-Cap raises her downcast eyes, she has—in her imagination—already stepped off the path. Instead of grave stillness, "she saw the sunbeams dancing here and there through the trees, and pretty flowers growing everywhere [and] she thought: 'Suppose I take grandmother a fresh nosegay; that would please her too. It is so early in the day that I shall still get there in good time.' " Light, sight, sound, smell, dancing, growing—life—come flooding in, and with the word *suppose*, Little

Red-Cap begins to tell her own story. She will incorporate the world of the wood into the task taking her from village to cottage. She will bear the beauty of the wood flowers with her to share with her beloved grandmother. She will not be out after dark, but she will take pleasure in the life of the day. She does for a time, going "deeper and deeper into the woods," forget her grandmother, but she doesn't forget entirely. And carrying safely not only the cake and wine but also an armful of flowers, she steps back on the path and arrives at Grandmother's cottage. For a space of time, she has successfully told her own story. She has done what she imagined. She has integrated the wood and the village. She has disobeyed, stepped off into self-discovery, and safely returned to the mother's path.

Meanwhile, the grandmother has let into the cottage too much of the wood in the form of the creature whose very home is the unbounded outdoors: the wolf. He cannot enter the cottage—which, after all, is a structure of safety, even within the wood—without invitation. Too weak to take proper care, the grandmother tells the wolf to "lift the latch." "The wolf lifted the latch, the door sprang open, and without saying a word he went straight to the grandmother's bed, and devoured her." Red-Cap is right to be surprised and alarmed that the cottage door is standing open when she arrives. The human psyche must have barriers against limitlessness; otherwise, the cunning and dangerous wolf will walk in and lie in wait, in clever disguise, in the very bed of one's night-imagination. Actively attempting to use her newfound senses, her curiosity, and the creative "forming" power of her imagination, Red-Cap, in her well-known exchange with the wolf, tries to make sense of "her grandmother with the cap pulled far over her face, and looking very strange." She comes close to discovery, but before she can put the whole picture together, the wolf, "with one bound . . . was out of bed and swallowed up Red-Cap."

The huntsman provides a model of a mature, fully integrated man. He is at home in the wood where he hunts dangerous creatures like the wolf, in effect, extending the limitations of society into the boundless woods. He is active, aggressive, independent, and logical; but he also participates in human relationship and community. Passing by the grandmother's house, he says, "How the old woman is snoring! I must just see if she wants anything." His impulse is helpful and neighborly. At the same time, when he sees the wolf, he recognizes him immediately for what he is: the "old sinner," the outcast from society, the masculine unintegrated into the feminine. Reasoning that Grandmother may have been eaten, the huntsman cuts open the belly of the sleeping wolf, now as inattentive to his danger as the grandmother had formerly been to hers. First Little Red-Cap springs out, still wearing her red cap, crying, " 'Ah, how frightened I have been! How dark it was inside the wolf'; and after that the aged grandmother came out alive also, but scarcely able to breathe." The huntsman is a facilitator, a true father figure, providing the protection and occasion for Little Red-Cap to emerge fully into the next stage of her development — the next chapter of her story. Thus, Red-Cap can imagine, initiate, and execute the plan that ends the wolf: "Red-Cap, however, quickly fetched great stones with which they filled the wolf's belly, and when he awoke, he wanted to run away, but the stones were so heavy that he collapsed at once, and fell dead."

The wolf dead, "all three were delighted," and fellowship abounds. Each of the three responds in a way which ensures against further danger from "wolves." The huntsman draws off the wolf's skin and goes home with it, thus domesticating the "wolf" in himself. "The grandmother ate the cake and drank the wine which Red-Cap had brought, and revived," strengthened by communion with her daughter and granddaughter. Finally, Red-Cap thinks to herself: "As long as I live, I will never by myself leave the path, to run into the wood, when my mother has forbidden me to do so." This statement does not represent the simple, contrite return to obedience that the moralists wish to conclude is the case. Red-Cap has moved from feeling no fear of the wolf because she "did not know what a wicked creature he was" — a dangerous stance indeed — to being devoured by the wolf, to executing his demise. Her conclusion, arrived at on her own rather than being given to her by someone else, is not to avoid the wood or even to avoid wolves. Rather, she decides to abide by the caution, appropriate for her age, not to leave the path by herself when her mother has told her not to. It may be that sometimes her mother will not forbid it, or it may be safe to leave the path with someone else. Her promise — to herself, this time — is not the promise of a frightened, chastened child. Instead, it is the reasoned conclusion of a maturing person. The "mother" who forbids her is really she herself.

The story proper ends here, but the coda functions as a validation of the growth and maturation, the experience and knowledge and self-integration, that have occurred. Once again, Red-Cap is taking cakes to her grandmother when a wolf says "good morning" and tries to "entice her from the path." Wiser now, she sees his "wicked look" and hurries on to reach her grandmother's cottage before the wolf. This time, Grandmother, well and strong, knows what to do. Rather than inviting the wolf to lift the latch, she says to Red-Cap, "Well . . . we will shut the door, that he may not come in." The split mother figure is thus appropriately reintegrated as an active, imaginative protector who can see "what was in [the] thoughts" of the wolf and, therefore, can change the direction of the wolf's story. The end of this wolf is comic. Rather than being filled with stones, the wolf, waiting on top of the roof, is tempted to edge farther and farther down the side of the roof, lured by the smell of sausage water Red-Cap — at the direction of the grandmother — has poured into a stone trough at the front of the house. Finally, "he sniffed and peeped down, and at last stretched out his neck so far that he could no longer keep his footing and began to slip, and slipped down from the roof straight into the great trough, and was drowned." This wolf, slipping and sliding down the roof, fooled by the smell, is more silly than dangerous. Red-Cap, self-reliant and sure of her self, "went joyously home, and no one ever did anything to harm her again."

# References

Bettelheim, Bruno. 1976. *The Uses of Enchantment*. New York: Knopf.

Dinnerstein, Dorothy. 1976. *The Mermaid and the Minotaur: Sexual Arrangements and Human Malaise*. New York: Harper and Row.

Gilbert, Sandra M., and Gubar, Susan. 1979. *The Madwoman in the Attic: The Woman Writer and the Nineteenth-Century Literary Imagination*. New Haven, Conn.: Yale University Press.

Grimm, Jacob and Wilhelm. 1944. *The Complete Grimms' Fairy Tales*. With introduction by Padriac Colum and illustrations by Josef Scharl. New York: Pantheon Books. The text is based on the translation by Margaret Hunt, revised, corrected, and completed by James Stern.

Kolbenschlag, Madonna. 1979. *Kiss Sleeping Beauty Good-Bye*. New York: Doubleday and Company, Inc.

Opie, Iona, and Opie, Peter. 1974. *The Classic Fairy Tales*. New York: Oxford University Press.

Tatar, Maria. 1987. *The Hard Facts of the Grimms' Fairy Tales*. Princeton, N.J.: Princeton University Press.

von Franz, Marie-Louise. 1972. *Problems of the Feminine in Fairy Tales*. Zurich: Spring Publications.

Watson, Jeanie. 1990. *Risking Enchantment: Coleridge's Symbolic World of Faery*. Lincoln, Neb.: University of Nebraska Press.

Zipes, Jack. 1984. *The Trials and Tribulations of Little Red Riding Hood*. South Hadley, Mass.: Bergin and Garvey Publishers, Inc.

# "Speak I Must"

## JANE EYRE AND THE DISCOURSE
## OF DISOBEDIENCE

## Lena B. Ross

*Suddenly, without warning, Jane Eyre stole upon the
scene, and the most alarming revolution of modern
times has followed.*

Mrs. Oliphant (1855)

$J$*ane Eyre* has been viewed from a great number of vantage points, many of
which have taken note, in particular, of the way the text progresses, as well
as Jane's growth (e.g., Gilbert and Gubar 1979, Peters 1991, Kadish 1987). I
propose to look at the story of Jane Eyre primarily as a psychological tale in
which Jane is able to constellate an identity and grow through disobedience.[1] Whether spoken, silent, or enacted, disobedience constitutes a particularly feminine discourse, made necessary in a patrifocal (or phallomorphic) culture where a woman's identity is defined and shaped through
her relationship to the male world, and a man's to a single standard of
masculinity.[2] Within that definition, a woman's "no," particularly in service
to her own needs, both intellectual and sexual, can only be defined as

" 'Speak I must': *Jane Eyre* and the discourse of disobedience" is part of
*First Voice: Disourse in the Feminine Mode*, a larger work in progress
which seeks to illuminate how ancient texts express a feminine voice compensatory to the consolidation of masculine consciousness. *Jane Eyre* is
presented as a descendent of these ancient voices.

[1]As I hope will become apparent through this paper, I am viewing Jane's
development metaphorically, as an embodiment of a complex shift taking
place on the archetypal level through which long-denied energies may
incarnate.

[2]A patrifocal orientation refers to cultures whose structure derives from
the father. Etymologically, father relates to preserving, since the Latin
*pater* is from the Sanskrit *pa* (to protect) and protection is for the purpose
of preservation. I prefer to use the word *phallomorphic* because it implies

disobedient, certainly not seen as creative. In comparing *Jane Eyre* to *Wuthering Heights,* Adrienne Rich notes that Jane's is "the life story of a woman who is *incapable* of saying *I am Heathcliff* (as the heroine of Emily's novel does) because she feels so unalterably herself" (1973, p. 68). How did this "singular integrity" (Zeiger 1960, p. 457) grow, given the conditions that obtained then (1847) and now? Psychologically, what are the larger implications of Jane Eyre's tale?

In her essay, "The Power of Discourse," Luce Irigaray says that "what is important is to disconcert the staging of representation according to exclusively 'masculine' parameters. . . . It is not a matter of toppling that order so as to replace it — that amounts to the same thing in the end — but of disrupting and modifying it, starting from an 'outside' that is exempt, in part, from phallocratic law" (1985, p. 68). *Jane Eyre* provides for those who follow a *Bildungsroman*, literally a formation-novel, of an inner as well as outer journey. It also highlights a feminine discourse about the growth of the individual self out of disobedience, not by overthrowing the established order, but through subverting it in Irigaray's sense.

## First Voice

Jane Eyre is an orphan, perhaps the first condition that places her "outside" of "phallocratic law." Gilead characterizes Jane as comprising a "particularly potent liminal configuration: victimized and illegitimate, she is severed from a mysterious past and denied an imaginable future" (1987, p. 304). Jane was taken in by her uncle, Mr. Reed, when her parents died in her infancy. Her uncle, too, dies soon after, exacting a deathbed promise from his unwilling wife to raise Jane. Jane is an alien organism in the family body within which we first meet her. As Jane herself tells us,

> I was a discord in Gateshead Hall; I was like nobody there; I had nothing in harmony with Mrs. Reed or her children. . . . I know that had I been a sanguine, brilliant, careless, exacting, handsome, romping child . . . Mrs. Reed would have endured my presence more complacently; her children would have enter-

the form imposed by the hierarchical power of patriarchy. (From an etymological standpoint, matrifocal culture, related to the Sanskrit *ma*, to make, presumably would have more to do with construction or creating.)

Additionally, for the purposes of this paper I will show an aspect of the single standard of masculinity as it is represented through the character of Rochester.

tained for me more of the cordiality of fellow feeling; the servants would have been less prone to make me the scapegoat of the nursery. (Brontë 1946, p. 21)[3]

The first disobediences are outside of Jane's ego control. She could not be "handsome": fate has handed her a slight, plain, drab look, so that the first disobedience is to a collective which celebrates physical beauty in a woman as primary. In myths and fairy tales, plot developments often spring from the fountainhead of a girl/woman's beauty, as with Scheherazade of the *Arabian Nights* or Psyche, from Apuleius's *Cupid and Psyche*.[4] In these earlier tales, fundamental change is initiated through the effect of the woman's beauty on the man. But Jane is plain (and poor), so her story begins in a condition which is outside the conventions of the collective masculine discourse *about* the feminine.

C. G. Jung spoke of the archetypal layer of the psyche, where there are primordial, preexisting archaic structures, drawn from the collective unconscious (1921, pars. 746 and 747). More recently, Daniel Stern, speaking from clinical observation of infants, notes that "infants begin to experience a sense of an emergent self from birth" and are *"predesigned* (my emphasis) to be aware of self-organizing processes" (1985, p. 10). He comments that "infants consolidate the sense of a core self as a separate, cohesive, bounded, physical unit" (ibid.). Although we only know her from the age of ten, there are many textual allusions that indicate Jane has always felt alien in the Reed family. An autonomous energy moves Jane, the necessity to disobey for survival of the Self/self.[5]

The early part of the book is replete with words and images of Jane's rebellion, often couched in terms of her inability to resist the push to self-assertion: in the first few pages, she attempts to hide from her tormenting cousins. She leaves her hiding place when she is found and attacked by

---

[3]All quotes from *Jane Eyre* are taken from the 1946 edition.

[4]The centrality of female beauty seems undisputed in myth and literature universally. It's effect on the patrifocal world can differ in cultures, however, as *Taketori Monogatori*, the oldest piece of Japanese fiction extant, demonstrates. Here, the men of Japan are crazed by their desire to possess the beautiful Kaguya-hime, though none have ever seen her. She causes havoc by refusing union with men and making clear her disdain for them.

[5]I am using the uppercase "S" to stand for the larger self, an ordering and directing principle in the psyche, which, according to Jung, "designates the whole range of psychic phenomena in man. It expresses the unity of the personality as a whole" (1921, par. 789). I use the lowercase "self" to indicate individual identity. These seem to run parallel in Jane's psyche, an unusual though desirable phenomenon in everyday life.

her older cousin, John Reed. "Wicked and cruel boy!" Jane says. "You are like a murderer—you are like a slave-driver—you are like the Roman Emporers!" When he attacks her in a fury, she tells us "he had closed with a desperate thing" (p. 16). Dragged away to the red room as punishment, Jane tells us "I resisted all the way . . . like any other rebel slave, I felt resolved in my desperation, to go to all lengths" (p. 17). In chapter three, referring to a servant's opinion of her, she says, "Abbott, I think, gave me credit for being a sort of infantine Guy Fawkes."

In chapter four, Jane, continually bullied by her cousin John, "instantly turned against him, roused by the same sentiment of deep ire and desperate revolt" which she had felt before. He runs away to complain to his mother; Mrs. Reed stops him "rather harshly," declaring Jane "unworthy of notice" and of their association. Jane, overhearing this exchange, "cried out suddenly and without at all deliberating on [her] words—'They are not fit to associate with me.'" Mrs. Reed rushes up the stairs and descends upon Jane, ordering her to say nothing the rest of the day, whereupon Jane immediately replies as follows:

> What would Uncle Reed say to you, if he were alive? was my scarcely voluntary demand . . . it seemed as if my tongue pronounced words without my will consenting to their utterance: *something spoke out of me over which I had no control.* (p. 34, my emphasis)

Jane's disobedience may, in the beginning, be a preexisting structure in her psyche which will not let her adapt through a false self, for example, or through death, silence, or madness, often alternatives for women in her miserable situation, and all of which are presented through figures in the text (e.g., Georgiana Reed, Helen Burns, Miss Temple, Bertha Mason Rochester) as possibilities at one point or another. Often seen as aspects of Jane, these figures may also be taken as representations of various forms of rebellion or adaptation which are not-Jane.

This scene is soon followed by the fateful meeting with the Rev. Mr. Brocklehurst, the director of the Lowood School, to which Jane is to be sent. As others have noted, Jane's spiritual allegiance seems to be to nature rather than to the prevailing collective sentiment, which is Christian.[6] In her interview with Mr. Brocklehurst, Jane clearly shows her natural nonallegiance to conventional 'Christian' sentiments (and Brontë her sense of

---

[6]Perhaps Jane's non-Christian sentiments were what led Queen Victoria, who liked *Jane Eyre* very much, nevertheless to label the novel "peculiar" (Myer 1987, p. 107).

humor). When he asks her what she must do to avoid the pit of hell, Jane replies, "I must keep in good health and not die" (p. 40).

In the meeting with Mr. Brocklehurst, Mrs. Reed brands Jane a liar and makes sure that she will receive harsh treatment at Lowood. After the meeting is over, all of Jane's resentment and anger over her treatment at Gateshead fills her and she thinks, "*Speak* I must: I had been trodden on severely and *must* turn" (p. 44). She then confronts her aunt with her cruelty and lets Mrs. Reed know her feelings. Her aunt, appalled, asks Jane how dare she say such things? Jane replies:

> How dare I, Mrs. Reed? How dare I? Because it is the truth. You think I have no feelings, that I can do without one bit of love or kindness; but I cannot live so. . . . People think you are a good woman, but you are bad, hardhearted. *You* are deceitful! Ere I had finished this reply, my soul began to expand, to exult, with the strangest sense of freedom, of triumph, I ever felt. It seemed as if an invisible bond had burst, and that I had struggled out into unhoped-for liberty. (p. 45)

"The development of one's inner voice constitutes the counterpart to one's inner vision, and both the inner voice and the inner vision incarnate in the world through the development of a core self (Ross 1991, p. 74). In the early stages of the book, Jane's task is clearly the development of what Hélène Cixous refers to as woman's "privileged relationship with the voice" (1981, p. 251).[7]

## Jane and Not-Jane: Sorting Out

Shortly thereafter, Jane is sent to Lowood. Her significant meetings there are with Miss Temple and Helen Burns, two of the women representing alternatives or possibilities. From these women she receives love and instruction; she feels love and admiration in return, but ultimately rejects both of their examples. Helen Burns, whose doctrine of endurance enables her to bear the humiliation she suffers daily at the hands of the instructor

[7]The importance of the voice becomes clear in clinical work. Many of my female patients have related how, beginning in childhood and continuing into adult life, an attempt to convey a strong emotion or thought articulately would be stopped by tears which choked them, leaving them, in essence, mute. The central part of the work in these cases has been to recapture the inner voice that was stifled or distorted in an attempt to get anything out into the world.

Miss Scatcherd, tries to impart to Jane the importance of the next life and the negligible worth of this one. Although Jane loves and admires Helen, she cannot accept her belief that whatever happens is fated and must be born stoically. Of Helen, Jane thinks, "I could not comprehend this doctrine of endurance." The dialogue between them shows where each stands on the issue of endurance as an answer to life:

> "But I feel this, Helen: I must dislike those who, whatever I do to please them, persist in disliking me; I must resist those who punish me unjustly. It is as *natural* [my emphasis] as that I should love those who show me affection, or submit to punishment when I feel it is deserved."
>
> "Heathens and savage tribes hold that doctrine; but Christians and civilised nations disown it . . . It is not violence that best overcomes hate — nor vengeance that most heals injury."
>
> "What then?"
>
> "Read the New Testament and observe what Christ says and how He acts. . . ."
>
> "What does He say?"
>
> "Love your enemies; bless those that curse you . . ."
>
> "Then I should love Mrs. Reed, which I cannot do; I should bless her son, which is impossible" (p. 68).

Helen "lives in calm, looking to the future" (p. 69). She represents a path with which many of us are all too familiar. (After all, many of our mothers endured, some courageously, lives which they felt incapable of changing.) Helen is committed to substituting, in Rich's words, "a masculine God for the love of earthly men (or women)" (1973, p. 70). For Jane, it is clear that this cannot work. Her allegiance is to nature and to life — *her* life, in *this* world. Similarly, the model Miss Temple represents, one of fairness, grace, learning, and kindness, but well within the collective Christian framework, is also not-Jane.[8] Miss Temple offers Jane a shelter difficult to find within a patrifocal culture. She is a diminished deity within the sanctuary which Lowood becomes (once the power of Mr. Brocklehurst wanes): the ancient powers of anger and passion are not lived by her, only

---

[8]Miss Temple's is actually the more collectively acceptable Christian life. Helen Burns, like her kindred spirit St. John Rivers, represents the uncomfortable alternative of the passionate spirit wanting to die for Christ. Rich compares Helen to women like Simone Weil or St. Theresa, "certain gifted imaginative women in the Christian era" (1973, p. 70).

the capacity for endurance plus a propensity for subversion. She practices the latter through such acts as feeding the girls, particularly Jane and Helen, to whom she dispenses "tea and emblematic seedcake, nourishing body and soul together despite Mr. Brocklehurst's puritanical dicta," his "sanctimonious stinginess" (Gilbert and Gubar 1979, p. 345).

During the years at Lowood, Jane studies and becomes skilled in the teaching profession. Miss Temple provides sanctuary but eventually marries and leaves. Up to this point, Jane had found a home and a mode of being, Miss Temple's mode. She describes her years at Lowood in this way:

> [Miss Temple's] friendship and society had been my continual solace; she has stood me in the stead of mother, governess, and latterly, companion . . . I had imbibed from her something of her nature and much of her habits; more harmonious thoughts . . . I was quiet; I believed I was content (p. 98).

But all of this proves to be a fiction. For when Miss Temple leaves Lowood to be married, Jane quickly reverts to the impetuous, fiery core self that is truly her own: "I had undergone a transforming process . . . my mind had put off all it had borrowed of Miss Temple . . . and now I was left in my natural element" (p. 99). Jane takes the daring step of advertising for a position as a governess. When her advertisement is answered, a new chapter in her life begins. She now goes to Thornfield. With her identity defined, she knows who Jane is and who she is not. She is now ready for her greatest test.

## Jane in Love

As others have noted, Jane's first encounter with Mr. Rochester, the master of Thornfield and her employer, is an odd one. Out of the lonely night, he appears on horseback, preceded by his dog, Pilot. Jane fantasizes at first that it is the Gytrash, a mythical north-of-England spirit from her childhood tales. This romantic image is soon dispelled when Jane perceives it is only a traveler on a horse; even more so when the man slips on the ice and sprains his ankle, crying, "What the deuce is to do now?" The scene is comic in its contrast to Jane's fear of the supernatural and serves several functions. One is to foreshadow the equivalency of their future relationship: Rochester is brought down, literally, to a level where he must lean on Jane. The ridiculous nature of his meeting with Jane signals the future, necessary puncturing of his inflation as a master of his world. Also, his initial minor pain foreshadows the severe maiming he will experience: as central representative of the masculine energy in this book, Rochester will suffer before he can achieve union. Although his story is much the smaller part of this book, Rochester's meeting with Jane and his development constitutes an integral piece in Jane's growth.

As Rich notes, when Jane leaves Lowood for Thornfield, she is not longing for a man, yet that is what she finds (1973, p. 98). Jane grows to know and admire Rochester—his intellect, his passion, and his wider knowledge. She, in turn, becomes to him the symbol of all the truth and honesty, intelligence and integrity which has been lacking in his life. However, his position as a man of wealth and family has meant leading a life of deception and decadence. He cannot consciously relinquish his power attitude, although he yearns for Jane. Irigaray says, "In our social order, women are 'products,' used and exchanged by men. Their status is that of merchandise, 'commodities.' How can such subjects of use and transaction claim the right to speak and to participate in exchange in general?" (1985, p. 84).

While Rochester does recognize her worth—when he proposes, he says, in part, "my equal is here and my likeness. Jane, will you marry me?" (p. 286)—he also tells her, "I love you as *my own flesh*" [my emphasis]. Jane is apparently "equal" because she *is* him—right at the moment of the proposal we see foreshadowed his inability to perceive her equality as one of equivalence of being. Jane must *be* him—she cannot be both loved and different. When he asks her to marry him, she returns his love and agrees to be his wife. Although consciously she feels happy, she also feels increasingly disturbed by his tendency to treat her as a possession. There are several allusions in the text to "harem" and "seraglio," and though Jane continues to let him know in very straightforward terms that she will not be his plaything, Rochester never really hears her.

As the appointed day of the wedding approaches, Jane's qualms mount. She has two dreams, both on the same theme: she is carrying a small child, she is looking for Rochester; although she can see him at a distance, he is heading away; she tries to follow but cannot reach him. Jung's work on dreams shows them to relate in symbolic language the attitude of the unconscious, which compensates for the one-sided attitude of consciousness (1945, par. 101). Here, though Jane for the most part consciously trusts Rochester and looks forward to the marriage, the unconscious makes a profound statement. Rochester, in the dream, represents a *compensatory* symbolic figure, the animus, which Jung believed to be the counterpart in women to the man's anima, or soul. As Kathrin Asper explains:

> If C. G. Jung laid the foundations of this genial concept . . . then the credit goes to Emma Jung for depicting the animus in a more differentiated manner than Jung had originally done . . . Contrasting it with the anima, which Jung called "she that must be obeyed," [after H. Rider Haggard's *She*] Emma Jung

> cautioned women against regarding their animus as
> . . . "he that must be obeyed." For too long, women
> had accustomed themselves to obeying men and had
> internalized this hierarchical order. (1991, p. 121)

The Rochester figure in the dream represents a negative internal component of Jane's unconscious towards which all of her energy could be guided with disasterous results, energy that belongs with the child — the symbol of her core self. The unconscious might be said to be striving to let Jane know that this aspect of her psyche needs to be regarded as "he who must *not* be obeyed."[9]

She tells Rochester about the two dreams, as well as a strange visitation in the night. Although he explains them all away, their wedding the next morning is stopped by the revelation that he has a wife, the mad Bertha Mason Rochester, who had in fact visited Jane's room the night before. Jane knows she must leave him. Their parting is wrenching, as they love each other passionately. He begs Jane not to leave, but she makes it clear that his marriage (and his failure to be truthful) form an insurmountable obstacle to any relationship: he says, "It would not be wicked to love me"; she says, "It would be to obey you" (p. 353). Although her stand seems firm and her mind made up, she is in danger of being misled by pity for his wretchedness and the feeling that his very salvation depends on her. That night she has the following dream:

> *I dreamt I lay in the red-room at Gateshead . . . The light . . .*
> *seemed glidingly to mount the wall . . . [the moon] broke forth*
> *as never moon yet burst from cloud: a hand first penetrated the*
> *sable folds and waved them away; then, not a moon, but a*
> *white, human form shone . . . inclining a glorious brow earth-*
> *ward . . . it spoke to my spirit . . . it whispered in my heart —*
> *"My daughter, flee temptation!"*
> *"Mother, I will."*

The moon, which is present at key moments throughout *Jane Eyre*, represents an archetypal level of the feminine which compensates in a major

---

[9]The scope of this paper does not allow a full discussion of this revisioning of Jung's concept of the animus; from clinical work, however, I would observe that, since women grow up internalizing patrifocal directives, a dream image of the animus leading or guiding a woman has a negative cast. Instead, a more propitious dream image in terms of the growth of a woman is one which signals an inner union between the ego and animus where the ego is not led but met.

way for Jane's susceptibility to the demands of a patrifocal culture. The dream, not bound by time or space, compensates for her coming weakness when she arises and flees. She feels greatly torn as she walks past Rochester's door and hears him pacing restlessly into the night:

> There was a heaven — a temporary heaven — in this room for me, if I chose: I had but to go in and say — "Mr. Rochester, I will love you and live with you through life until death," and a fount of rapture would spring to my lips . . . My hand moved towards the lock [of his door]: I caught it back, and glided on. (p. 357)

Even while Jane is in the process of running away, she thinks "I longed to be his; I panted to return; it was not too late . . . I could go back and be his comforter — his pride; his redeemer from misery; perhaps from ruin" (p. 358) . Supported by the unconscious in the form of the archetypal feminine, however, Jane does not return.[10]

She eventually finds her way to Marsh End, where she is rescued by St. John Rivers and his two sisters, Mary and Diana. The sisters take her in and her life with them is good, in some ways not unlike her life with Miss Temple, though perhaps intellectually broader. The sisters represent another alternative that, like Miss Temple's life, is viable. This book is about difference, not sameness, and one woman's choice may not be another's. The Rivers might very well represent "the ideal of female strength for which Jane has been searching" (Gilbert and Gubar 1979, p. 365), except for one fact: at this late point in the book, Jane's identity has coalesced and that identity is not like the sisters, women for whom the peace and unity of each other's intellectual and sympathetic company provides what their nature needs. That is simply one decent model, but not Jane's, whose tempestuous and fiery nature seeks elsewhere for completion. Through Jane, a change in psychic structure manifests, one that symbolically demonstrates the potential to radically change the relation of women to the world.

Likewise, Jane rejects St. John's plans for her to join him as a missionary. Gilbert and Gubar comment that "St. John's attempts to

---

[10]Jane's extreme feeling that only she can save Rochester from his imminent ruin would constitute a dangerous inflation, if acted upon. Under the guise of selflessness and pity, women often avoid personal growth. While patrifocal civilization supports and even encourages such erasure of the needs of the woman in service to the development of a man, certain types of men are also prone to this psychological makeup with regard to women. Whether in women or men, this is not to be confused with a genuine recognition of the need to put someone else first (e.g., a child or elderly parent).

'imprison' Jane may seem the most irresistible of all" (1979, p. 366), since they come on the heels of Jane's vaunted adherence to "principle and law." However, his blandishments are necessary to highlight how little any collective principle and law have to do with Jane's actions.[11] Jane's adherence is to the development and maintenance of her core self, which flows from an archetypal base that requires attention to her inner voice and cares little for collective rules of right thinking. Although St. John appeals to her urge to serve (in this case the patriarchal religion), he deeply offends her natural affiliation to a different religion, that which addresses spirit in body. He will allow her to serve only if she marries him, and as Jane says: "Can I . . . endure all the forms of love (which I doubt not he would scrupulously observe) and know that the spirit was absent?" (p. 451). (In different ways, both St. John and Rochester want to colonize Jane's body; at least Rochester's is the more honest passion.) Although Jane tells St. John that she scorns his offer as well as his idea of marriage, he, like Rochester, fails to hear her. Nevertheless, Jane is thrown into inner turmoil by his offer, and finally asks Heaven to show her the way. At that moment, she hears the voice of her beloved, Rochester, calling "Jane! Jane! Jane!" in a voice filled with "pain and woe." It is not heaven that answers her: "It is the work of nature. She was roused, and did — no miracle — but her best" (p. 467).

Jane immediately leaves for Thornfield but finds it in ruins. Jane's reunion is with a Rochester who has experienced pain and loss and has found humility. Through a terrible fire, in which Bertha died, he has lost one eye (toward the end some vision comes back in the other) and one hand in an attempt to rescue her. These wounds have had the effect of liberating Rochester from the constraints on his vision imposed by phallocratic culture; the liberation allows him to achieve union with Jane. This release could not happen without the experience of pain and loss equal in many ways to her's. He is softened and tempered by his experiences so that his soul "calls" to Jane over the miles, although she knows nothing about the fire. His blindness is like Gloucester's, as Gilbert and Gubar have noted: he sees more clearly now than he could before. His ability for deception of self and others is stripped away. He has undergone a profound change in personality and circumstance.[12] It is this change which opened him to the

[11]Such "principle and law" would be an example of directives from the animus.

[12]Jane and Rochester undergo analogous but quite different forms of growth. Jane listens to her inner voice, sacrificing her love willingly but with great pain. Here, the ego acts in harmony with the Self. Rochester, on the other hand, has no way consciously to lose his arrogance, as it was fated by his birth into a phallocratic culture; he does, however, through

extrasensory connection with Jane. His newfound humility allows him what he had wished for earlier in the tale: to wipe the slate clean and begin anew. Eventually, Rochester and Jane marry and have a son. Together, they symbolize a new possibility of union, stemming from development of a feminine discourse of disobedience.[13]

Irene Taylor calls "most troubling . . . the end of the 'wild, free thing' in Jane: 'she went out with Bertha's fires' " (1990, p. 177). I read the union of Jane and Rochester rather differently. "Reader, I married him" begins the last chapter, and as one writer comments, "The tacit message is that *I* married him—not that *he* married me" (Oates 1988, p. 167). The birth of Jane's baby indicates the possibility of new life out of this completely new union. But more striking for me, Jane is only twenty at the novel's end. It is difficult to conceive of the idea that Jane Eyre, who has developed a core self and fought against all the world to retain it, who has by her adherence to her inner voice, which has required that she attend to it and in so doing disobey the world, could simply cease to grow. Jane begins her tale as a motherless child but she ends it as our imaginal mother, in her turn giving birth to and nurturing us. Perhaps it is the energy of Jane Eyre that gave birth to Charlotte Brontë, who then returned the favor and gave birth to Jane.

# References

Asper, K. 1991. Fitcher's Bird: Illustrations of the negative animus and shadow in persons with narcissistic disturbances. In *Psyche's Stories.* Wilmette, Ill.: Chiron Publications.

Brontë, C. 1946. *Jane Eyre.* Cleveland, Ohio: The World Publishing Company.

Cixous, H. 1981. The laugh of the Medusa. *New French Feminisms.* New York: Schocken Books.

Gilbert, S. M., and Gubar, S. 1979. *The Madwoman in the Attic.* New Haven, Conn.: Yale University Press.

Gilead, S. 1987. Liminality and antiliminality in Charlotte Brontë's novels: *Shir-*

his experience of great pain at the loss of Jane, make himself open to the searing transformation that will allow him to regain her. Together, they represent the possibility of an equiarchal union, on the inner as well as outer level.

[13]That the new union embodied in the text has always had a fascination for men as well as women is exemplified by a charming review that appeared when *Jane Eyre* was first published. A man, reading *Jane Eyre* for the purposes of review, stated that he was not prepared to enjoy the book; however, he found himself so completely enthralled that he read all night until, he said, at four a.m., he finally married Mr. Rochester!

*ley* reads *Jane Eyre. Texas Studies in Language and Literature.* 29(3): 302–322.

Irigaray, L. 1985. *This Sex Which Is Not One.* Ithaca, N.Y.: Cornell University Press.

Jung, C. G. 1921. *Psychological Types. CW*, vol. 6. Princeton, N.J.: Princeton University Press, 1971.

———. 1945. On the nature of dreams. In *CW* 8:281–300. Princeton, N.J.: Princeton University Press, 1974.

Kadish, D. Y. 1987. *The Literature of Images: Narrative Landscape from Julie to Jane Eyre.* New Brunswick, N.J.: Rutgers University Press.

Myer, V. G. 1987. *Charlotte Brontë: Truculent Spirit.* London: Vision Press.

Oates, J. C. 1988. *(Woman) Writer: Occasions and Opportunities.* New York: E. P. Dutton.

Peters, J. D. 1991. Finding a voice: Towards a woman's discourse of dialogue in the narration of *Jane Eyre. Studies in the Novel* 23(2):217–236.

Rich, A. 1973. Jane Eyre: Temptations of a motherless woman. *Ms.* (October), pp. 68–107.

Ross, L. B. 1991. Cupid and Psyche: Birth of a new consciousness. In *Psyche's Stories.* Wilmette, Ill.: Chiron Publications.

Stern, D. 1985. *The Interpersonal World of the Infant.* New York: Basic Books, Inc.

Taylor, I. 1990. *Holy Ghosts: The Male Muses of Emily and Charlotte Brontë.* New York: Columbia University Press.

Zeiger, A. 1960. Afterword. In *Jane Eyre.* New York: New American Library.

# TO SPEAK OR BE SPOKEN

## SOME WOMEN IN AFRICAN LITERATURE

## Marjolijn de Jager

*To my daughter, Claudia Jane; grateful for all she has taught me and for, perhaps unwittingly but so truly, her following in the footsteps of her great-grandmother, Cornelia Jane.*

In *Sundiata, An Epic of Old Mali* (Niane 1965), Sogolon is the Buffalo Woman and Oulamba is the hunter who has killed the buffalo of Do. Sogolon is first described to Oulamba as "a very ugly maid — uglier than you can imagine . . . (who) is called Sogolon Kedjou, or Sogolon Kondouto, because she is a hunchback. . . . She will be an extraordinary woman if you manage to possess her." Earlier, it had been foretold to the king of Mali, Maghan Kon Fatta, by a stranger and a soothsayer that, although the king already had an eldest son, "your successor is not yet born. I see two hunters coming to your city; they have come from afar and a woman accompanies them. Oh, that woman! She is ugly, she is hideous, she bears on her back a disfiguring hump. Her monstrous eyes seem to have been merely laid on her face, but mystery of mysteries, this is the woman you must marry, sire, for she will be the mother of him who will make the name of Mali immortal for ever" (p. 6). Indeed, some time later, Oulamba — "the conqueror of the buffalo (who) had not been able to conquer the young girl (and) only as an afterthought . . . had the idea of giving her to the king of Mali" (p. 11) — comes to offer Sogolon to the "handsome Maghan." During the preparations for the wedding of Maghan and Sogolon, we are told that "Sogolon wept softly" and "never uttered a word" (p. 10). The king, too, is unable to conquer her and consummate the marriage. It takes a full week, followed by the king's decision (revealed to him by his jinn) to sacrifice Sogolon and spill her virgin blood, the news of which causes her to faint, before he is able to possess her during that fainting spell. She conceives and will, indeed, become the mother of the great Sundiata. So reads the text of the Mali epic, centuries old.

Werewere Liking (from Cameroon) is a poet, musician, novelist, playwright, performer, and painter and is also the artistic director of her own theater troupe, which works and lives together at the Villa Ki-Yi in Abidjan (Ivory Coast). In her last "roman-chant" (novel-song/chant), *L'Amour-cent-vies*, she gives us her version of Sogolon:[1]

> The king of Do decided . . . to seek new blood and chose the daughter of a powerful marabou-hunter. . . . Alas, the young girl had already chosen another man, a blacksmith, master of fire, and was expecting a child by him. The enraged king had the blacksmith banished and took possession of the young woman, pregnancy and all. . . . And the child was born. A girl. A relief. No problems of succession, of land, which a woman always finds through marriage.
>
> The little girl did not resemble the king at all; the insinuations and rumors created just a bit of embarrassment, which were removed as soon as she began to grow up: they would marry her off as quickly as possible and put an end to all this! Is that why she grew to have such an open aversion to marriage which, in her eyes, became a rejection of her personality, sexual segregation, and masculine domination? In any event, she swore that she would never marry anyone at all unless she herself had chosen him. But how? She was beautiful and growing up fast, and women were given away in marriage according to the interest and the alliances of families, her opinion would not be asked in those days.
>
> She told herself that it would be enough to discourage suitors, to find some way of not pleasing them. . . . So they watched her neglect all those household tasks that validated womanhood and devote herself to the most difficult of masculine tasks, even those that require a previous initiation such as the hunt. . . . Very soon she was rumored to be a sorceress. . . . And she would have wept with joy: the timid and the conform-

---

[1]All the quotes from this novel that follow are from a translation in progress and not yet the definitive version. The title literally means *Love-One Hundred-Lives*; phonetically, however, there is a second meaning. As titles can be quite complex, it must, for our present purposes, be left in its literal version only.

ists would thus automatically be eliminated from the list of suitors!

One day, as she was tracking a herd of buffalo, she witnessed a scene that sickened her permanently of the masculine tribe: a pregnant female was obviously having great difficulty giving birth; it was very clear that she would never manage all by herself. . . . She was rolling on the ground, biting trees in order not to bellow so violently as to lose herself. Throughout all this, the rutting male was running after all the young females in the group, making revolting orgastic noises! Reveling and wantonly romping around the mortified laboring female who was desperately struggling. The male, blinded by his rut and not managing to catch up with a young female, brutally jumped on the female in labor, who was crazed with pain and pointed her horns into the male's belly, literally disemboweling him! In one irresistible leap, forgetting all caution, our huntress pounced upon the male and finished him off, dispersing the rest of the herd. Then her eyes met those of the laboring female and she sensed the encounter. . . . And softly she began to speak to the animal as if to a friend and helped her through the delivery And the miracle occurred: the animal spoke to her and asked her what she might do for her to give proof of her gratefulness. . . .

"Pass some of your appearance on to me so that the ordinary mortal will never be able to find me beautiful and desire me, so that I may be free to marry only him whom I will have chosen, him who will be able to look at who I really am inside." So the female buffalo passed her hump, her blackness, and her terrifying ugliness on to the young woman, as well as part of her strength. She in turn gave some of her golden blood to the animal and so it is that the beast found herself with a golden tail. The golden tail by which the buffalo could be described who ravaged the country of Do, killing all the males that came across its path, males both animal and human.

The young woman hoisted the male buffalo on her back as if he were a simple gazelle and went to the king to offer him her first true big game. Everyone fled before her, taking her for a sorceress who had failed in a metamorphosis, for she was now as ugly as a buffalo. And they called her Sogolon, the buffalo-woman. A great emptiness was created around her and, having thus eliminated from her life all "people in rut," as she used to call them, she was at leisure to seek and discover those who were preoccupied with other things, those who were preparing the rebirth, and they were not among the nobles of the royal court, alas! (Liking 1988, pp. 41–43)

What concerns us here, as in the other contributions to this collection, is the particular form that "disobedience" takes in this work by Liking. One of the most sought after characteristics of womanhood, sought after by the male first and by the female as a consequence of this, is physical beauty. Traditionally, woman suffers in the male-dominated society if she is anything less than somewhat (and therefore acceptably) attractive, suffers from earliest childhood on, will pretend not to be terribly clever in order to be popular, will spend more time and money on hairdos and makeup than on discovering her inner self, her intelligence, her dormant gifts. Similarly, the pretty girl (and who defines beauty?!)[2] suffers albeit in very different ways: first she learns to compete with other attractive girls, later vying with young women for the attentions of the male, leading not toward solidarity and sisterhood but away from it, to every level of envy, jealousy, and to insidious resentments and anger. Either way, both if present or absent, physical beauty is more often than not a handicap, unless the female has learned to cut through the "cover of her book" to a discovery of its contents, that is, her spirit, her intelligence, her soul, her inner needs and desires. Only then can she be free enough to conquer her physical beauty if she is so endowed, or to conquer her sense of loss if she was born "ugly" and then begin to find herself and be free to develop that self.

If the act of being visible is disobedience, then the conscious act of rendering herself not only visible, but visible in a hideous way is a double disobedience on Sogolon's part. Yet, it is her only way out of the literal and figurative imprisonment of male domination, expresssed from the moment of her birth as, on the one hand, "a relief . . . no problems of succession" since she was the king's eldest but not his child and her femaleness sets her free from the throne (or from death, as a boy child would not have made it to that throne in all probability). On the other hand, she is in every other way enslaved, since she has no right to make any decisions about her own life. In Sogolon's case, beauty is equalled, if not surpassed, by her desire for freedom, by her intelligence which leads her to find a way to that freedom. Yet, she must pay a terrible price: she not only willingly sacrifices her physical beauty, but lives in the "great emptiness (that) was created around her" by the mere fact of her ugliness. Even those who knew her when she was still beautiful never knew her well enough to have retained a memory of

---

[2]On the anecdotal plane: a personal friend, who is a teacher in the New York City public school system, was recently offered a one-day modeling job for which she would receive *as much* remuneration as she normally earns for a full month's work in the classroom; once again, and still, the physical aspect is valued far higher than is any other real contribution women (and sometimes men, e.g., in the world of sports in particular) make.

her inner self and, therefore, must have *always* judged her by her appearance alone. When she *spoke* and stated that she wanted to choose her own marital partner, she had been silenced or simply not heard; in order to accomplish her own goals, she must render herself ugly so that silence is no longer imposed but, in fact, is now the response from the previous dominator. During her period of beauty, she was made not to speak; now that she is ugly, she may do what she will but the others will not speak to her. Either way, her action, admirable though it may be, is a *re*action to a male-dominant culture, society, class. And here lies the tragedy, for it is tragic that in both the old epic of Sundiata and Werewere Liking's (very feminist) depiction of Sogolon, the buffalo-woman was never *born* to be herself from the beginning. Liking's Sogolon makes herself free, whereas the epic's Sogolon is never free, recognized and validated only after her son, Sundiata, grows to be a heroic king. But even Liking has, must have, her Sogolon buy into the *value system* of the patriarchy, rejecting (one of) the most sought after female characteristic(s) in order to allow herself true equality and freedom. Her act of courage is, of course, an act of disobedience from the patriarchal point of view.

How can this ever be altered as long as the ground rules are set by the patriarchy? And how do we change the roles of those who set the rules? And, last but perhaps most important, how do we make sure the rules themselves will be altered in order to be, indeed and truly, equal for all humans, female and male alike? Primarily, it seems to me, the roles and "rules" of nurturing and protecting must inform the value system to be. In *Wild Women in the Whirlwind*, speaking of Momma Henderson: "Maya Angelou invites others to follow her grandmother's model — to stand courageously and full of faith — not to turn back and not to falter. In the role of nurturer and protectress, Momma, in the words of critic Stephen Butterfield, both protects and 'inspires the urge to protect' " (Braxton and McLaughlin 1990, p. 303). If models can be emulated and the models are protectresses and nurturers, they will indeed inspire the followers to similar behavior.

This, too, happens in *L'Amour-cent-vies*, where one of the great figures is Madjo, the grandmother of the young male protagonist, Lem. Without going into a detailed synopsis of the novel, Lem is about to commit suicide by hanging himself from a tree with a rope he is knotting of umbilical cords, when he hears:

> . . .grandmother's crystalline laughter like a voice in a canyon, a pebble on a lake, echoes and vibrations. . . .
>
> "What are you doing up there, Lem? I know that you 'have a habit of throwing bridges.' But I didn't think you'd be

throwing bridges of meat to the heavens at midnight. Do you know I've been looking for you since noon?"

Just imagine Lem, clutching his rope like a life-jacket, with his look of mature adult-child, when he came up against this obstacle to his suicide:

"Madjo, I might as well tell you right away: there's nothing you can do for me anymore, and you won't convince me any longer. I've made my decision, and I'm going all the way. My rope is ready, I'm going to hang myself."

Do you hear Grandmother Mischief's laughter as it stealthily slips in the soft and sticky rope, as in the hoop of a child, as into a lightweight toy . . .?

"But that rope is much too long and too heavy for this little tree. You'll never go all the way with that. Come to your father's plantation, where there are many taller and more sturdy trees. At this hour there's nobody there, you know."

And look at Lem, disappointed in that hope we always have of finding resistance so that we can fight all the more and show the strength of our willpower, so that we can still play at being the stubborn child. . . . (p. 13)

In fact, the novel-song is told in several (female) voices, of which Madjo's is the main one, geared toward recounting the history of Lem's immediate and not-so-immediate ancestors while he continues to knot his cord and listen and reflect upon what he is hearing. At one point in Lem's story when he is a nine-year-old child, even Sogolon is superimposed over his grandmother's being, when in one of his favorite games (the buffalo hunt) with Madjo, he sees and *smells* her as a woman turned buffalo, suddenly hideous, then "grandmother's face continued its metamorphosis and became the face of a young woman so unusual she seemed extra-terrestrial . . ." (p. 21). The boy speaks to her with a voice he doesn't recognize himself and

his own voice frightened him so much that he screamed out and closed his eyes tightly. . . . Then Madjo's voice clothed itself in its usual mischievousness only to say to him: "You're not going to start that again, are you?" And the enigmatic look she had, left him with a taste of forbidden fruit which he would chase after always. . . . And I believe [says Lem] it is shame that makes me cry out. As I see it coming I dread the moment that I'll jump on her and be swallowed up by her, as I believe I have done at other times, in other places. . . . And she was singing the same lullaby to him there underneath his rope of umbilical cords, with

a voice like the original sound, while he was weeping over his
weakness, over what he used to think of as his powerlessness.
. . . (p. 22)

In the end, Lem comes down from the tree to hear Madjo's voice up
close. First he hears his own sobs, then hears only his grandmother's voice
and "he said to himself that the original sound had probably not been a sob;
creation would surely have been aborted. . . . The original sound was a
voice" (p. 79). For Lem, his grandmother's voice has become the cosmic
voice, filled with vibrations and intonations and music, of which he is and
always will be a part.

And so, he decides not to take his life. Instead, having learned the
lesson his grandmother has been teaching him all along, having lived vicari-
ously through the experiences of courage of his ancestors as told to him by
Madjo, he finds the courage to live the life he is meant to live, that of the
sculptor-artist which he was afraid to become. It is only Madjo's nurturing
and protection that leads him to this point, and when he reaches it Madjo
has disappeared.

We see the reverse result in Ken Bugul's *The Abandoned Baobab*
(1991). Renée Larrier summarizes the situation well:

> Ken Bugul's mother's absence had a profoundly det-
> rimental effect on her. In *Le Baobab Fou* (1982) she
> associates absence and silence with her mother who
> used to leave her alone playing under the baobab tree
> when she was only two years old, a scene which
> would haunt her throughout her life. They would
> later be separated. Ken was also estranged from her
> grandmother, an unfortunate occurrence in that it is
> she who would ordinarily provide direction. . . . As a
> result of being abandoned, of this lack of bonding,
> Ken dreamed of her "ancêtres les Gaulois" (her ances-
> tors the Gauls) and a Europe she read about in maga-
> zines. In Belgium on a scholarship, she dropped out
> of school, drifted, and experimented with drugs. Ken
> Bugul was searching for an identity that she was
> denied growing up. (Larrier 1991)

In Ken Bugul we have the incorporation of the two issues discussed
earlier: first, she has no protectress, no nurturer during her formative years
and is doomed to look for those everywhere she goes as she grows into
adulthood, finding herself silent and abandoned despite her "popularity";
second, she *is* "popular" as always for the wrong reasons—she is beautiful,
and, once in Belgium, she finds herself in a double bind. "Because she was

Black, and also because she hung on and she was daring, out of sheer despair. She dared to be transparent, she dared to disguise herself, she dared to laugh, she dared to weep, but deep down she was bitter" (1991, p. 85). As she describes it: "Never had I been able to talk about myself. Faced with Laure and François, I based myself only on references. I would listen, I'd follow along, I'd participate, but it wasn't me. They were stripping me, emptying me out, displaying me" (ibid.).

Where Sogolon is *surrounded* by emptiness once she has taken on ugliness as part of her being, Ken *is left* empty on the inside as members of her society suck her dry, wanting her beauty and "exotic" aspects for their own gratification, in a vain attempt to fill their own emptiness. But Sogolon is whole within the surrounding emptiness, while Ken is (almost) destroyed, an empty shell surrounded by a crowd of grasping, needy, exploitative strangers. In trying to be "obedient" to the societal structure and its expectations, Ken Bugul loses sight of her freedom and her self. Sogolon finds her freedom and self through the very act of "disobedience" to the societal structure and its expectations. Both were born into a patriarchal society and culture that would by necessity require they wage a battle for their free existence. Neither of them would have had to wage the battle had the structures within which they lived been more protective of their being and of their right to a free existence from the moment of birth onwards. So the structures must be undone. Never will they be undone by those who have written the present rules and abide by them, which is to say that the way must now be indicated by the protectresses/protectors/nurturers and those who follow their lead.

Kimiko Hahn, in a poem called "Her First Language," writes, "It occurs to you / only women and wounded soldiers / writhe" (Hahn, Jackson and Sherman 1988, p. 41). If the act of being visible is disobedience, if the act of being audible is disobedience, they are so only from the viewpoint of the patriarchy. If women want to stop writhing under the lashes from the patriarchs who punish us for our disobedience, we will have to turn the patriarchy around. Or, as Trinh T. Minh-ha has already put it so eloquently:

> In trying to tell something, a woman is told, shred-
> ding herself into opaque words while her voice dis-
> solves on the walls of silence. Writing: a commitment
> of language. . . . She has been warned of the risk she
> incurs by letting words run off the rails, time and
> again tempted by the desire to gear herself to the
> accepted norms. But where has obedience led her? At
> best, to the satisfaction of a "made-woman," capable
> of achieving as high a mastery of discourse as that of
> the male establishment in power. . . . The more one

depends on the master's house for support, the less
one hears what he doesn't want to hear. Difference is
not difference to some ears, but awkwardness or
incompleteness. Aphasia. Unable or unwilling?
Many have come to tolerate this dissimilarity and
have decided to suspend their judgments (only)
whenever the other is concerned. Such an attitude is a
step forward; at least the danger of speaking for the
other has emerged into consciousness. But it is a very
small step indeed, since it serves as an excuse for their
complacent ignorance and their reluctance to involve
themselves in the issue. You who understand the
dehumanization of forced removal-relocation-
reeducation-redefinition, the humiliation of having
to falsify your own reality, your voice—you know.
And often cannot *say* it. You try and keep on trying
to unsay it, for if you don't, they will not fail to fill in
the blanks on your behalf, and you *will be said*.
(Minh-ha 1989, pp. 79–80, emphasis mine)

For a long time, Ken Bugul *was said*. Until she spoke and told her
story. Even so, her publishers urged her to use a pseudonym (Ken Bugul is
Wolof and means "the person nobody wants") rather than her own name,
Mariétou M'Baye, in an attempt to avoid possible scandal because of the
explicitness of her disclosures—not tolerated, unacceptable, when coming
from the African woman. It goes without saying that many of the reviews of
her book in Senegal were negative precisely because of those disclosures,
pseudonym or not.

Madjo speaks *herself* and in so doing makes a (hu)man, a real man,
out of her grandson, opening the door one more inch onto a society that will
not be patriarchally dominant, but that will be populated by a race, the New
Race, the "Blue Race . . . of children of breath and fire, of jasper and coral"
(Liking 1983).

# References

Niane, D. T. 1965. *Sundiata: An Epic of Old Mali*. G. D. Pickett, trans. Essex:
    Longman Group Ltd.

Liking, W. 1988. *L'Amour-Cent-Vies*. M. de Jager, trans. Paris: Editions
    Publisud.

Braxton, J. M., and McLaughlin, A. N., eds. 1990. *Wild Women in the Whirl-
    wind*. New Brunswick, N.J.: Rutgers University Press.

Bugul, K. 1991. *The Abandoned Baobab: The Autobiography of a Senegalese
    Woman*. M. de Jager, trans. New York: Lawrence Hill Books.

Larrier, R. 1991. Reconstructing motherhood: Francophone African women autobiographers. African Literature Association Annual Conference, March, New Orleans.

Hahn, K., Jackson, G., and Sherman, S. 1988. *We Stand Our Ground*. New York: IKON, Inc.

Minh-ha, T. T. 1989. *Woman Native Other*. Bloomington, Ind.: Indiana University Press.

Liking, W. 1983. *Elle sera de jaspe et de corail*. Paris: Editions L'Harmattan.

# APPLE, NABILA, AND RAMZA

## ARAB WOMEN'S NARRATIVES OF RESISTANCE

### Miriam Cooke

I teach a class on women's feminist writings in the Arab world. At the beginning of the course, many students are skeptical, not quite sure why they are there. Their parents and their friends have discouraged, even mocked them, asking whether any of those black bundles haunting TV screens and newspapers are educated enough to write their own names (do they have names?), let alone poetry and novels. Jennifer confided: "At work, I was telling my colleagues about my class. Someone asked me, Are there women in Arab literature? Aren't they all dressed in black and hidden in veils? I found myself struggling to explain what I am reading and learning in this course. I felt as though I was describing mythical or imaginary aspects of women's writings. The people I work with looked at me in disbelief. 'Really. Is that so?'"

I have come to acknowledge that this attitude is not so surprising in view of the stereotypes we Americans hold of Arab women. Although all women outside the Euro-American sphere are, in general, perceived to be victims, Arab women are more than victims. They embody silence, the prohibition on language. They live apart, far from places that give space to speech. Their mouths are covered, their voices are strangled.

Soon, the students learn that the Arab woman myth mirrors not

I want to thank the faculty of Asian and African Languages and Literature at Duke for reading through an early draft of this paper and for their helpful suggestions. Their comparative perspectives allowed me to situate Apple, Nabila, and Ramza beyond their immediate Arab context.

I owe a major debt to all the students in my Fall 1991 Women in Arab Lit course who have taught me so much. Their comments and activities in class, their written reactions to the readings, and their criticisms of this paper have been invaluable in helping me think through some difficult and critical issues. Thanks particularly to Scheherazade, a consummate storyteller and lover of language.

reality but the desires of those who have constructed the myth in the first place. As Elaine said, "At first, I thought of these women as children; now I realize that they know more about feminism than I ever shall." Inara elaborated, "I could not think of them as women like myself. I feel very differently now. I feel a deep answering vibration in my soul each time I read one of our books or stories. I find myself believing in a worldwide community of women in a way I never knew existed, or even had any inkling that should exist. And this awakening feminism comes not only through an acknowledgment that, wow, women, really have it bad in the Middle East, but an understanding that what powers the men and women in the Middle East powers us all. I cannot shrug off their lives as unconnected from my own, because they are women and men, just like the people in this country." Christine was even more emphatic: "Arab women reflect our inner fears and our own encounters in society. They remind us of ourselves. But we don't like to look at ourselves as disempowered. If we can categorize Arab women as wholly 'other,' we don't have to face our own struggles. We can escape looking at our shared problems and feel good that our society is different."

Arab women not only write today, they have been writing out forcefully since the nineteenth century. They certainly experience oppression, but they do not accept their lot passively. They have resources to draw on to help them overcome their fate. Reva's reaction encapsulated that of others: "After reading three stories about disobedience, my fear is not of being a 'bad girl'—but of not being bad enough. How can I ask Arab women to become activists, to break out of oppressive patterns, when I can hardly think of a time when I've done that. Sure, I make little leaps forward—I call myself 'a woman,' I volunteer to carry heavy things, I stick with my math major—but I do all this in a very accepting and liberal college environment."

Precisely. However, this accepting and liberal college environment is not that of the protagonists of most Arab women's literature, and certainly not of the two Arabic short stories, "A Girl Called Apple" (Badran and Cooke 1990) written in 1981 by the Lebanese Hanan al-Shaykh, and "House of Obedience" (ibid.) written in 1962 by the Egyptian Ihsan Assal, and the Francophone novel, *Ramza*, written in 1958 by the Egyptian Qut al-Qulub (ibid.).[1] How is it that these women who had no access to a validating, supportive community could find the strength to say no to institutions and behavior patterns that no one else had thought to question? How could each protagonist, caught in a web of relationships and social codes, attain a

[1]Several writers have dealt with the topic of house of obedience, including Mahmud Tahir Lashin in 1928.

sense of self that would not allow her to capitulate? Like the proverbial fly, each one shudders and shakes as she senses the web's tightening grip. Yet, unlike that hapless fly, each one persists in her struggle long after other flies would have died.

Hanan al-Shaykh's "A Girl Called Apple" is a fantasy story set in a remote desert tribe. Its remoteness suspends disbelief at the emergence of radically different social systems. It follows, at a step removed, the confused life of a Bedouin girl called Apple. In her oasis, all girls are given the names of fruits—delicious, sweet comestibles. This desert island with its women-fruits is reminiscent of the fabled island of Waqwaq of which medieval Arab philosophers like Ibn Tufayl and geographers like Yaqut have written. The trees of Waqwaq were women-trees who produced women-fruits, some with huge buttocks and vulvas. Fedwa Malti-Douglas has written that these women-fruits were famed for giving men, particularly those from outside the island, pleasure such as they could not experience elsewhere. But once they had fulfilled their mission, they died. Their survival depended on their silence; when these women-fruits uttered a sound, they were ripped from their branches and died. Malti-Douglas concludes that this is an early example of the prohibition on women's speech (1991, pp. 88–90).

"A Girl Called Apple" responds directly to the *raison d'être* and fate of the women-fruits of Waqwaq. It sets up an almost identical situation: an isolated site and women with names of fruits at the disposal of men, especially outsiders. Their commodification is signaled by the hoisting of a flag that announces to all, including chance passersby, that there's a girl for sale: "Surely the idea of marriage would not occur to anyone in such a short period, and yet the flags fluttering above the roofs would tickle the men's hearts, enticing them to marry in the oasis" (Badran and Cooke 1990, p. 157). The first tender years are marked by a red flag, the more mature by blue, and the drying up by yellow. Thereafter, the flag disappears and with it the hope for marriage. Before Apple, all had accepted the necessity of the flag: "The importance of raising the flag had not been explained to them, but they knew as well as they knew their own faces that the flag was probably the only way to get married. Indeed, this oasis was the only one that had not relied on the services of a matchmaker for generations" (ibid., p. 156).

Apple knows that this is the way that marriages are brokered; she longs for marriage and for children, yet she says no to the flag. Although baffled by this unprecedented rejection of the system and its symbol, her father never really protests. Whenever she sees him about to take the flag up on to the roof, Apple stops her father. He folds up the flag, prepared to wait for her to change her mind. However, the years slip by and with them the flags and the opportunities for marriage and happiness in the only way conceivable for the oasis women. Throughout the years, Apple herself is perplexed by her rejection of what others have always accepted. Perhaps she would be embarrassed to have the flag flutter above her house, or she may fear leaving the oasis if bought by a stranger; but these reasons prove hollow. Her father's solution for each anxiety is one that allows Apple to retain her dignity and her place in the society. However, as soon as she hears the solution, Apple remonstrates but without explanation. Even at the moments when she longs most intensely for the comfort of a family of her own, she cannot entertain the thought of the flag.

Finally, when even the yellow flag approaches the end of its appointed time, Apple seems to change her mind. The story ends with her climbing up the stairs to hoist herself the flag she had not allowed others to touch. We leave her in the middle of the night, awaiting a knock at the door. But is this the end? When we reread the pattern of Apple's behavior, we see constant vacillation between reluctant acceptance and reflex rejection. Is this conclusion not another stage in Apple's struggle to reconcile her desire for what the flag may bring and her simultaneous revulsion at what it symbolizes? The logic of the story, it seems to me, militates against capitulation. The story may have ended but not its writing (see Cixous 1981).

This end, which my students construed as a beginning, illustrates the dynamics of resistance.[2] At every instant, Apple was torn between acquiescence to "tribal" expectations and uncompromising rebellion. But the struggle was her own, no one was forcing her to comply with the rules. No one blamed her for her rebelliousness, no one called her mad. Her recalcitrance brought pain to her family, but they did not punish her. The use of the flag precluded the need to introduce matchmakers and suitors into Apple's life. Apple was not rejecting specific individuals her family was proposing, as would Nabila and Ramza. She was rejecting the kind of future her society considered appropriate for her. Apple was not resisting a person but rather a symbolic system. Herein lay her problem, but also her power. It was a problem because targeting and attacking an individual as the source of oppression is much easier than confronting the multiple forces at work in an oppressive structure. However, this diffuse rejection was also empowering because it allowed her to function against the grain of accepted practice. Her inarticulate resistance precluded dialogue and thus subverted the dominant logic. Inarticulateness saved her life, as silence had saved the lives of the women-fruit of Waqwaq.

Whereas Apple has no specific target, Nabila in Ihsan Assal's

---

[2]The students reenacted this story so that its ending should be activist. In their version of the ending, Apple allows the flag to flutter to attract customers, not for her body but for the carpet that she had been weaving throughout those anguished years.

"House of Obedience" does: the husband. Nabila has been married off underage to a man she dislikes. She escapes and returns to her childhood home where the law catches up with her. She is taken to court and learns that Islamic law dictates that she must go back to her husband as a prisoner. When she enters the place where she is to be held, the "house of obedience," she sees that it is next to the Cairo prison, and she smiles to herself at the irony (Badran and Cooke 1990, p. 162). Her husband, as holder of the key to the rooms that constitute the "house of obedience," now has total power and rights over her body. Nonetheless, Nabila does not give in. Although she would seem to have no recourse, she is able, after a struggle, to prevail upon him to leave her alone. Adil does not wish to believe that she refuses to be his wife, so she announces categorically: "You think that the obedience verdict means that I have to give myself to you against my will? Adil, whatever you do I shall never in my whole life be yours" (ibid., p. 163). Twice, she seizes on a slip of attention to escape her prison and return to her parents' home. Although her father and mother are sympathetic, they are weak. They make little or no effort to help her, even though they perceive the injustice of her husband's claim. Again, he drags her back but this time threatens her with *nushuz*. *Nushuz* means recalcitrance and its pronouncement allows the husband to hold his woman in limbo so that she is neither married nor divorced, a nonperson. Nabila becomes desperate to leave the house of obedience and will accept anything that will make this possible. When Adil shows her the *nushuz* papers, she realizes that he has inserted a clause that would make it possible for him at any time to reimpose the house of obedience. While he is not looking, she tears up the papers. This act convinces him that Nabila truly does not want to be with him. He grants her the coveted divorce. In court, he admits defeat but he asks one last favor: he wants to spend a few minutes with her alone. She agrees even though she fears some form of retaliation. Far from it. Having officially lost all power and rights over her body, he concedes that he had never really controlled her. In fact, he admits that he had been controlled by her, at least, by his love for her. Yet, he says tellingly, he had not known how to convey this love. He has been trained to act in a certain way that renders expressions of tenderness taboo. To be a man, he has to assert himself as master. Otherwise, his masculinity is in danger.

"House of Obedience" demonstrates how the gender roles society enjoins destroy the possibility of understanding between women and men. The husband has not invented the house of obedience, it is there as a religiously sanctioned prop for those men who are "not man enough" to control their wives singlehandedly. This house of obedience oppresses the men almost as much as the women, for it signals a change in identity from spouse to enemy. The house of obedience cannot but highlight the irreconcilable difference between the enforcer of obedience and the agent of disobedience. His declarations of love at the end — "Good bye, Nabila. I had wanted you to be with me forever. It looks as though I didn't know how" (p. 167) — signal his own disobedience to the code of masculinity. But it is too late. Society has intervened and gender roles have lost any flexibility they may have ever had. Each must live with the outcome of disobedience. For Nabila, this outcome is a victory; for her husband, it is irredeemable loss. Nabila has been "bad enough" to challenge and overcome the strictures that society had placed around her. Adil does not even know until the end that he, too, is functioning within such strictures, hence he does not know how to challenge and overcome them.

Ramza's story emerges out of the very same logic that drives Nabila. Say no to oppressive social institutions and their representatives without counting the cost. However, Ramza's no, unlike Nabila's and Apple's, is not portrayed as instinctive, irrational, impossible. In 1958, thirty-five years after the first public unveiling in Egypt launched feminism as a self-conscious ideology in the Arab world, Qut al-Qulub authored a woman whose education and sophistication opened up new horizons that forced her to question the authority of received tradition. She cannot but disobey the father she loves and who had nurtured her mind and her will.

Like many upper-class women in turn-of-the-century Egypt, Ramza enjoys a privileged relationship with her father, particularly after her mother's death. But also like them, she finds that when she becomes nubile, her father no longer fosters her freedom, particularly where marriage is concerned. At first, he refuses to believe that Ramza has actually chosen Maher, preferring to impugn the young man for improper behavior. Surely, his daughter is not disobeying his explicit instructions to marry the highly eligible Midhat. He has chosen carefully and lovingly, convincing himself that he is enlightened and that he is not blindly following repressive Eastern customs. Certainly, they are living in the East, but he wants to persuade her "as you would expect any European father to do." Yet, in the same breath, he adds, "even if I had wanted to refuse Safwat Pasha's request I could not. We are committed to the family" (p. 247). Early into the novel, we are put on notice once again that men may wish the best for women in their charge, but that they do not know what this best might be, and even if they did, the society that they helped construct does not allow them to exercize full freedom. Ramza's father can only choose the best among the limited options that society provides. Ramza understands precisely her impending fate, like Apple she is "to be passed on like an inherited good." However, unlike Apple, she eloquently articulates her refusal of this commodification and announces her determination "to marry the man I have chosen freely, the man I have loved" (p. 246). Helpless in the face of his daughter's defiance, the father forbids her, or tries to forbid her, from seeing Maher again. Sensing his helplessness, Ramza is galvanized into action. She disguises herself in her maid's wrap and goes off "to get married right away" (p. 247).

The father declares war on the eloped couple. Ramza is undaunted, but she very soon detects less resolve in her new husband. She fears correctly that he cannot disobey his disapproving father as she had hers. Interestingly, at the point when she fears that she is losing her husband's support against both their fathers, Ramza refers to the letters she was receiving from "young girls in the harem congratulating me on my courage and pleading with me to carry on" (p. 248). With this support network behind her, her battle is reinforced: she has become a role model and has a duty to these more timid women to keep on fighting.[3] Her newfound role and goal make her persist despite the fact that the pretext, her attachment to Maher, is becoming secondary to the fight for the sake of fighting. In stark contrast with Apple and Nabila, Ramza knows, studies, and then devotes her entire energy to learning the law, trying to beat the system that is trying to cow her into submission. She is satisfied that her marriage to Maher conforms to the letter and the spirit of the law. As they await the trial, they plan their future beyond what they anticipate to be a favorable verdict. The surprise negative outcome changes everything. Ramza understands how difficult it has been for Maher "to be accused of every possible beastliness" and to hear that "a marriage between us was an aberration because we were not of the same social class" (p. 249). She anticipates that the public ignominy may make him hate her. Yet, she also knows that what was at stake in this trial was a principle: the public condemnation of "the freedom of choice of marriage partners by the younger generation" (p. 250). With a mixture of pride and trepidation, she describes the impact of the case. The Khedive and Lord Cromer become involved, and Ramza finds that the public has elevated her "into the role of a national heroine fighting for Egyptian independence" (p. 251).

News of her father's growing inflexibility inspires Ramza while it weakens Maher. Ramza has taken refuge with the family of a wealthy shaikh, and it is there that she meets with Maher. Although he seems cold and distant, when pressed he does assure his wife that "his love was stronger than ever" (p. 251). He explains that his father does not want them to meet. Ramza predictably is incensed that he should put his father's pleasure before hers. She reminds him of her own rejection of her father. Exasperated, she bursts out: "Can't you see how we are struggling to liberate women? Do we have to do the job for men as well?" (p. 252). It is not at all clear who is meant by we, but what is clear is that it does not include Maher. This indeed is the crux of Ramza's story, but also of Apple's and Nabila's

---

[3]Ironically, the judge of her case was hardened against her because he "had daughters and feared that I would set a precedent if I won" (p. 248).

stories as well as of countless other Arab women protagonists. Women have found a way to speak and to act against received traditions, men have not.

Although stung by the insinuations of weakness, Maher is not goaded into action. He wants Ramza to be patient (weak?) like him and to await the outcome of the appeal so that they may then reenter their fathers' good graces. He does not recognize that Ramza's action and his passive acquiescence have driven them beyond the pale of social acceptance. Ramza is clear about their ostracism. She has not anticipated the waves that her decision would make, but when they happen she does not hope to roll them back. She proposes that they leave for Sudan, or at least move into an apartment together, have a baby, and to hell with society. Maher runs as fast he can.

Maher's weakness and the continuing pressure of society's disapproving attention begin to take their toll. Ramza sees herself cooped up in the shaikh's house in the harem and surrounded by uneducated women whom she superciliously presumes not to understand her predicament. She even lashes out at her host and storms off. She finds alternative accommodations—as Virginia Woolf reminds us, money is the key to a woman's freedom—and establishes herself comfortably with two servants. Although she complains about the expense involved in prosecuting the case, her decisions never plunge her into dire economic straits.

When the appeal also fails, they have to accept that in society's eyes their marriage is null and void. Why? Because of a difference in class! The authorities have placed class above God and religion and love. Ramza refuses such prioritization, Maher accepts. When she follows him to his military post in the south, he urges her to return to Cairo so as to avoid a scandal. In light of his determination to accept the court's ruling, Ramza reviews her relationship with Maher. She realizes that it was she who had always initiated action, Maher had at best obeyed her. In fact, it becomes painfully clear that Maher had always tried to obey both her and his father as long as the two were not in irreconcilable conflict. But when he had to choose whom to obey, it was to his father that he gave real allegiance. Ramza now understands that the two of them have been her opponents all along. Maher is not her opponent out of maliciousness, because she knows that he loves her in his own way, but out of weakness because "his love was not enough to surmount the prejudices and the obstacles which assailed him. He was afraid of public opinion" (p. 254). Like Apple's father and Nabila's husband and father, Maher is not strong enough to stand up to society's rules and censure. However, social censure has an even more insidious outcome: it makes Maher afraid of Ramza. As a strong, disobedient woman, she will always elude his control. Additionally, the death of Ramza's father closes off a major route to patriarchal forgiveness, to reacceptance into the society that ostracized them. Without his social moorings, Maher flounders.

Ramza finally accepts Maher's inability to work outside the social structure into which his father had initiated him. She leaves but pronounces her decision to be hers alone. She is not acceding to fathers or their surrogates, and she wants a divorce as proof that society cannot dissolve their marriage without their consent. Reluctantly, Maher gives her the divorce that allows her to maintain control over the entire process. Although she knows that in the eyes of the world she has lost, Ramza feels that she has won. To win is to have held on to her principles, obeying them alone. To lose is to have obeyed men who restrict women's rights to disobey. She emerges out of the struggle alone but strengthened and determined to fight.

None of these women can obey those whom society has named as her guardian. They cannot compromise their conviction that the program that society has set for them is unacceptable. Each one is forced into multiple disobediences. Apple acts to stop the perpetuation of the cycle. Her action causes consternation but does not invoke sanctions. Nabila acts to prevent further abuse being enacted on her body. She resists her husband's need to possess her even when she is physically confined and in his custody. Her action announces not madness but strength. Ramza's case becomes a *cause célèbre* because of her social standing. Her life suggests that resistance to society is possible if not always successful in the traditional sense of the term. As Jennifer reminded me, she wins freedom *from* restrictions if not freedom *to* make a positive change. Yet, her recalcitrance is not punished by marginalization. Amends are sought by trying to enforce conformity. In contrast with many rebellious heroines in nineteenth- and twentieth-century Euro-American women's texts, these Arab women protagonists' "assertion, ambition, self-interest, and outrage," particularly in reaction to marriage norms, are not labeled insane (Showalter 1985, p. 72).[4] They are sometimes controlled, but most often pronounced dangerous. They thus retain agency and control.

Apple, Nabila, and Ramza demonstrate women's ways of resisting a system that somehow succeed. In the Arabian desert, Apple is allowed to stay at home and to oppose, virtually without opposition, her tribe's conception of conventional matrimony. She is not punished. In Cairo in the 1960s, Nabila opposes a legally and religiously sanctioned institution of married life, and her husband—struggling to regain her—locks her into a prison over which he presides. By all rights, he is her lord and master, yet when she resists his advances, he does not force himself on her. Finally, he

---

[4]"Women who reject sexuality and marriage (the two were synonymous for Victorian women) are muted or even driven mad by social disapproval" (Showalter 1985, p. 63). Madness is seen to stem from "the limited and oppressive roles offered to women in modern society" (ibid., p. 213).

acknowledges that he had not known how to make her love him nor how to make his love known to her. Her determination and wit liberate her from his control. Ramza has an advantage over Apple and Nabila because, as a wealthy woman, her rebellion is always financially underwritten. Her decision to defy her father and society does not hold the risks that Apple and Nabila face in their rebellions. She has money, influential friends, servants and, in the last resort, jewelry she can sell. Her disobedience wins her the status of enemy. She is a force to be reckoned with and has ceased to be the obedient, dismissable object of patriarchal whim she was expected to be. The whole of the social apparatus is arrayed against her; she may not be able to win on their terms, but she can and does on her own.

Success is, of course, relative. The students conceded that reading these women's writings had radically challenged their notion of success. Success may be no more than "buying time so as not to get sucked into the system," said Pat, "so as to demand attention and consideration. Once a woman has an audience — whether it is a father, husband, brother, mother, or a larger extended audience — she has a chance to initiate change." Inara added, all of these women "are punished, all have to sacrifice to gain success."

Each of these resistance narratives portrays a woman who finds a way of saying no to people and institutions that would silence and crush her into uniformity. None of these women is trapped by her sexuality, for even in captivity agency is retained. Apple retains control of her life through emancipatory practices that no one, not even she, can understand. All are enmeshed in a system that regulates the formation of relationships. The tribe long ago had devised a system it believed superior to other systems. How then could it accept such a flouting of its rules? Is it perhaps an indication that the tribe, or at least certain members of it, were themselves not quite convinced that their ways were the best ways? And if this is indeed the case, then Apple's rebellion falls on fertile ground. In "House of Obedience," Nabila never once gives in to Adil and her father.[5] But is it Adil who is the enemy? I submit that Adil is as much a prisoner as Nabila. As a man, he too is trapped in role play. He has been taught from the earliest age that there are certain ways of dealing with women. If he violates these rules, he may cease to be truly masculine. As Chris commented, "because he does not have the courage to risk his place in the system, he has less freedom than Nabila." Ramza rebels out of a clear understanding of what her rights should be. Although she blames her father for opposing her after having supported her early in life, and she berates Maher for his cowardly obedi-

---

[5]"He charged me, in front of my husband, to look after the house of obedience" (Badran and Cooke 1990, p. 162).

ence to his father and society, she knows that neither is driven by hate or the wilful desire to oppress her. Each is caught in prescriptive formulations that leave little room for individual initiatives. She may be surprised and impatient when they succumb to conforming social pressures, but she is never unaware of those pressures. Her final attitude is contempt rather than hate. The respect inherent in hate has gone.

As I read these narratives of resistance, it seems to me that the men have as little and sometimes even less freedom than the women; men act in reaction to women's actions. Each story indicts a patriarchal order that assigns gender roles; it also rejects institutions that oppress both men and women. What am I saying? Are my interpretations exonerating men? Are Arab men not, as Carrie mentioned, like "slave owners. Is it enough to say that they lived in a time when the system of enslavement was espoused by the government to excuse them from any reproach? They also benefited from the system as do the men in the stories we have read"? Cathy's question elaborated Carrie's doubt: "If men and women are both trapped within a system, then what are the origins and dynamics of that system. Who created it? If it was men, did men trap themselves unintentionally? Are men cognizant of being trapped?" My only answer to such questions is to say that I am not in search of reasons, motivations, or conclusions. I am trying rather to understand how resistance can be imagined against the grain. How it is that the powerless can strike fear in the hearts of the so-called powerful. It is the women who seize the initiative to break the mutually disempowering hold of gender roles. It is the women who open up a space in which power relations can be analyzed, shown to be mutually harmful, and then renegotiated. Ramza speaks for Apple and Nabila and all those groping, tongue-tied rebels when she explodes: "We are struggling to liberate women. Do we have to do the job for men as well?" And now we know to whom the "we" refers.

"A Girl Called Apple," "House of Obedience," and *Ramza* illustrate a consciousness that pervades Arab women's writings. Men alone are not at fault, but rather men and women together are complicit in a world construction that constricts and alienates individuals from each other. These stories depict women empowered by hopelessness; women, who have less at stake in the maintenance of a miserable *status quo*, are the ones to break its hold. These stories do not deal with the struggle to redefine only women's place in the social order. To redefine women's place entails the simultaneous redefinition of men's places. In twentieth-century Arab women's writings, gender roles and places exist both in tension and in tandem. Is there not, then, a potential for harmony?

# References

Badran, M., and Cooke, M. 1990. *Opening the Gates: One Hundred Years of Arab Feminist Writing*. Bloomington, Ind.: Indiana University Press.

Cixous, H. 1981. Castration or decapitation? A Kuhn, trans. *Signs* 7(1):41–55.

Malti-Douglas, F. 1991. *Woman's Body, Woman's Word: Gender and Discourse in Arabo-Islamic Writing*. Princeton, N.J.: Princeton University Press.

Showalter, E. 1985. *The Female Malady: Women, Madness, and the English Culture, 1830–1980*. New York: Penguin Books.

# Staying in the Place of Danger

## The Disobedient, Poetic "I" of Dahlia Ravikovitch

### Nili Rachel Scarf Gold

Flirting with danger and the wish to remain a child are dominant characteristics of Dahlia Ravikovitch's poetic "I." These traits, at times intertwined, are her form of rebellion, her expression of disobedience.

Dahlia Ravikovitch was born in 1936 in Ramat Gan, near Tel Aviv. Her poetic work, which thus far spans a period of about thirty years, established her as the leading Israeli woman poet. She published her first book of verse, *The Love of an Orange*, in 1959, and her fifth one, *Real Love*, in 1986. Two collections of her poems have appeared in translation in the United States: *A Dress of Fire* in 1978 and *The Window* in 1989. She belongs to a handful of Israeli poets who have had complete books of their verse translated into English, and she is the only Israeli woman poet to have received such acclaim in North America. In this article, I will discuss Ravikovitch's early work, her first three books (1959–1969).

After *The Love of an Orange* (1959) and *A Hard Winter* (1962), her third book (1969) marks, according to some critics, a turning point in her career.[1] Although this observation is correct regarding form, idiom, and grammar, it seems to me that the deep structure or the story behind this poetry remains the same.

Courting catastrophe—attempting to stand in a place of danger while refusing to grow up and be careful and responsible, to obey adult norms and rules—is the route chosen by Ravikovitch's lyrical voice in creating its poetic world. Whether she weaves webs of gold in a legendary, dreamlike landscape, "chants" magical incantations, or tries to reconstruct a traumatic situation, the careful reader can always discern a rebellious, childish thread intertwined with tendencies of self-destruction and walking on the edge.

---

[1]See, for example, Robert Alter's introduction to *The Window* (Ravikovitch 1989, p. x).

This article addresses the question of how flirtation with danger functions for the poetic "I." Is seeking danger a way of identifying and thus reuniting with the lost object through self-destruction? Is it an attempt to encounter danger and master it as if to recreate the catastrophe but this time to overcome it? Another possibility is that it is expression of longing for the pretrauma existence, a kind of yearning for being a carefree child, oblivious to danger and immune to it for that reason. This is analogous to the child who does not need to watch for cars coming, because she is holding the parent's hand that will guide her to safety.

Although it may at times be a boy's behavior, the refusal to accept the adult world by not growing up is often a particularly feminine response. This is similar to anorexia nervosa, where menstruation stops as a result of self-starvation and enables the adolescent girl to return to an earlier state of development (see Woodman 1980, 1982).

The emergence of the disobedient, childlike poetic "I" may be explained by a close reading of Ravikovitch's most self-revealing poems, analyzing linguistic traces, literary and syntactical qualities as well as psychological phenomena.

In his article in *Contemporary Psychoanalysis*, entitled "Paternal Absence," Owen Lewis uncovers an intriguing psychological mechanism, namely the internalization of an abandonment story. This mechanism can be useful if it is applied to the interpretation of Ravikovitch's verse. Lewis discusses three case histories of boys who were abandoned by their fathers at a young age. He notes a similarity between the abandonment story of each one of these patients and the eventual development of their personalities. He posits that "the void of their conscious experience of the loss of their fathers is unconsciously no void at all" (Lewis 1991, p. 272). Furthermore he adds that "their personalities evolved from the particulars of how they lost their fathers, thus allowing their fathers a permanent place in their lives" (ibid.). One of the children, for example, who was rejected earlier on by his father, grew up to be pathologically shy, as if forever afraid of rejection.

In the same fashion, I would like to suggest that Ravikovitch's poetry is an eternal attempt to fill the void created by her own loss, with a content that bears similarity to the details of her own story. It is an artistically sophisticated reworking of the trauma of losing her own father at the age of six. He was killed by a drunk driver. The violent aspect of this death seems to resurface in her poetry. There it takes the form of an unusual fascination with danger and violence. Perhaps there is also a fantasy of him not having been careful; therefore *she* stops being careful.[2] This may coincide with the Jungian theory of the contrasexual component of the psyche (the animus for a woman), which compensates for the loss of the father by appearing intrapsychically as an aspect of the poetic voice that constantly courts disaster.[3] She deals openly with the naked event only in two texts, one of which is an admittedly autobiographical short story, and the other a poem from her first collection.[4]

Chanah and Ariel Bloch, Ravikovitch's translators, chose this poem to open the book *The Window* (1989, p. 3). This poem, titled in English, "On the Road at Night," serves as a key to Ravikovitch's complex inner world:

> On the road at night there stands the man
> who once upon a time was my   father.
> And I must come to the place where he stands
> because I was   his eldest daughter.
>
> And night after night he stands alone on the road
> and I must go down to that place   and stand there.
> And I want to ask the man how long will I have to.
> And I know, even as I ask, I will always have to.
>
> In the place where he stands there is a fear of danger
> like the day he was walking along and a car ran him over.
> And that's how I knew him, and I found ways to remember
> that this very man was once my father.
>
> And he doesn't tell me one word of love
> though once upon a time he was my father.
> And even though I was   his eldest daughter
> he cannot tell me one word of love.

[2]Ravikovitch describes how, in 1942, when her father wanted to go and fight the Nazis, her mother "prevented him from going, therefore . . . he found his death in a meaningless way" (1977, p. 145).

[3]See, for example, E. Harding's discussion of the ghostly lover (1970), chapter 2 throughout, but in particular pp. 37–39.

[4]The story is titled "Esrim Vahamesh Shana" ("Twenty-Five Years"). It appears in Ravikovitch's only collection of short stories, *Death in the Family* (1977). The story is an attempt to draw a portrait of her dead father. The description is direct and lacks any "literary disguises."

The colloquial, almost childish diction of the poem comes through even in translation, but some of the nuances and intertexts unfortunately get lost. The poem's main concern is "*Abba sheli*," translated as "my father" but more accurately "my dad" or even "my daddy." This emphasizes the speaker's childish or even helpless voice. Furthermore, the Hebrew text carries with it associations to the tenth plague, "*makat bekhorot*," the killing of the firstborn in Egypt. But unlike the biblical text, here it is the father who dies, while his firstborn, his "*bekhora*" must "come to the place where he stands." The inevitability of the tragic events and their nocturnal nature, however, are common to both texts.

Textual traces of the Exodus story seem to surface in a few of the poems depicting the moments of the ultimate trauma, which is sometimes portrayed as a kind of "fall." Linguistic remnants of "that night," of the dramatic night, in which the firstborn were dying, serve as a marker of tragedy and emotional crisis in Ravikovitch's verse. This is the case even in poems which completely disguise their matrix, such as "The End of the Fall" and "Clockwork Doll." These poems contain references to "that night" or to elements belonging to its descriptive system, such as references to a "miracle" and the words *blood* and *signs*, drawn from the scriptures (Exodus 11–12).[5]

The textual signals to the plague in "On the Road at Night" include the repetition of the word *bekhora*, "the firstborn," and the idiom *latet simanim*, meaning "noticing marks of identification," which in the Passover Haggada introduces the mnemonic device by which to remember the plagues. The same idiom is also traditionally used as a legal term, concerning the identification of a lost article. Ironically, the lost item in the case of the poem is no other than the father.

The last, but definitely not least, linguistic echo to be mentioned here is the saying of the sages: "*Al tadin et khaverakh ad shetagi'a limkomo*." The literal translation of the idiom is: "Judge not your fellow man or woman until you have reached his or her place," meaning that one can only judge the other if he goes through similar experiences (a more ominous variation of the American "don't judge me till you've walked a mile in my shoes").

In other words, this poem, and perhaps others as well, may be an

---

[5]The poem "The End of the Fall," for example, directs the Hebrew reader to the story of Exodus. It does so by repeating the word *blood* ("*dam*") which evokes the blood marking on the Hebrews' houses, signaling to the angel of death to pass them over. Other key words are "the middle of the night" ("*emtza ha-layla*"), *signs* ("*otot*"), "with clumsy movements" ("*bikh'vedut*"). These words are clearly associated with the intertext.

attempt of the poetic "I" to reach the same place, to relive the father's experience, standing in the place of danger.

This emotional journey may have multiple purposes. It may be a wish to touch death in order to disarm it, or an attempt to identify with the father, to literally stand in his place, in order not to judge him too harshly for having withheld his love. He is dead and therefore excused; as she says, "He *cannot* tell me one word of love." In a poem written ten years later, called "The End of the Fall," God's withholding of love is ascribed to his sensitivity: "He does not want to alarm man with signs of love."[6] Despite the fact that this poem discusses a man falling from an airplane and his soul or spirit saved by God, it seems that the underlying trauma is Ravikovitch's original fall, namely her father's death. The flight which takes place in "the middle of the night" is a variation of the play with danger. In the poem "On the Road at Night" the obsession of returning to the place of danger is intertwined with the childish voice of the poetic "I." This voice speaks in simple syntax and seemingly basic vocabulary. It reiterates the childish expression "my daddy." Assuming this childlike persona may be a way of defying the most painful adult truth, namely that death is final. The wish to remain a child, or the refusal to grow up, is the refusal to see the truth and to accept the sentence of logic and of common sense. Internalizing the place of danger, weaving it into the poetic text and into the voice speaking in the poem, is parallel to the developmental reworkings of the abandonment story.

It is also difficult to ignore the element of doom, of desperate fatalism, as the poem reads: "And I must go down to that place and stand there / And I want to ask the man how long will I have to? / and I know even as I ask, I will always have to." The encounter with danger has therefore become an inseparable part of the lyrical self.

In a poem published in 1969, one can discern a similar substructure even though the details of it seem to be entirely different. Again we encounter the defiant and disobedient childlike voice who against all common sense is attracted to danger. This time, however, a great distance is created between the original trauma and the events in the poem: the danger seems to involve a romantic connection, and the Jewish intertexts, such as the Bible or the Haggadah (the traditional nonbiblical text retelling the story of Exodus), make room for the fatalistic echoes of a Greek chorus.

The translator's insight should be noted again, as she chose the title of the poem "A Dress of Fire" to be the title of the first collection of Ravikovitch's poems that she translated (Ravikovitch 1978). This poem,

---

[6]The Hebrew *otot* for "signs," rather than the more common *simanim*, is a recognizable reference to the story of Exodus.

which begins the volume, is a powerful poem in its own right, but it is also
representative of some dominant traits of Ravikovitch's writing. The translated version presented here is taken from *The Window* (1989, p. 57) as it is
closer to the original than the earlier translation.

### A Dress of Fire

You know, she said, they made you
a dress of fire.
Remember how Jason's wife burned in her dress?
It was Medea, she said, Medea did that to her.
You've got to be careful, she said,
they made you a dress that glows
like an ember, that burns like coals.

Are you going to wear it, she said, don't wear it.
It's not the wind whistling, it's the poison
seeping in.
You're not even a princess, what can you do to Medea?
Can't you tell one sound from another, she said,
It's not the wind whistling.

Remember, I told her, that time when I was six?
They shampooed my hair and I went out into the street.
The smell of shampoo trailed after me like a cloud.
Then I got sick from the wind and the rain.
I didn't know a thing about reading Greek tragedies,
but the smell of the perfume spread
and I was very sick.
Now I can see it's an unnatural perfume.

What will happen to   you now, she said,
they made you a burning dress.
They made me a burning dress, I said. I know.
So why are you standing there, she said,
you've got to be careful.
You know what a burning dress is, don't you?

I know, I said, but I don't know
how to be careful.
The smell of that perfume confuses me.
I said to her, No one has to agree with me,
I don't believe   in Greek tragedies.

But the dress, she said, the dress is on fire.
What    are you saying, I shouted,
what are you saying?
I'm not wearing a dress at all,
what's burning is me.

It does not matter whether this is an inner dialogue between a superego, an internalized parent, society, or common sense on the one hand, and a disobedient, careless, passionate, and childish "I" on the other, or an actual dialogue between a superior adult, such as a mother, a friend, or a nursemaid, who faces an irresponsible other. The reader's first impression of the poem is that of a verbal exchange in which one voice is pleading desperately, warning the other against some grave danger. The exchange is recorded, however, by one who refuses to heed the warning. The repetition of "she said," "I said," can be likened to a child's manner of reporting events. The familiar, simple, childlike syntax and vocabulary reappear, and so does the flirtation with danger.

The dialogue form illuminates the inner tear, or rather, the dual nature of the "I." But it is also fitting for a poem that so bluntly alludes to Greek tragedy. The drum sounding warnings brings to mind the voice of reason of a Greek chorus. The opening lines introduce Medea, who destroyed her rival-in-love with a burning dress, in a quasi-intimate tone: "Remember how Jason's wife burned in her dress? It was Medea, she said, Medea did that to her." The facts are told as if they happened to a next-door neighbor. This tone erases boundaries of time, place, and culture, and it intimates that we all are manipulated or motivated by the same laws or passions — just like mythological women. The myth therefore functions as a kind of shorthand, directing the reader to a realm of jealousy, betrayal, self-destruction, and doom.

Medea's presence also alerts the Hebrew reader to the pun in the original title: "HaBeGeD," literally "The Garment," but also containing the root letters "B.G.D." which mean "to betray." Furthermore, in Jewish mysticism the soul is often likened to a garment that a person weaves throughout life. The texture of the garment is made up of the person's deeds. These will determine his or her fate in the world to come. In addition, the tearing of the garment is a Jewish custom of mourning, which emphasizes the relationship between the attire and the self.[7] This, of course, is spelled out at the poem's closure. The image of the dress is then charged with meanings:

[7]In Ravikovitch's first volume, there is a poem titled "Tearing." There, without a mention of the garment or of death, the tearing represents mourning.

the garment (*BeGeD*), which was supposed to protect, betrays (*BaGaD*). The image of the *BeGeD* (garment, dress) is central in the interplay between ancient Jewish texts and concepts and Greek tragedy.

The poetic "I" continually refuses to listen to the voice of reason, which warns against the approaching dangers of fire and poison. It becomes clear in the poem's third stanza that courting danger and disobedience are character traits, imprinted in the poetic "I" at an early age. As children, many of us were told not to leave the house with wet hair, lest we get sick. Oddly enough, the poetic "I" is reporting that, at the age of six, she disobeyed this rule. She was also six when her father died, according to her autobiographical story. Playing with the dangers of rain and water at an early age is parallel to ignoring the burning dress later on. The core story keeps on reworking itself. The unnatural quality of the perfume can be attributed to the speaker's internalized tendency to live on the edge (which is, of course, at least rationally unnatural) and to ignore repeatedly the collective knowledge reflected in her mother's voice or in Greek tragedies. The disobedient "I" follows its desires to the bitter end, like Icarus who is evoked in the above-mentioned poem, "The End of the Fall."

The unnatural perfume also suggests magic and thus connects the six-year-old girl to Medea, the betrayed woman whose supernatural powers could not prevent, and perhaps contributed to, the catastrophe. At the outset of the poem it seems that the "you" is identified with Jason's wife: "You know, she said, they made you / a dress of fire. / Remember how Jason's wife burned in her dress?" But as the poem unfolds, the ambiguity grows, until, contrary to appearances, the poetic "I" can be seen as Medea, whose passions consumed her and drove her to madness. The poem's closing lines associate the poetic "I" with Medea's fiery origins and nature: "I'm not wearing a dress at all, what's burning is me."[8]

"A Dress of Fire" is unique in Ravikovitch's writing in terms of its self-awareness and self-exposure, states Openheimer in his article in the Hebrew literary quarterly *Siman Kri'a* (1991, p. 418). He highlights the disintegration of the self evident in this poem and compares it to the early "Clockwork Doll" (Ravikovitch 1989, p. 7), which retells the story of the night of the fall of a wound-up doll.

### Clockwork Doll

That night, I was a clockwork doll
and I whirled around, this way and that,

---

[8]Mythologically, Medea is the daughter of King Aeëtes, who is himself the son of Sol, the sun god (Ovid I. 69, 96).

and I fell on my face and shattered to bits
and they   tried to fix me with all their skill.

Then I was a proper doll once again
and I did what they told me, poised and polite.
But I was a doll of a different sort,
an injured twig   that dangles from a stem.

And then I went to dance at the ball,
but they left me   alone with the   dogs and cats
though my steps were measured and rhythmical.

And I had blue eyes and golden hair
and a dress all the colors   of garden flowers,
and a trimming of cherries on my straw hat.

Disintegration is not at the core of this poem, but rather, the reworking of the trauma of the fall and, more importantly, the aftermath of the fall. As in "On the Road at Night," the sense of doom overshadows the details. What was broken is not to be mended. The daughter will forever relive her loss, the doll never again be a first-rate doll. The opening "That night . . .," echoes the initial night of the deaths of the firstborn in Egypt.[9] There is no healing of the wound nor can it be camouflaged by a garment or by trimmings of cherries on a straw hat.

"Clockwork Doll," however, goes beyond the fall to examine the nature of existence after it. The quest for danger continues and so does the disobedient childish behavior. The duality between logic and desire in "A Dress of Fire" is present here, as well as the inability to control one's own passions and tendencies toward self-destruction. The doll is not allowed, not even for one night, to follow her heart. She, who was meant to be an obedient "clockwork doll," is punished for trespassing (she was not supposed to whirl around). Disobedience results in a fall, as the myth of Icarus clearly states.

The poem "Clockwork Doll" has the appearance of a sonnet (in

---

[9]"Mechanical Doll" (which is the title of an earlier translation) opens with "*balayla haze*" ("in that night"). This is reminiscent of the "*ma nishtana*," a very well known part of the Passover Haggada in which the expression "*halaya haze*" ("this night") repeats in every verse. It is worth noting that the *ma nishtana* is the only part of the Haggada traditionally recited by children. In both "The End of the Fall" and "Clockwork Doll," as well as in "On the Road at Night," the night is the temporal landscape for catastrophe.

Hebrew). It has the appropriate number of lines and stanzas as well as a perfect rhyme. This rigid form is in itself an ironic statement about the constraints imposed on the self. The poem strikes a tragic chord: it portrays the second-rate life ("they left me alone with the dogs and cats") inflicted on the passionate self.

In discussing this poem in *The Modern Hebrew Poem Itself*, Sachs notes the childish voice of the speaking doll "And I . . . and I fell . . . And I tried . . . and I did . . . and I had blue eyes . . . and a dress . . ." (1965, pp. 186–187). This linguistic and syntactical mechanism is reminiscent of the language used in the poems discussed above. The simple vocabulary and uncomplicated syntax are the poetic realization of the child's position, namely, that of being oblivious to danger, responsibilities, and rules. The identification of the child persona with the doll takes this existence *ad absurdum*, as though to say "I would rather be a complete robot with perfect features than do what they want me to do."

At the beginning of this article, I asked how living on the edge and choosing to remain a disobedient child function for the poetic "I." That question can now be answered: all the threads reunite, weaving themselves into "the garment" of the creative process. In other words, the place of danger is the place of writing. In order to write, the poetic "I" needs to maintain the tension of the threshold.

Courting danger is an inherent trait of the lyrical self. It may be connected to the creative process. Writing is then the ultimate place of danger, since it obliges the writer to touch the most intimate and raw regions of pain. It makes it necessary to relive and rework the traumas, and, in the case of a woman writer, it may involve the danger of defying the rules of a society inclined to listen to male voices.

In the opening poem of the Hebrew volume, *The Third Book* (1969), Ravikovitch paints a writing scene ("Surely You Remember," 1989, p. 41).

> Maybe it's nice after all to write poems.
> You sit in your room and the walls grow taller.
> Colors deepen.
> A blue kerchief becomes a deep well.

While the kerchief's metamorphosis may represent the intensity of the experience, one may not ignore here the suggestion of deep water alluding to suicide. The poem continues:

> Narcissus was so much in love with himself.
> Only a fool doesn't understand
> he loved the river, too.
> . . . . . . . . . . .

> You wish you were dead or alive or
> somebody else.

The identification with Narcissus, the attraction to the river, and the deep well are variations on the theme. Writing is then the ultimate place of danger that may lead to self-destruction.

Ravikovitch uses the qualities of the Hebrew language to embody the inner conflict of a woman writer. In the writing scene that is set at the beginning of the poem, it is stated three times: *"ani nish'ert"* ("I remain"). This is the feminine form of the verb, implying that the speaker, or rather the writer, is a passive woman:

> After they all leave,
> I remain alone with the poems,
> some poems of mine, some of others.
> I prefer poems that others have written.
> I remain quiet, and slowly
> the knot in my throat dissolves.
> I remain.

The feminine presence disappears, however, as soon as the creative, life-threatening but empowering process emerges (the eleventh line). At that point in the poem, the text turns to the masculine: *"ata yoshev"* ("you sit"). The *ata* (masculine singular) form replaces the feminine speaker for the remainder of the poem, the last twenty-four lines, culminating with the confident promise of "sun and moon, winter and summer / will come to you / infinite treasures." The shift in gender reflects a view of the creative self as an internalized masculine other who represents the lost object, the risk-taking father. The process of writing, like the river, is at once luring, seductive, and dangerous.

# References

Harding, E. 1970. *The Way of All Women*. New York: Harper and Row.

Lewis, O. 1991. Parental absence. *Contemporary Psychoanalysis* 27(2):265–287.

Openheimer, Y. 1991. Keshirut politit [Ravikovitch's ability as a political poet]. *Siman Kri'a Literary Quarterly*, pp. 415–430.

Ovid. *Metamorphosis*. F. J. Miller, trans. Cambridge, Mass.: Harvard University Press, 1916.

Ravikovitch, D. 1959. *Ahavat Tapu'ah Hazahav* [*The Love of an Orange*]. Tel Aviv: Mahbarot Le'sifrut Publishing.

_____. 1969. *Hasefer Hashlishi* [*The Third Book*]. Tel Aviv: Levin Epstein Publishing.

_____. 1977. *Mavet Ba-Mishpaha* [*Death in the Family*]. Tel Aviv: Am-Oved Publishing.

_____. 1978. *A Dress of Fire*. C. Bloch, trans. New York: The Sheep Meadow Press.

_____. 1989. *The Window*. C. and A. Bloch, trans. New York: The Sheep Meadow Press.

Sachs, A. 1965. "Clockwork Doll." *The Modern Hebrew Poem Itself*, Burnshaw et al., eds. Cambridge, Mass.: Harvard University Press, 1989.

Woodman, M. 1980. *The Owl is a Baker's Daughter: Obesity, Anorexia and the Repressed Feminine*. Toronto: Inner City Books.

_____. 1982. *Addiction to Perfection: The Still Unravished Bride*. Toronto: Inner City Books.

# TRANSFORMING

*a*

# WORLD

# WOMEN WHO DISOBEY

## EXAMPLES FROM INDIA

## Manisha Roy

This paper tells stories of women of nineteenth- and twentieth-century Bengal, India, who disobeyed their society and culture, which had always emphasized conformity. The women paid heavily for such defiance, yet they had to do what they did. But why?

I shall try to explore this question, first historically and culturally, then psychologically, using some mythological examples.

A short story titled "Letter from a Wife" written in 1912 by the literary genius of India, Rabindranath Tagore (1961), captures a wife's need to disobey her husband, her family, and the social expectations of a woman. Here I have translated short excerpts from the letter the wife writes:

> In your family, I have never known suffering in its usual sense or felt any deprivation of food or clothing. Unlike your brother, your character is faultless. If you were unfaithful like your brother, I might have taken recourse to blaming my fate and lived as a mindless and suffering wife who is silent and obedient. Therefore, this letter is not to accuse any of you, but just to tell that I am not coming back to the family. (p. 260)

In the same letter, the disobedient wife tells us why all women of all societies may have difficulty doing what she did.

> I ask God, why do the most trivial things in life become the hardest obstacles? Why does the insignificant, joyless life of the walled-in house on an old city lane pose such a hurdle that I cannot cross the little threshold even for a moment? Why must my soul, also a part of your beautiful and free creation, die slowly in the secret shelter of bricks and wood? (Ibid.)

The story behind this letter of defiance is simple yet immensely complex. Mrinal, the wife, is a beautiful and intelligent young woman whose physical beauty was the main consideration in being selected for her negotiated marriage. No one inquired about her intelligence or how she felt about anything. Soon after her marriage, she began to question many of the family customs and decisions, including silent compliance by her sister-in-law whose sister was married off to an insane man by the family. The family was trying to get rid of an unwanted guest. Mrinal failed to understand why the victim's own sister, who loved her, would not confront such cruel and unjust behavior.

Was fear of confrontation the only reason not to fight such cruelty? Or was it just the habit of performing the long-learned duty of being quiet, something women learned well and unquestioningly? Mrinal could not remain silent; she voiced her objections to the whole family and helped someone who had no one. She also had to leave the security of her marriage, which was suffocating her authentic self. Unlike the protagonist of this story, not all women who dare to make waves and break rules are fortunate enough to be able to leave their security with dignity.

Let me turn to history for some examples of defiant women in the eighteenth and nineteenth centuries. Their stories come from their autobiographies, either written or spoken to family members who published the narratives later. In order to place these women in the right historical and cultural contexts, a brief sketch of Bengali culture is necessary.

The State of West Bengal lies on the eastern part of the Indian subcontinent, with Bangladesh to the east, the Bay of Bengal to the south, and the East Himalayan ranges to the north. It contains one of the largest deltas in the world, is criss-crossed by many rivers, and has heavy rainfall due to monsoons. Water plays an important role, not only in rice and jute agriculture but also as a natural boundary and as a cultural symbol in art, literature, and religion. Thus somewhat isolated from the rest of India, West Bengal has developed a unique language and culture of its own. Along with the rest of north India, Bengal (the undivided state which included West Bengal and present-day Bangladesh until 1947) also faced a series of invasions—Pathans (twelfth century), Moghuls (seventeenth century), and the British (eighteenth century)—all of which contributed toward political, cultural, and religious changes and enrichment.

Nearly six hundred years of Moslem rule (1190–1750) in north India had its impact on undivided Bengal, mostly in the conversion of lower-caste people and its cultural impact on upper- and middle-class women. Women became more segregated due to the Moslem custom of *purdah*, which found support in the already established belief system of the orthodox Hindus. Medieval Hindu family law prevented a woman from education and independent thinking, although she was entitled to her dowry or a small portion of her parental property. Women receded into the walled interior space of the house, being literally and figuratively cut off from the outer world.

The lowest point in the life of Hindu society in Bengal was reached at the end of the eighteenth century when European contact began. Polygamy and the proliferation of meaningless forms of religious rituals along with the utter degradation of women had become institutionalized through the practice of *Kulinism*. *Kulinism* was a device introduced by the orthodox Brahmins to maintain purity of the upper castes through strict marriage restrictions. This system led to a high rate of polygamy and the rites of *Sati* (first recorded in the fourth century B.C. by Alexander the Great when he invaded India), an ancient practice of self-immolation of wives on their husbands' funeral pyres. Although voluntary in theory, records tell us that the family and social pressure made it virtually obligatory among the higher-caste women.

The Bengal renaissance of the nineteenth century was an inevitable outcome of a century of constant resistance to orthodox Brahmanical Hinduism by the modern radicals and Westernized social reformers. It was in Bengal that British rule was first established, Western education was introduced, and a new economy gave birth to a group of middle-class intellectuals who led many cultural and religious movements for next two hundred years.

Bengal's contact with the Western world during the eighteenth century was crucial in inspiring a sense of individualism among men against the strict dictation of the oppressive *Kulinism* described above. In 1828, a religious reform movement called *Brahmo Samaj*, led by an outstanding man, Raja Rammohan Roy, fought openly against the degradation of women. The followers of the movement established an alternative religious system based on the uncompromising monotheism of Islam and the proud rationalism of modern Europe, promoting individual freedom to live and act according to one's own judgment. Their pressure succeeded in mobilizing their British government to abolish *Sati* in 1829 and to establish legal sanction for widow remarriage in 1856.

But all these legal changes took at least another hundred years to be implemented in reality. The life stories of many women during this era show that, perhaps more than anything, the extreme social adversity created the challenge for them to rebel.

We learn about the social situation from Nistarini's verbal account, which was recorded and published later by her nephew (Dev 1984, pp. 17–20, 33–35). She was born in 1833 to a well-known family in which the men were all highly educated. Her great-grandfather married 106 times and her grandfather 58 times! Marriage, for the *Kulin* men, was a means to make money, since the bride's family gave cash to the groom as a gift. He went around during various festivals collecting money from all his in-laws. While the age of marriage for men had no limit, extending to very old age, it went down to age four or five for girls, producing a high number of young widows. Many of the brides never went to live with their husbands and some never even met them. The married girls lived with their fathers or brothers the rest of their lives and often became nothing but glorified or not-so-glorified servants to the family.

Married women lived in such an oppressed state in their own homes that some tried to escape by going to the city in search of a freer life. Usually they had little choice but to join the oldest of professions. They preferred prostitution to staying in their families. Also, an independent profession, no matter what, had a semblance of economic freedom for them. We learn about their deplorable situations from the anonymous letters written by some of these "fallen" women in the literary journals of Calcutta. According to the 1853 Calcutta *Gazette*, a majority of the prostitutes of the city were widows and wives of *Kulin* Brahmins. These women not only acted, but they also broke the silence. The social reformers of *Brahmo Samaj*, learning about some of the atrocious cases from these published letters, tried to rescue some of the women. In some cases, young men willingly married the widows to set examples to the rest of the population and suffered major insults, including excommunication from the society at large.

Parvati was married when she was two-and-a-half years old and became widowed at five! She belonged to a living hell of a family, ruled by a cruel stepmother. A couple of gentlemen helped her escape on a boat, but her family was informed by a neighbor and she was found and brought back by force. But one young man did not give up. He arranged again for a boat to wait and sent word to her to escape while the whole village was preoccupied with a sick woman. When the family discovered that she was missing, they decided she was eaten by a tiger. Someone found a basket she was carrying to pick flowers. Later she married a young man from the *Brahmo Samaj* and lived outside the Hindu society and far away from her village (Dev 1984, pp. 38–40).

Rashsundari Devi was born in 1809, married at the age of twelve, and gave birth to twelve children. She died at the ripe age of ninety-one. This busy housewife and mother defied the social custom all on her own and learned to read and write and even wrote an autobiography in verse (Dev 1984, pp. 118–130).

As a child, she heard the boys in her family read aloud and imitated the sounds and tried to remember what she heard. Since girls were not allowed to learn how to read or write, she kept her desire to herself. After her marriage, when she was fourteen, she began to steal pages from her husband's and sons' books and hid them under her sari veil. She tried desperately to read the words while cooking meals for her large family. With the help of her childhood memory of the sounds of the alphabet, she began to learn how to read slowly but surely. No one knew about this secret adventure, and one day she succeeded in reading the book she so desperately wanted to read. It was a biography of a devout disciple of Vishnu, the god she herself worshipped every morning.

Let us listen to her own words. "I was afraid to tell any one about my secret readings except a few very close friends. We had great fun keeping this to ourselves like children who break rules imposed by adults. When my sisters-in-law were busy with household rituals, we would lock ourselves inside a room and read to them. One of my friends stood guard at the door to warn us if anyone from the family approached" (Dev 1984, p. 43). Nearly forty years later the first school for girls was founded in 1849.

In spite of the official opening of girls' schools, the social objection to women's education continued inside the middle-class families. They were concerned that education would make a woman independent in her thinking, and she would question the old traditional virtues of gentleness and obedience. They would behave like the Western women and try to rule the men, as Queen Victoria was ruling the British Empire. Strangely enough, some of the men in these families were pioneers in the efforts to introduce education to their daughters, sisters, and wives, something historically quite unique to India. This phenomenon of Indian men pioneering women's education and liberation is quite unusual in the patriarchal history of the world. More on this situation will be discussed in the concluding section.

Krishnabhabini Das had such a husband who encouraged her to pursue her interest in studies and even took her with him to England. Born in 1868, she was married to an educated man of a well-known family at the age of nine. She left her young daughter in care of the family when she accompanied her husband to England. While in England, she wrote several books and articles, all dealing with women and their deplorable condition. Her book titled *Bengali Women in England* (1885) was banned from sale in India because of her courageous stand on the topic of women's liberation (Dev 1984, pp. 54–56, 108–117, 139).

Back at home, her husband's family had arranged a marriage for her ten-year-old daughter without the parents' permission. Krishnabhabini had no means to stop them from the very act she herself stood up to change. When the couple returned after eight years in England, they were renounced by the family and were not allowed contact with their daughter. Her husband tried to make a living by establishing a college and by writing.

Krishnabhabini suffered further from the two untimely deaths of her husband and her unhappy daughter within a month of each other. This extraordinarily brave woman lived another twenty years, dedicating herself to social reform toward liberation of women. She was instrumental in starting schools for women prisoners and shelters for destitute widows in Calcutta. Krishnabhabini Das left an autobiography written in Bengali.

## Conclusion

I could continue with many more life stories similar to the ones above. The number of women who tried to break away from the rigid and life-negating social norms in nineteenth-century Bengal was not insignificant. As we read about them or read their own autobiographies, a few observations can be made regarding the circumstances and contributing factors, as well as the nature of rebellion and the rebels.

To begin with, the foreign contact with Indian society seemed to have created the grounds for both oppression and the consciousness to change it. The extreme fossilization of the orthodox Hinduism could have taken place as a reaction to the Moslem conversion and other modern trends, which in turn helped the individual women and men break away from the rigidity of the old system. Introduction of English education, which in itself had become a symbol of defiance against the traditional culture, plays a vital role not only in the women's courage to break the age-old prohibition against education but also in their independent thinking. A few upper-class families employed British women to coach their girls. These tutors, along with the English books, also brought new ideas inside the walled homes.

The fact that many of these women were helped by their husbands and other men in their defiance had also to do with Westernization to a great extent. Men who became educated in the English system also began to realize that it was to their benefit to bring women out of the inner home to the world of ideas and consciousness. They began to appreciate how totally one-sided and dull the male world had become because of the strict segregation between the outer and the inner parts of the house.

Although this practice of inviting the women to "come out" of the inner house first began among a small group of revolutionary men, slowly the others followed. It was as if men were trying unconsciously to educate their anima, their inner women.

Women who had received no support from their men, as we saw in some cases, must have had exceptionally strong needs for psychological survival to sacrifice the social security in order to embrace what to others were shameful and ignoble lives. For these women, the easier choice would have been to be mindless, compliant, and silent. Their sacrifice of the security of social protection meant total excommunication. They and often their families were excluded from all social and religious rituals including their own funeral services. The only psychological explanation for such risk-taking rebellion must be an uncontrollable inner dictation from the Self, as C. G. Jung formulates the concept. Their moral strength in listening to the Self offered them the additional courage to sacrifice the persona of the "good woman" which was the only identity available to them.

Like the protagonist of the story "Letter from a Wife," women who sacrificed their good names also voiced criticisms of the world they left. To be able to speak up for something one believes in is not easy, especially if such words create dangerous reactions. Making the first move of defiance seems to go hand in hand with breaking the silence. That is why so many women in Bengal, as elsewhere in the world, wanted to learn how to read and write. Written words can replace unheard voices, both unspoken and spoken. Thanks to the research by determined women scholars, we are discovering essays and autobiographies of early women writers which had been lost from sight.

From the above examples we also see that some women learned to use words more for self-expression than to protest. Like Rashsundari, I was told, my great-grandmother used to practice writing poems with a piece of charcoal on the mud floor of the kitchen as she cooked the family meals. When she heard the footsteps of men approaching, she would wipe the words with a wet rag. I wonder if those unpreserved words had not been handed down to the generations after her. Every woman in my family seems to have a need to use words for self-expression.

This urge to express in words or in any other form of symbols comes from that basic instinct to express oneself and to connect with the *other*. Even today in village India, illiterate women paint simple and primitive pictures on the grounds in front of their homes every morning. These drawings can be simply geometric forms or images of gods and goddesses. I believe my great-grandmother was trying to connect with her own inner self, the self which had not learned to speak to the world yet. Composing one's thoughts in words may be the very first step toward a life apart from that defined by the culture. In a time and culture when the persona became the only identity for women, they desperately needed to know how to define themselves more authentically. Thus words—both spoken and written— become one of the means to self-knowledge and psychological consciousness.

In Hindu mythology, the story of Durga's defiance of her father, a powerful king, in her choice of husband is well known. Durga chose Shiva, a rather unconventional god who creates as well as destroys. He was a householder without a home but a committed and a loving husband. Durga's father never forgave her for this act of disobedience and punished her not only with his disapproval of her husband but also by totally neglecting her. Unhappy and angry, Durga tried to win the father's acceptance and failed. Out of frustration and suffering, she died.

In his enormous grief, Shiva mourned his beloved wife in a cosmic dance with her dead body on his head. The gods in heaven became scared of Shiva's dance of grief which could destroy the universe. The god Vishnu used his circular weapon to cut through the lifeless body of the goddess to distract Shiva from his dance. Wherever in India the parts of her body fell, that place became a pilgrim center.

Even the gods and goddesses cannot escape the punishment for the disobedience to the king, the power of the collective consciousness. However, the goddess's act of disobedience eventually led to the creation of sacred places where the mortals can worship her.

In a widely known folk tale of Bengal, a poor man obtained the position of the wisest counselor in the king's court by repeating his daughter-in-law's words. His envious colleagues discovered the truth and told the king. The king summoned the daughter-in-law to the court. In order not to put the father-in-law to shame, the woman cut off her tongue, and thus achieved immortality. Her words live even today in the form of proverbs and wise sayings. This woman was rewarded for her ultimate obedience as a good daughter-in-law.

In India, even today, a little girl is brought up to be obedient: obedient to her parents, to her teachers, to all her elders, and, of course, to her "roles" prescribed by her culture. Yet, as we have seen, many women also disobey just like the goddess Durga whom they are brought up to worship as well. While her society and culture punish her if she goes against the expected norm, her mythology, on the other hand, offers the model for such behavior. Thus, the conscious and the unconscious worlds are kept together, despite being contradictory to each other. And, within this contradiction a woman's selfhood is born, her personality matures, and she becomes herself. Some women, not only in nineteenth-century India but at all times and in all places, may be ready to pay anything to achieve this.

Tales and legends of disobedience exist in the Western tradition as well. The story of Genesis itself tells us how God's punishment for an act of disobedience created the possibility of human consciousness of both good and evil. In defiance of the Egyptian edict that all her children must be killed, Moses' mother Jockabed put Moses in a basket and let him live. Moses grew up to be the child of two cultures and led his people to the holy land. King David's defiance of Bathsheba's marriage resulted in his sin against God and the punishment of losing his first child, yet his second son, Solomon, was a wise prophet. According to another version, David and Bathsheba also gave birth to a daughter Sophia who represents wisdom.

The paradoxical outcomes of the acts of disobedience, therefore, exist in both Eastern and Western mythology. The practice of disobedience in both human and divine lives seems archetypal and acts as a compensatory opposite when we obey one idea or one authority or even one god too one-sidedly.

# References

*I thank Ms. Colleen Bryant and Mr. Russell P. Holmes,*
*O.C.D., for their help with the biblical references.*

### Bengali Sources

Das, Krishnabhabini. 1915. *Jeebaner Drisyamala*. Calcutta: publisher unknown.

Dev, Chitra. 1984. *Anttapurer Atmakatha*. Calcutta: Ananda Publisher's Private Limited.

Tagore, Rabindranath. 1961. Strir Patra. *Rabindra Rachanabali* 23:247–261.

### English Source

Roy, Manisha. 1975. *Bengali Women*. Chicago: The University of Chicago Press.

# THE WHIRLWIND AND THE SPIRAL

## STATE-SPONSORED TERROR
## AND PSYCHIC RESISTANCE
## IN MARTA TRABA'S
## *MOTHERS AND SHADOWS*

### Teresa Anderson

The original Spanish title of Marta Traba's novel, *Conversacion al Sur* (1981), is more revealing of its substance than the English translator's concept (1986). In 1973, a conversation takes place between two women, Irene, age 40, and Dolores, age 28, in Montevideo. This dialogue, which is interrupted by numerous flashbacks and psychic journeys throughout the novel, is described by Irene as "more of an excavation than a conversation." The "Sur" of the title refers to South America's Southern Cone, the nations of Uruguay, Argentina, and Chile, which during the late sixties and seventies suffered under a widening reign of terror imposed by the totalitarian regimes that came to dominate their governments.

The dialogue between Dolores and Irene remains the axis around which all the interior action revolves. Although its events can be viewed as proceeding in a linear progression toward a climactic ending, the real work of the novel consists of the uncovering of the psychic motivations for Irene's resistance to the State. By moving along the spiraling path of memory, the reader discovers the source of Irene's compassion as well as her alienation from a middle class which remained loyal to the terrorist regime. Traba challenges her readers to examine "both sides of an issue and conveys them with emotional power. Refusing to choose between sides Traba obliges the reader to bear the tension between them" (Chevigny 1985, p. 99). In Irene we find operating simultaneously a fear of speaking out countered by a clear vision of reality that requires her to oppose the self-inflicted blindness, silence, and passivity many choose as defenses against oppression. As we examine the world from within Irene's psyche, we are always aware of this struggle between awareness and what Bell Chevigny has termed the will to ignorance.

Traba alternates continuously between third-person narration coupled with dialogue in the present tense and interior monologue in order to evoke the active presence of memory at work beneath the observable action. Irene works at uncovering pieces of a puzzle she insists upon solving, spiraling down time and time again into the well of her psyche and resurfacing with more fragments to be added to the composite mosaic of herself. The result is a profoundly moving and resilient image of a woman fighting to maintain her dignity and sanity in a world maddened by blind terror. The fact that she expresses her resistance to state terrorism through participation in *collective* action is relevant to Traba's worldview and to her idea of woman as always part of a community.

From the beginning, the fear is overwhelming and omnipresent. Before we know the origin of her pain, we learn that Irene is having trouble controlling her shaking hands while pouring coffee for Dolores. The objective reality so well evoked by Traba can best be imagined as an expanding whirlwind of terror which enveloped the citizens of South America's Southern Cone during a period of nearly a decade. In the path of its blind destruction lay thousands of victims who were kidnapped, tortured, murdered, and made to disappear. After hearing Dolores's account of her brutal torture at the hands of the regime in Uruguay, Irene raises questions concerning the origins of the cataclysmic changes in her world.

> The outside world of war, earthquakes, changes of government, trips to the moon or Mars or whatever had ceased to exist for them. . . . Dolores droned on mechanically about how she'd got off lightly because at least they hadn't tortured her but had only made her have a miscarriage by stamping on her belly. So that doesn't count as torture? Are you living in cloud-cuckoo-land or something? (Traba 1986, p. 42)

For Dolores, who has survived torture and lost her unborn child and husband to the torturers, the dilemma is one of struggling to reconcile highly incompatible psychic needs. She longs to find respite from the torment of memory while seeking with the same intensity a way to avenge the deaths of her loved ones and friends. Her renewed contact with Irene results in the opening of the door to memory.

> For years she'd refused to let herself think about Enrique or the baby (a little girl, the nurse had said) they'd made her miscarry by stamping on her belly. But today she had thought about them and had talked openly about Enrique. . . . [Irene had] made her see clearly for the first time that this jumble of blood and horror and teeth and claws was part of her life, something she had to accept as part of herself; and that the unfeeling salvation she'd

been clutching at desperately would be meaningless if she pretended that the unspeakable suffering she'd experienced had never happened. (p. 96)

As both women struggle to come to terms with the enormity of the changes brought about by terror, we travel with them toward the source of their anguish and their resistance. Irene expresses a sense of solidarity with the suffering of others which enables her to endure her own:

> . . . going back in time would throw some light on her present situation . . . talking about things was not an escape from the present. On the contrary, it was a kind of peg on which the present hung and which somehow made it possible to cope. The fact that others had been through the same hell gave her the strength to endure it. (p. 68)

Irene traces the beginnings of her political education to a night in Montevideo five years before the conversation begins. She is a well-known actress who has come to Uruguay from Buenos Aires at the request of a director-friend to give a benefit performance. The timing of this performance falls during the first days of Uruguay's state of siege. During the first night of rehearsals, she meets Dolores, a student-activist and poet, who becomes infatuated with the older, celebrated woman. The next evening, Irene inadvertently finds herself caught up in a police charge directed against a group of activists during the funeral of one of their martyrs. During that night of headlong flight from police tear gas and gunfire, Irene is aided by Dolores and her friends, who lead her to the burned-out ruins of a local theater which serves them as a temporary refuge and later to the sumptuous home of Luisa, a very wealthy woman who has made room in her life for these young activists. Irene meets Dolores's husband, Enrique, and their friends, Andres, Juan, and Tomas. Five years later, all of these young men will be dead at the hands of the regime that came to power in Uruguay in 1967. Luisa's sexual alliance with Montevideo's Commissioner of Police leads to a disastrous conclusion to the evening when the young people and Irene are detained by the police. Irene loses her passport and, in order to retrieve it, is forcibly returned to Buenos Aries.

Prior to that night, Irene had managed to create for herself an ordered, predictable world far from the working-class, precarious existence she experienced in childhood. By means of her marriage to an influential man and her successful career as an actress, she had removed herself from the turmoil of the workaday world. She expresses annoyance at finding her rehearsal canceled and consequently running into the police charge:

> Her whole life had been devoted to organising the world around her, and nothing exasperated her more than something refusing to fit in. (p. 22)

The shock of experiencing firsthand the indifference of Montevideo's police to her inconvenience brings Irene into contact with the reality of a regime dominated by brutes in the service of totalitarianism.

> No matter who I might be, I simply didn't exist for them. Or rather; they decreed who could exist and who could not. And who were they? The scum of the earth, the bottom of the heap; we'd never noticed them til now but they must always have been there in our midst, waiting for the day they could exact their revenge. (p. 44)

Irene also begins to understand the seeping terror that, within a few years, would come to dominate her life:

> . . . the cold she felt as she left the police station was a different kind of cold . . . this was an internal, organic cold, that stemmed from being at the mercy of something or someone you can't pin down; something that was beginning to take shape, threatening her when she'd thought she was free and immune, how wrong she'd been! (p. 46)

In an interior monologue, which is really her imagined dialogue with Dolores, the one she cannot bring herself to speak, Irene reveals the depth of her bewilderment at the profound changes in her concept of the world, her anxiety, and her sense of mourning for what has been lost. There follows a passage that illuminates the source and nature of Irene's compassion, her deep understanding of Dolores's childhood in which "resignation was handed down to you by your parents, who from the moment of birth had expected to die and had made ready for the eventuality so it wouldn't catch them unprepared" (Traba 1986, p. 50). Irene knows this fatalistic worldview from the lessons of her own youth spent among members of the working class in the southern section of Buenos Aires.

> . . . I've never met your parents, but I can imagine them looking at you. I can see them, their lives taken up with earning a meagre living, queuing to claim their state benefits, making regular visits to the hospital to get their money's worth . . . dressed all year round in sensible colours that wouldn't show the dirt. . . . (p. 50)

The reader from this point on remains steadfastly allied with Irene. Her compassion and humanity transcend that privileged class position from which she had previously observed the world.

A scene crucial to Irene's realization that she must remain alienated from those members of Argentina's middle class who continue to support the state throughout this period takes place on a bus filled with tourists returning from Iguazu Falls. Irene is going back to Buenos Aires to visit her friend, Elena, whose daughter has recently disappeared at the hands of security forces. She remains thoroughly repulsed by the "bourgeois smugness" of her fellow passengers.

> . . . with everyone downing kilos of sirloin and mountains of ravioli, overflowing with pride; in the national flag, football, the Malvinas, whatever was held up to them as an example? An entire nation cavorting after the carrot dangling in front of their nose, while at the same time people were literally being hacked to pieces, with everyone pretending it had nothing to do with them. (p. 59)

When, during a rest stop, a young girl approaches Irene, saying, "We're the champions," she responds with a question, "Champions at what?" One of the mothers replies, "Champions at everything. The best football, the best meat, the best education system." Irene's lukewarm response does not go unnoticed. She realizes all the children are wearing "little flags, badges, T-shirts, caps saying I LOVE ARGENTINA. WE ARE THE CHAMPIONS." The passengers begin singing patriotic songs, such as "Argentina the Brave," and Irene does not join in. She feels she has become "the Jew on the coach. I'd sown discord and unrest amongst them" (Traba 1986, p. 61). Irene realizes that the bus trip is forcing her to take sides. She does not side with the passengers.

> Boring people who before I'd dismissed as inoffensive now turned out to have a hidden, dangerous side; beneath the painted hearts, the flags of victory, the innocent T-shirts, a sinister symbolism was at work. (p. 63)

During her visit to Elena, Irene participates in a demonstration of "the Madwomen of the Plaza de Mayo." This weekly series of demonstrations, organized and carried out exclusively by women, became a wellspring for political activists throughout the Americas and beyond. Begun by mothers and grandmothers of the thousands of young people tortured, murdered, and made to disappear at the hands of Argentina's military, these demonstrations continued throughout those years of terror and have been credited with forcing Argentina's present government to bring to trial those generals responsible.

Traba's description of the psychological process involved in Irene's participation in this act of collective disobedience forms the radiant core of the novel. Elena is Irene's best friend from girlhood days. She has been participating in these demonstrations since her daughter, Victoria, disappeared. The Plaza de Mayo is the central square in Buenos Aires, marked at one end by the cathedral and at the other by the Casa Rosada (what North Americans would see as Argentina's "White House").

As she and Elena arrive at the plaza, Irene is struck immediately by the fact that this usually very busy section of the city is completely devoid of people.

> No sightseers were standing around, no school children or men going about their daily business were hurrying across it, no old people sunning themselves on the park benches . . . her mind was completely taken up with the fact that at half past four in the afternoon, there was not a single person there except the women taking part in the demo. (p. 85)

When Irene notices that the usual grenadier guards posted on sentry duty at the gates to the Casa Rosada are also missing, she is given insight into "the enemy's machinations":

> . . . every Thursday, for the two to three hours during which the demonstration took place, the Plaza de Mayo was wiped off the map. Their ploy was simply to ignore them; to ignore the existence of the square and of the madwomen stamping their feet. (p. 87)

The women carry photos of their vanished loved ones to hold up during the demonstration. These, accompanied by lists of all the missing, they hold high as they begin to wave them from side to side. Irene is surprised by the silent grief shared by these women, wondering if that was the only purpose of the demonstration. Immediately after Irene's speculation, the collective shouting begins. Irene struggles to describe the overwhelming power of the experience:

> How can I find the words. I could say that suddenly someone started to shout and everyone started shouting and in a matter of minutes the whole square was one single shout. But that wouldn't begin to tell you what it was like. . . . it was as if the words were severed from one another by sobbing and howling.

Every now and then I thought I heard the words "Where are they?" "Where are they?" but it may have been my imagination. And yet they have been voicing some demand that served as a focus for the general mood of anger, because the crowd of women surged forward like a tide. (p. 89)

Irene, who had become separated from Elena by the crowd, finds her in the middle of a circle of women chanting in unison, "Where are they? Where are they?" The image of Elena's face twisted by rage and grief is one Irene will not be able to forget.

As the wave of rage and anguish begins to subside, Irene's reaction to the complete lack of response by government officials and the public at large reveals the degree of her frustration. Just after rejoining Elena as the demonstration is breaking up, she does something she views later as "awful, really awful."

I broke away from her and ran out into the middle of the road shouting how was I supposed to feel, for Christ's sake, how was I supposed to feel, and why didn't those bastards hiding behind the curtains come out into the open . . . I created a real scandal. And do you think anyone came out to see what was going on, do you think anyone looked out of the window? Not a soul. (p. 91)

Irene returns to the square to witness its "return to normalcy." At this point, we understand clearly that Irene's rebellion is against complacency and willful blindness. She feels betrayed by those Argentinians who refused to acknowledge the terror that was controlling them.

Following her participation in the madwomen's expression of collective outrage, Irene will carry within herself the tension between her certainty that witness against oppression is a necessity and the knowledge that the majority of her countrymen and women will not be willing to risk their individual safety for the sake of that principle. Unlike Dolores, who entered the world of political activism from an ideological position that recognizes the fundamental complicity of the middle class with those in power, Irene remains continually shocked by what she views as the betrayal of her brothers and sisters.

In spite of her deep fear of losing everything, Irene becomes a part of the "madwomen" who dare to confront the regime with the names of its victims. Her particular struggle is carried out not only against the architects and practitioners of terror but also against the self-satisfied members of her class who refuse to acknowledge its realities.

At the midpoint in the novel, the focus of attention gravitates to Dolores, working class, politically radical, and a victim of state torture. For a brief period, the two women separate, and we enter the dark pool of Dolores's memories. For the younger woman, Irene was initially an object of infatuation when they first met in Montevideo where they shared arrest. Now, years later, Dolores returns to Irene in order to share her loss. For Dolores, being with Irene "made you feel like a disconcerted sailor who, after a long and stormy crossing, suddenly catches sight of the longed-for haven. Nothing was quite like being with her, nothing in the world" (Traba 1986, p. 96).

Dolores imagines Irene's life as a fantasy of luxury and delight in contrast to the repressive world of her childhood. She understands that such images constitute her "nocturnal apparitions, the unexpressed passion that runs through the lines of my poems, the irremediable suspicion that my slice of the cake is the worst of all possible worlds" (Traba 1986, p. 118). The debate between Dolores and Irene reflects not only generational and class differences but also an essential difference in temperament. Bell Chevigny has noted that "Irene and Dolores cannot agree about the psychological preconditions of survival. For Irene survival depends on the identification of life with happiness and the refusal to come to terms with death, but Dolores dares not live without anticipating the worst, controlling horror by imagining it in advance. While Irene believes her equilibrium would be betrayed by unflinching realism, Dolores fears most the temptation of happiness." (Chevigny 1985, p. 100)

During their last revealing dialogue, Irene and Dolores discuss the very different motivations for their political commitment. Their disagreement clearly represents one with which the author is familiar. Irene explains the way she arrived at her position:

> . . . I feel that I've got there by an independent route. That I got involved on my account, not because I approved of what you were doing . . . but because of the change I was just talking about: I mean the question of compassion and solidarity with others. Has the notion of pity been lost irrevocably? Because if it has, it means our society has lost all sense of humanity, that's what worries me. (p. 173)

Dolores has returned very late to Irene's apartment, having fled her parents' house after learning of the unexpected death of her father. Dolores's mother, a bitter woman for whom life has held few joys, begins pouring out a diatribe of complaints against Dolores for her neglect and the shame which her political activism brought upon the family.

Dolores returns to Irene as to a place of sanctuary where her grief and anger can be given a voice, where she can be accepted. After her anguish has subsided, Dolores falls asleep, and Irene, watching over her, remembers all the years she watched over her son in the same way. Just after the women have created a new emotional habitation, there is a brutal knocking at the door; "we listen with them to the shattering of locks and panels that closes the novel and becomes an invasion of the reader's space, bringing an end to quiet certainty and distance" (Chevigny 1985, p. 100). The end of quiet certainty and distance is exactly what came about for Irene as we journeyed with her through this novel of oppression.

The experience of reading *Mothers and Shadows* requires us to accompany Irene and Dolores on their spiraling journey into the well of memory from which both women generate their strength to resist the overwhelming force of a terrorist regime. The horror left by the whirlwind remains vivid and continues to fill us with revulsion long after we have finished the last page.

However, what triumphs in the final analysis here is the spirit of compassion, courage, and self-sacrifice embodied for us by the examples created in the characters of Dolores and Irene. Speaking in 1982 at a symposium on literature and violence at New York University, Traba explained that her novel arose from desperation, from a feeling of guilt and impotence. After reading reports brought to Washington by representatives for the Mothers of the Plaza de Mayo, she found herself incapable of writing about anything else.

In Latin culture, the figure of the *mater dolorosa* has a power that informs the consciousness of Catholic believer and nonbeliever alike. That single image of the pure mother offering oblations for the sins of the people has been appropriated by both rightist and leftist movements. In spite of the traditional machismo which allocates to men supremacy in the public arena, the power of the mother in family life and in the household remains undisputed. When these grandmothers and mothers left their homes to protest publicly, in the names of their children, the repression of the state, they drew upon very powerful psychic forces embedded in the public consciousness. The terrorist state invokes the forces of "moderation and reason" to put down what it views as insurrection and threats to established order. Such repression is best carried out against men or groups of armed peasants or workers, who can be viewed as controlled by incendiary subversives. To mow down a few thousand women armed with photographs and lists of those who disappeared would have been a tactical error for which the state could have created no palatable justification.

Why these women chose to risk so much during this time of violent repression remains the central preoccupation of *Mothers and Shadows*. Traba strives to celebrate their courage which rose from the ache in the womb every mother feels when her child goes out one morning never to return. At the same time, she grieves, through the character of Irene, over the silence of those who chose self-imposed blindness. This unremitting tension between the angry, shattered women who spoke out and those who chose complicity with the assassins is the source of the novel's tragic clarity as well as its enduring strength.

## References

Chevigny, B. 1985. Ambushing the will to ignorance: Elvira Orphee's *La Ultima Conquista del Angel* and Marta Traba's *Conversacion al Sur*. In *El cono sur: Dinamica y dimensiones de su literatura*, Rose S. Minc, ed. Upper Montclair, N.J.: Montclair State College, pp. 98-104.

Traba, M. 1981. *Conversacion al Sur*. Mexico City: Siglo Veintiuno Editores, S.A.

_____. 1986. *Mothers and Shadows*. Jo Labanyi, trans. London: Readers International.

# AT WAR WITH HOME IN SOUTH AFRICA

## WRITING BY ELLEN KUZWAYO
## AND LAURETTA NGCOBO

## Jane Foress Bennett

### Introduction: The South African "Home"

For most of the twentieth century (and with particular specificity since 1948), the legal and economic interlock of the system known as "apartheid" has carved out conditions of survival for black South Africans so dehumanizing that one might want to claim all memory of their living bodies and voices as the incarnation of political transgression.

Internationally, "apartheid" has been sometimes understood more readily as systematized racism than as a mode of labor control which engages racism as one of its most powerful tools. The state policy of "separate development" for peoples of different ethnicities has, over the years, ratified the "legal" separation of the land into "South Africa" (of which only white people are citizens) and ten "bantustans" (13 percent of the land, of which people classified as "Xhosa," "Zulu," and so on are voting citizens).[1] Movement from the bantustans has been pitilessly controlled to secure men for labor within "South Africa" and to define the immobility of those left behind — women, children, the old, and the ill. The state's term for these bantustans is "homeland," and these "homelands" have worked with

[1] The bantustan system of labor control has been endlessly restructured by the state; certain bantustans have "achieved independence" in the later 1970s; currently De Klerk's proposed "white paper," which seeks to abandon the legalization of this system, is under state discussion in South Africa. Whatever the process of this, the economic realities entailed by the praxis of this system will be with the lives of all South Africans for a long time.

macabre efficiency, not only in the production of people as "laborers," but in the reproduction of labor at very little cost to the state.[2]

Within "reproduction" lurks very particular implications for the lives of black South African women. In 1987, 63 percent of black women were confined to bantustan territory, together with some eight million children.[3] The word *homeland* cannot be thought of simply as a tidy state euphemism: the name embodies (a literal embodiment) black women's coercion into a role designed to maximize the success of apartheid. "Homeland" is a bitterly accurate term for the state's laws of re/productive control— peopled by starving women and children, the bantustans replenish and nourish the public (white) wealth of South Africa. Black women's bodies bear the next generation of "laborers," while a current generation wrestles for both subsistence and "family" in an arrangement that splits men between their own economic survival and their children, forces women into alienated, claustrophobic relations of endless, impossible "caretaking," and structures the possibility of a living standard for white South Africans that is almost the highest in the world.

The malevolence of legal "homes" for black South Africans (wound so closely into the plush material lives of most white South Africans) has forged another meaning for the word. Whereas middle-class American and European feminists have characterized "home" as a trap in the means of production from which women need escape, the struggle of South African black women to *own* control of their "homes" and children, to wrest them from the interests of the state, has been germane to the narrative of South African resistance. "Home," simultaneously exploited and sundered by apartheid policy, signifies also one of the most revolutionary desires of black women speaking from beneath apartheid—a ferocious demand for a family's safety, space, and right to constitute itself as a community (or a process) in its own terms of allegiance.

The focus of black women's rebellion here is not connected to idealism about "precolonial" family structures nor is it wedded to any particular tolerance for assumptions of male authority; it is, primarily, a visceral political rejection of state interests which have both devoured and defined "home" for thirty million South African black women and men. The reclamation of "home," its language, complexities, and future, is one argument shared by the work of the two writers discussed in this piece. It is

[2]The term *homeland* was part of the policy drafted by one Professor F. R. Tomlinson, in 1949, whose commission's agenda was to streamline labor control after World War II.

[3]These figures come from the publications of the South African Institute of Race Relations.

also the site where literacy can envisage a theory of both South African economic history and the narrative of revolution against state interests as rooted within black women's experience.

Ellen Kuzwayo was 71 in 1985 when her autobiography, *Call Me Woman*, was published. In Bessie Head's foreword to the book, she predicts, "Books like these will be the Bible one day for the younger generations." The second author whose representation of the meanings of "home" for black South Africans deepens an illustration of "woman's place" in the history of South African resistance is novelist Lauretta Ngcobo. *And They Didn't Die*, her second novel, tells a story of rural women's lives where any assumption about freedom, gender, or the meaning of reproduction is a semantic and political warzone.

Reading both autobiographical and fictional writing by black women in South Africa, it is possible to think not only of their rebellions against the gridlock semantics of "home," but to consider the formal subversions feasible in women's use of genres like the novel or autobiography. If black South African women's work demands a radical reconceptualization of the word *home* within the politics of representation, perhaps it demands also a refusal to settle for distinctions between "self," "history," and "imagination" conventionalized by the notion that autobiography entails the fiction of authorial visibility while novels encourage the allure of authorial suppression. I am compelled, in this brief piece, by the way these writers may explode predictions for "a woman's place" both at the intersection of language and experience, and at the level of a literature and history.

## "Does It Make Sense to You?"

### *Ellen Kuzwayo's* Call Me Woman

> Ellen Kate Cholofelo Nnoseng Motlalepule are all names I answer to. Please do not ask me why so many. . . . I am the author of this book. (Kuzwayo 1985, p. 55)

Ellen Kuzwayo divides her autobiography *Call Me Woman* into three sections: the first sketches Soweto as a window into the history of capricious state brutality and its effects on half a century of black women's experience; the second traces "my own story in detail"; and the last four chapters, entitled "Patterns Behind the Struggle," collect in a third section a web of observation about the extraordinary achievements of black South African women's lives. The broad structure of the book thus embeds the birth of the author on June 29, 1914, into Kuzwayo's presentation of black women as her mentors, challengers, inspiration, and genealogy. The (perhaps not) parenthetical placement of the "personal" resonates in fact throughout the text. The design of the chapters in sections one and three plots the languages of anecdote, introspection, historical explanation, philosophy, and testimony into one another so that the "I" who is the author is often encircled by other subjects, who sometimes comment directly on "I's" partiality, class, or limitation. (When, for example, Kuzwayo asks women who work as vegetable vendors in Soweto whether she should accept on their behalf an offer from "well-intentioned people with money" to build them shelters, their negative reaction is presented as a lesson to Kuzwayo on the details of vending permits and the elderly women's solidarity, which refuses the possible strife concrete shelters would bring (Kuzwayo 1985, p. 38).)

The quotation above exemplifies the exchange of communal and individual identities Kuzwayo explores as a woman. She describes the genesis of her names and their salience to family members, and from the fluidity of a history in which she means different things to different people, she testifies at once to an identity and a responsibility: "I am the author of this book." Attention to the implications of a name ("author," "Cholofelo") opens the section Kuzwayo claims as personal autobiography, but the initial chapter is entitled "Coming Back Home" and demands the meaning of "home" for every black South African. The letter that begins *Call Me Woman* was received by Kuzwayo in 1978 from Debra Mabale, imprisoned under South African security laws for her work in the YMCA's Youth Association. "Debs" describes how:

> Except for the natural consequences following the denial of basic human needs, viz. Fresh Air, Sunshine, Essential Vitamins, Communication, Love, Movement, Security, to name a few, I remain unscathed . . . I don't have to tell you how life is at the Fort. You've been here before . . . All I can say is I am at home. Enjoying the clean peaceful atmosphere prevailing in this place . . ."

In a move analogous to that which subverts the privacy of a letter between women into a historical document and a representational key, Debra's words assume the reality of a South Africa in which antonymy functions as subterfuge. The "clean peaceful atmosphere" describes the monotonous, deadly deprivation of Johannesburg Fort, part of Kuzwayo's own story in chapter fourteen. The implications of "I am at home" spin and widen across the connections between incarceration and black women's lives in South Africa. State policy entails everywhere an identity between restraint and familiarity; state intentions could easily be read as seeking to name prisons as "home" for black South Africans. The refusal to be intimidated by state power, and the insistence on claiming an autonomy, a people, a "home" for oneself while within the concrete of a jail is a frequent gesture of detainees' protest. With deceptive simplicity, Kuzwayo's use of this letter introduces the politics of verbal ambiguity as a production of a system which has lost the right to reference, to self-representation. Kuzwayo moves on, valorizing Debra's courage, to ground the exploration of South African "sense" in her answer to the explicit question: "Where is home for a black person in South Africa?" (p. 4).

She seeks the answer through an outline of black women's historical survival as endless legislation pits men against their families, "resettles" millions of people, forces desperate women looking for work onto the fringes of cities, and attempts to control reproduction. She tells how Soweto (which she claims as "my home," a city now of two million people) had its beginnings in the settlement in the 1920s of mineworkers on the edges of Johannesburg. Later, thousands of women (left behind to the ravages of pitiless hunger in the bantustan "reserves") streamed to these "location" communities. Other women had to stay in the rural areas, becoming "without warning . . . overnight mother, father, family administrator . . . and overall overseer of family and neighborhood affairs" (p. 13).

Across decades, the "homes" in which black women live are the shacks of Sophiatown and early Pimville, the bitter huts of the "homelands," the eventual chaos of Soweto's grid of boxlike housing, and the isolated rooms built outside white houses where "the girl" sleeps. The configuration of each "home" involves black women's desire to resist the state: to endure, to work, to create themselves and their children. Each different "home" is a space where a black woman fights the daily intent of the state to erase and exhaust her, to soak her life of labor in the interests of white wealth. Kuzwayo's opening voice uncovers the surface of domesticity to reveal a fierce network of historical relations, relations she perceives as integral to the very possibility of her autobiography. "Still," she writes at the end of this chapter, "the black people of South Africa have not . . . attained their rightful homes" (p. 15). Placed "at home" in Soweto as a writer, she links herself first to the huts or shanties of her mothers and sisters and, at the end of the chapter, to the final logic of these dwelling places, the fact that black South Africans are "homeless."

The chorale of testimony to black women's radical dedication to the dream of a freely chosen "home" which encircles part two of *Call Me Woman* supports the heartbeat of anxiety in Kuzwayo's own story, "the uncertainty about any place I could call home without hesitation for fear of being rejected" (p. 122). Although Kuzwayo's representation of black women's position on the frontlines of apartheid's malevolence is completely lucid about the revolutionary impulse fueling their desire for a home, she brooks no simplification of the difficulty she has experienced as a woman—a worker, a daughter, a student, a wife—in relation to her experiences of "home." Brought up on a farm (stolen in 1974 by a state decree that the area was a "black spot" from which her family should be forcibly ejected), Kuzwayo wraps the narrative of her youth into memories of a loving mother, her education, and her friends. "An innocent, respectable little girl" (p. 72), she drafts the first hint of a rebellious curiosity about the meaning of "home" for women. She describes the different dances performed according to gender by the Basotho people with whom her grandfather works on the farm and explains that "as a child from a Christian home, I was strictly forbidden to associate with the girls who had accepted *lebello* (a traditional ceremony of initiation into gender) as part of their lives" (p. 73). Kuzwayo, nonetheless, watches the girls' dancing, loving their agility, fearing the "wrath of her family" for her delight. While the narrative thus confronts the split between a "tribal" and a "Christian" home, Kuzwayo throws the fabric of her respect over the fissure, claiming traditional women's dance as a gift and highlighting black women's solidarity: "The mothers I saw and lived with in Thabo Patchoa, their involvement in their daily chores and outside in the fields and elsewhere, modelled the image I had of black women in rural areas . . ." (p. 75).

Kuzwayo's passion for the strength of this image is, however, challenged by tensions within her family home. Her mother's divorce alienates her slightly from her playmates, her mother's sudden death causes her deep shock, and the subsequent remarriage of her stepfather to Aunt Blanche leads to her eviction from the farmhouse under conditions which bewilder her: "My whole childhood had tumbled away . . . I lost all sense of personal direction and identity" (p. 107). Instructed by an inexplicably implacable Aunt Blanche to go and live with her natural father in Pimville, Kuzwayo is thrust out of her rural home into the railway station, crowds, and unemployment of Johannesburg. The trajectory from rural outcast to urban squatter is — as Kuzwayo has already illustrated — a leitmotif of black women's history under apartheid. Her own journey is one she presents as the outcome of being a young single woman whose options are organized as much by certain family systems as by state-directed ones (despite the fact that she is an accredited primary school teacher, her professional stature carries no power to protect her from Aunt Blanche's rejection).

The central chapter of part two, "A Home of My Own," takes on the triple discourse of heterosexuality, family structure, and the possibilities of working in an education system shaped by racism. This chapter begins with Kuzwayo's description of her efforts to invigorate the education of the girls she was teaching, and — with the expansion of her ideas about women's physical self-sufficiency — she "realizes" that "the answer to my feelings of homelessness was to find myself a life partner . . . I yearned for a home where there was peace and love" (p. 122). Kuzwayo marries and is plunged into the devastatingly traumatic sense of the word *home* already presaged by the image of her parents' divorce: "I went through both physical and mental sufferings. Day by day I realized I was being humiliated and degraded, an experience I have in recent years come to realize is suffered by many women the world over, within different races, cultures and religions" (p. 124).

In order to escape the violence of her husband, she has to abandon her baby sons, fleeing through the night for her life. Because she is the legal "property" of her husband, she avoids his "attempts to track her down"; when she reaches the only place she is entitled to go, her father's home in Johannesburg, "for a split second [he] did not recognize me" (p. 133). Kuzwayo's vision of a marital "home" is shattered by the meaning she discovers here for the term *wife* and this wounds her as bitterly as the later assault she suffers as a "mother" whose younger son is not permitted by apartheid law to live with her and whose elder son is banned and exiled to Mafikeng for organizing black adult literacy programs in 1971. In other words, despite an avowed dedication to political community with "our menfolk," Kuzwayo insists on narrating the complicity of state interests and the possibility of family coercion against black women's autonomous homes.

Her response to this complicity is not, however, a rejection of its various terms of definition: *worker, wife, mother*. Drawing on the names and life stories of other black women—Annie Silinga, Dr. Mary Xakana, Charlotte Maxeke, Winnie Nomzamo Mandela, Joyce Seroke—Kuzwayo summons herself into the revelation of her passion for her children, her commitment to activism as a youth organizer, her readiness to face the horror of detention "in the name of the black child," and her refusal to compromise the complexity of black women's imprisonments or the multiplicity of their strategies of resistance. As a formal resolution of the semantic abyss Kuzwayo faces ("home" as a term of state imprisonment of women; "home" as a place neither she nor any other black South African owns; "home" as the site from which she can be corralled or banished by her relatives), Kuzwayo's affirmation of her gender as a complex source of political strength strikes me more as a heuristic than a theorem. After her release from detention, she is greeted by scores of children calling "Umama! Umama!"—"the custom of my nation where every mother is every child's mother" (p. 217)—and it is clear that motherhood is a political affiliation whose terms change daily to accommodate the metamorphoses of apartheid. The autobiography began with Debra's greeting:

> Darling Mama,
>    It was so wonderful to see that familiar
>    handwriting. 'Twas like I've really come home . . .

Kuzwayo's autobiography meshes the words *Mama, home*, and *woman* into a kaleidoscopic celebration of black women's significance to the history of

South Africa. To call her woman is to accept that, indeed, "one is not born a woman, but there are some who may achieve it."[4]

## "Jezile, Life of My Life"

### Lauretta Ngcobo's And They Didn't Die

The complexity of the places defined as home by and for black women create the urgency of Kuzwayo's quest for autobiography. It is these roots of place which become the focus for Lauretta Ngcobo's story of Jezile in *And They Didn't Die*. The novel is (to my knowledge) the first written in English by a black South African woman which takes the experience of "homeland" people as the ineradicable source of resistance to the laws of apartheid.

> The dipping tank was empty. The dip mixture lay
> green, drying in trickles and splashes on the grey clay
> soil . . . For the fourth successive week the women of
> Sigageni had emptied the tank in spite of the threats
> . . . (Ngcobo 1991, p. 1)

The poisonous sludge of the dip hints at the terms of the civil war waged here. State efforts to control the lives of the people of Sigageni, a community of several villages in the so-called "homeland" of KwaZulu territory, commandeer drought, starvation, and the freezing winter winds as weapons. The people of Sigageni are, by and large, women and their children. Mr. Pienaar, the white officer in charge of getting the Sigageni cattle dipped, rails against them: "These women, this strange breed of womanhood, thin and ragged and not like women at all—they think they rule the world . . . if nobody stops them, they're going to ruin this country. In spite of what others think, it is the women we have to deal with, not those far away men in the cities" (p. 2).

The men of Sigageni are migrant laborers, living hundreds of miles away in mine compounds, returning once a year for two weeks. The women of Sigageni—some abandoned wives, some women clinging to the hope that the scrawled hurry of a letter which appears now and then (occasionally bringing money in its folds) means a marriage, many women with thin children and sickly babies, some mothers whose fraught relation to their

---

[4]A well-known article by the feminist theorist Monique Wittig (1980) suggests—after de Beauvoir—that "women" are the negative product of a socially coercive set of institutions and ideas.

absent sons' wives is their sole source of self-recognition—these women's interactions design the struggle for home rehearsed over and over by a century's worth of rebellion against state intentions. *And They Didn't Die*, as a title, announces the victory of this rebellion and locates its details in the body of Jezile's story.

Jezile, very young and a central instigator in the surreptitious weekly spilling of the cattle dip, is childless as the novel opens. Married to an adored, absent Siyalo, she lives under the scornful criticism of his mother, MaBiyela, and works "as a water carrier, a wood gatherer, a road mender . . . ploughing, sewing, weeding and reaping" (p. 5). Her narrative stretches across the interstices of state coercion and women's desire: she longs for pregnancy but Siyalo returns home only as the law permits and, during his whirlwind visit, Jezile does not conceive. Taking control of her own hopes, Jezile decides to travel to Durban, to Siyalo's barracks and love. In order to make the journey, she has to accept a "pass" permitting her legal exit from the KwaZulu territory into "white" South Africa. For years (the book spans the early 1950s to the 1980s), both rural and urban women have been resisting the government's attempt to extend pass law over their lives, simply by refusing to accept the tiny hated books. For Jezile to make an exception of herself constitutes a betrayal; Nosizwe, a doctor who inspires the women's solidarity, scolds her, "In fighting against the passes, can we allow exceptions? . . . there are as many special cases as there are these women" (p. 42). MaBiyela attacks her, not for political stupidity but on moral grounds—why is Jezile "jaunting off to Ixopo [to arrange the legality of her trip] like a trollop?" (p. 15). Snagged on the barbs of her competing priorities, Jezile nonetheless takes a bus into Durban and returns, "her future assured," with new life in her body.

Ngcobo permits no ease, however, with this passionate avowal of a desire for motherhood. Side by side with Jezile's determination, she introduces Zenzile, whose husband is also a migrant laborer, who rarely sends her money or any other sign of his affection. He does, every year, leave another growing child in her body, and Zenzile is surrounded by small, withered children. She droops with exhaustion and eventually dies, emaciated, in childbirth. The meaning of home is so much about the terrifying, thorny salience of children: "children were the insurance; mothers used them to keep the memory of home alive in their husbands, and husbands used them to fill the lonely existence of the wives they left behind. In this vicious circle many wives were trapped" (p. 15). At the same time children become the hostages of apartheid's exploitation of the family, it is the defense of children that propels Sigageni into an ever more poisonous struggle against the state. There are fierce community battles waged by the women in courts and prisons to keep control of the land out of state hands, and Jezile's own life escalates closer and closer to white men and women's violence—the book ends as she kills a white soldier raping her daughter:

"I've killed him, my child . . . Look, he's dead. It was bound to happen at some time or another; we have to fight back. I couldn't let him do it to you" (p. 242).

This final rebellion against the confluence of the state and the penis ripples beyond the immediate reclamation of black women from the greed of white men's institutional and literal grasp over their flesh. The retribution gives Jezile the courage to confront Siyalo who—according to custom—abandons her after she is herself raped earlier on in the novel (she gives birth to a light-skinned baby). She waits for him in the rising sun of the early morning: "That man, long ago, broke my life. And you never came to ask me . . . They broke our marriage, they broke our life here at Sabelweni, and they've broken all our children's lives and killed many . . . I had to defend her. We have to defend ourselves" (p. 245). (Siyalo is also presented as a man tortured by apartheid's hatred of a strong black family in one locale—he is "endorsed out" of his mine job because his supervisors dislike what they hear of his wife's activism, and he is later imprisoned for a decade for taking milk from a white farmer's full cow for S'naye, his starving baby.) Siyalo here responds to Jezile with the raw truth glimpsed in the face of an unspeakable future: "Jezile, life of my life." The novel here places genealogy into the name of a woman; her life is the language of all black survival, but this is no recuperation of a conservative domestic agenda for women. Jezile's transformation into a warrior takes its guidance from somewhere beyond the canon, somewhere almost unwritable.

*And They Didn't Die* thus reflavors and corroborates the premise of Kuzwayo's writing, i.e., the politics of black South African women's resistance revolve around the rich defense of reproduction as subjects, as humanity (rather than as labor). Home is presented as the arena in which the state works to eviscerate black strength, and such evisceration finds allies in community tensions of gender and generation. As most nakedly the "site" of reproduction, a black woman's body attracts the savagery of state attention so that her movement, relationships, and dreams are everywhere vulnerable. The gesture of subjective coherence (no matter what the surface appearance of disjuncture), the final indivisibility of identity is, then, a stunning spit of defiance.

I have abbreviated my reading of Ngcobo's creation of Jezile's subjectivity to talk about the relationship between autobiography and fiction, a relation on which this piece has presumed. I discuss Kuzwayo and Ngcobo as though the difference between autobiography (which privileges the separation of an authorial "I" from time) and fiction (which permits the fugitive authorial "I" in exchange for the panorama of her "imagination") was negligible. I want to suggest that in a context of black South African women's authorship, this distinction may in fact be negligible, *not* from a position which argues that the rareness of black women's writing entails the dismissal of literary fussinesses, but from one which takes the assumption of a black woman's authorial "I" as an act of extreme political courage. Whether figured as the qualifying presence of autobiography, or the enabling absence of fiction, this assumption is one of *body*, of substance. Modern theories of representation often note the difficulty of using "I" as referential, pointing to the intricate geology of erasure, context, and power that make any "I" resonant. These theories sometimes dismiss writing which claims historical verisimilitude for autobiography or fiction as naive. I am arguing that the pose of coherence, the assumption that one is "identifiable" under one's own terms of value, is a formally radical move under conditions of production which demand (and rely on) one's dispersal. At this formal level, Kuzwayo's autobiography and Ngcobo's novel draw on conceptions of "a whole self" which underlie both genres and create ineluctable reference for the black South African woman. To place this consciousness into negotiation with multiple perspectives on memory, "events," and so on—as both writers do—is nothing short of extraordinary.

Added to this motivation for taking seriously the connections between autobiography and fiction would be the context of black South African literature as a whole: many well-known "novels" take their author's life experience as a central theme and many "autobiographies" tell and retell the stories of South African history. This is a topic worth its own full discussion; with a wider lens, I think of other texts written from within the sites of intricate imperial violence. Harriet Jacobs's *Incidents in the Life of a Slave Girl* (written by a woman who escaped American slavery in the 1850s) or Michelle Cliff's *Abeng* (written about a 1960s Jamaican childhood) are both, for example, texts which integrate the meaning of authorial subjectivity into narrative convention from worlds deeply inhospitable to black women's self-representations. There is a clear thread of performative subterfuge to be found running from the plantation to the "colonies" and across the ocean to the work here of Kuzwayo and Ngcobo. I read their disobediences simultaneously as gauntlet and prophecy: "All over the country, at this moment, women are watching and thinking of us. Their hearts are with us."[5]

# References

Kuzwayo, E. 1985. *Call Me Woman*. San Francisco: Spinster's Ink.

Ngcobo, L. 1991. *And They Didn't Die*. New York: George Braziller.

Wittig, M. 1980. The straight mind. *Feminist Issues*.

[5]The quotation is taken from the Pass Petition of August 9, 1956, where thousands of women protested the extension of Pass Laws to black women.

# RAGE

## *and*

# DISOBEDIENCE

—

*Like a Raisin in the Sun*

# MEDEA'S FIERY
# CHARIOT

## Carol Savitz

*Ah, I have suffered*
*What should be wept for bitterly. I hate you*
*Children of a hateful mother. I curse you*
*And your father. Let the whole house crash.*

(111–114)[1]

One hundred lines into the text of Euripides' *The Medea*, Medea's voice is
first heard, proclaiming her suffering and rage at Jason's betrayal and
culminating in her thundering curse: "Let the whole house crash." Medea
speaks, unseen, from within the confines of the house and, from that still
interior space, calls upon the audience to witness her *internal* violence
before her bitter revenge becomes manifest. All is still interior, potential,
imaginal; destruction can still be reversed, rescinded, or redeemed. Yet, in
the drama, we see the enactment of a dark and bloody revenge that irrevers-
ibly crosses the threshold of illusion into life just as Medea herself will move
from the interior of the house to the visible stage itself one hundred lines
later. What begins as fantasy — annihilation of Jason for his ruthless
abandonment — ends in an unredemptive bloodbath in which sacrifice gives
way to murder, paradox to polarization, interiority to exteriority, Eros to
domination, and a creative flight of imagination to a deadly escape into the
chariot of the Sun and the paradisal garden of Athens.

Euripides' Medea is at once a complex and ambivalent figure:
betrayed and betrayer, victim and persecutor, poisoned and poisoner,
human and divine. With the sensibility of the Romantic imagination, we are
drawn to Medea: there is something grand and heroic about the power of

---

[1]All quotations from *The Medea* are from Rex Warner's translation in the
University of Chicago series, *The Complete Greek Tragedies*, ed. by D.
Grene and R. Lattimore, and are followed by their line numbers in
parentheses.

her language, her gestures of disobedience and refusal, her grasping toward the divine.[2] Yet, ultimately, we are forced to recognize the trail of self and other destructiveness that she leaves behind as she flees on the wings of her dragon-drawn chariot — her murder of her brother, of Pelius, of her two children, of Jason's bride. We begin to realize that a series of failures haunts the theatrical space of *The Medea*: the failure of Eros to result in the capacity for otherness, of the imaginal realm to hold suffering without a destructive enactment in life, and of an appropriate human–divine relationship. Especially, we are struck by Medea's failure to achieve psychic depth and integration through what might have been a creative act of disobedience to her father and Jason's world.

In this paper, I will argue that there is an intimate and necessary link between disobedience and sacrifice and that the tragedy of *The Medea* hinges upon the failure of her disobedience to be accompanied by this necessary sacrifice. Essentially, Medea refuses to exchange her flights in her fiery chariot and her refuge in Athen's paradisal garden for genuine suffering.[3] As *The Medea* unfolds, the chariot of the Sun gathers a multiplicity of symbolic meanings: of desire and rage, of disavowal of her father, of poisoning and murder. Ultimately, the chariot symbolizes her archetypal, inviolate sanctuary which is immune from human suffering and the tyranny of all that lies outside the self.[4]

*The Medea* begins with Eros's fateful arrow which awakens Medea's desire, merging the divine and human elements of her nature. "Her heart on fire with passionate love for Jason" (1.8), she disobeys her father by helping Jason steal the Golden Fleece and experiences a psychic shattering through Jason's subsequent abandonment. Although her disobedience has freed her from her father, Aeetes (a Sun god), still unwilling to relinquish her fury and fantasies of omnipotence, she remains trapped in psychic

---

[2]See especially Medea's speech to the women of Corinth in which she discusses the inequalities of male–female relationship and the lack of options for Greek women (215–266).

[3]For the description of Athens as the home of Wisdom, Harmony, and the Muses, see *The Medea* (825–856).

[4]Euripides' use of Medea's supernatural chariot has met with much critical controversy. Aristotle, in *Poetics* 54b1, (p. 20 and p. 111) has referred to the resolution of the plot as a "contrivance" — a *deus ex machina*. My reading differs as I see her refuge in the chariot as an integral part of the play from a psychological perspective. To avoid suffering Jason's abandonment, she opts to split off from the human realm and seek sanctuary in the archetypal realm. In that sense, Euripides has not avoided a resolution of plot, but describes a psychic process validated by clinical experience.

bondage to Jason; her revenge becomes an inadequate, retaliatory attempt to rescue her lost self from Jason's tyrannical otherness, a psychic failure to hold paradox and its accompanying suffering.

The Medea provides an archetypal ground from which we can envision the violence of betrayal and its aftermath of psychic fragmentation, rage, grief, and humiliation.[5] Seeking refuge from insufferable pain, Medea's psyche, as we will explore, polarizes into a split world of victim and persecutor, of human and divine, without an adequate ego space to hold these opposites, a pattern that we see clinically in both the internal world of the traumatized patient and in its transference manifestations within the analytic encounter. This psychic splitting helps us understand how Medea is able to murder her own children and why, refusing to sacrifice her rage and archetypal illusions, her disobedience cannot become a transformative act. Disobedience derives from the Latin oboedire "to hear" or "hearken" or "give ear to," and in The Medea we are forced to question not whom she "hears," but which aspect of her split self she "listens to" when she chooses to disobey.

Medea's split world is evoked through an image on a red-figure vase: here, Medea sits before us in her dragon-drawn chariot, encircled by the circumference and rays of the sun, hovering over the bodies of her two children, who lie dead on the altar where she has murdered them. To the right of her enclosed circle are the nurse and the tutor, who gaze in horror, with arms raised, at the bodies of the children. To the left of the altar stands Jason, looking upward at Medea as she escapes in her fiery chariot. Outside the solar circle, winged furies gaze at the catastrophe. Protected in her divine world, she has managed to find sanctuary from the consequences of her actions and the agony of the human condition. Let us briefly review the story of Jason and Medea before we turn to our discussion of psychic splitting and the failure of disobedience that follows.

[5]Medea is not a patient on the analytic couch (or in the Jungian armchair), and I hope to avoid the dangers of reification and view the characters symbolically, as metaphor that may illuminate our understanding of psychic process. I will use the terms masculine and feminine symbolically as well, rather than as references to actual men and women (see Ulanov 1971).

## The Myth of Jason and Medea

Jason arrives in Pelius's kingdom to win back the throne that his uncle Pelius had wrongfully usurped from Jason's father.[6] Pelius promises to yield the throne to Jason provided that he recover the Golden Fleece from Aeetes' kingdom of Colchis.[7] There, at the eastern edge of the Black Sea, Aeetes, the dark child of Helius, the Sun, kept the Golden Fleece hung high on a tree guarded by an ever-watchful serpent. Journeying with the Argonauts to Colchis, Jason must submit to a series of impossible tasks before Aeetes will give him the Fleece. Medea, daughter of Aeetes, and herself a granddaughter of the Sun as well as a priestess in Hecate's temple, is struck by Eros's arrow at the first sight of Jason and falls passionately in love with him. Filled with conflicting loyalties but driven by her desire for Jason, who has promised to marry her, she disobeys her father and procures the magic herbs that allows Jason to complete the tasks.[8] Then, putting the dragon-guardian to sleep, Medea enables Jason to seize the Fleece and flees with him from Colchis. She then murders her brother by dismembering him so that her father, needing time to gather the pieces of his son, is unable to pursue the escaping Argo.

When they return with the Golden Fleece, Pelius still refuses to abdicate the throne. Using her sorcery in an attempt to obtain the kingdom for Jason, she convinces Pelius's daughters that they can rejuvenate their old father to his original youth. She dismembers a ram and places him in a

---

[6]For a full description of the voyage of Jason and the Argonauts, see Apollonius's account. See also Ovid's version, pp. 153–167.

[7]A good description of the origins of the Golden Fleece can be found in Rieu's notes to his translation of Apollonius, p. 207. Briefly, the story is as follows: Phrixus was to be wrongfully sacrificed by his jealous stepmother who resented her stepson. He escaped on a magical, flying ram that was sent by Hermes. Phrixus landed in Colchis, where he sacrificed the ram to Zeus and left it in the keeping of Aeetes, Medea's father. The contrast of a wrongful and an appropriate sacrifice—to serve one's own ends instead of the divine force is at the center of the Medea and Jason story and emphasizes Medea's failure to sacrifice.

[8]See Apollonius, pp. 131–132. Medea teaches Jason to perform rituals to Hecate and gives him magic herbs that derive from the blood of Prometheus, who, punished by Zeus for stealing fire from the gods, was chained to a rock and bled each night as the eagle devoured his liver. The need for suffering to accompany an act of disobedience—precisely what Medea avoids—is symbolized in the Prometheus story. This myth is not incidental here, since the stealing of the Golden Fleece derives from a similar theme of the intersection of divine-human energies and the struggle for an appropriate boundary.

boiling cauldron until he emerges young again; when Pelius's daughters use Medea's magic to dismember their father, he does not return to life.

Jason and Medea escape to Corinth, and at this point Euripides picks up the story. Jason, to increase his power and prestige, decides to marry Glauke, daughter of Creon, king of Corinth, and abandons Medea and his two children. About to be exiled by Creon, she refuses to suffer further pain and humiliation and, in revenge, sends her children with a poisoned wedding gift to Jason's new bride—a golden dress and diadem that belong to her grandfather Helius, the Sun. Glauke dies a terrible death in the fiery dress in the arms of her father who perishes in the flames with her. To destroy Jason even further, Medea murders her two children and flees in her dragon-drawn chariot of the Sun to her premeditated sanctuary with Aegeus in Athens, leaving behind the wreckage and destruction she has both suffered and created.

## Medea's Split World and the Trauma of Betrayal

> Oh, I am forced to weep, old man. The gods and I,
> I in a kind of madness have contrived all this. (1013–1015)

An act of disobedience offers the potential for psychic integration, for a shift of authority from an outside order to a center inside the self. By its very nature, a gesture of disobedience forces us into a direct collision with the problem of otherness—of the tension that must always be negotiated in the space between self and other, ego and Self, inner and outer, the known and the mysterious. Through Medea's refusal to navigate this dark abyss, she remains locked in an omnipotent, hermetically sealed universe in which she has succeeded in annihilating the tyranny of the other. Unable to sustain the paradox of otherness, she cannot forge her disobedience into a creative act.[9]

*The Medea* calls into focus the ambivalence of otherness—the fascination and terror of the other who remains necessarily and insistently outside our grasp.[10] Otherness is always paradoxical; alluring in its potential

---

[9]See Benjamin (1988). I would state the paradox like this: if we annihilate the other, there is no one to know us; if we reveal ourselves to an other who violates us, we risk our own annihilation.

[10]Otherness was also a factor in Greek tragedy, since the actors were men and many of the protagonists were women. See Zeitlin's essay, "Playing the Other" (Winkler and Zeitlin 1990, pp. 63–96), where she discusses the theatrical and psychological implications of this masculine–feminine split in Greek theater. See also Pomeroy (1975).

to recognize the self, yet, when unresponsive to the needs of the self, this tenacity and separateness can create a terrifying abyss that may long to be bridged through merger of self and other or with a defensive self-sufficiency that denies otherness altogether. As analysts, we meet this problem in the entangled boundary of self and other in the borderline personality, in the glass wall that separates self and other in the schizoid world, or in the appropriation of otherness into the self that is characteristic of narcissism.

Otherness, as Jungians are aware, has an archetypal ground as well. As Otto suggests, the "wholly other" is the way we apprehend God, the numinosum that "has no place in our scheme of reality" and is "intrinsically other than and opposite everything that is and can be thought" (1958, p. 29). This archetypal "wholly other" can be experienced as an unknown region of one's own psyche or as the mystery of an other. With the awakening of Eros, the numinosity of "the wholly other" often erupts in a third space that holds the tension of both inner and outer — in the space between lover and beloved. Eros, we are reminded, was a god before we made him a complex, and in *The Medea*, Jason's "foreignness" from across the sea is originally what awakens her soul and shatters the enclosed containment in her father's world; ultimately his otherness results in a violation of the integrity of her self.

Following Jason's abandonment, Medea faces a chasm of anxiety, alienation, and despair. Having severed the thread to the sanctuary of her father's world through her act of disobedience, she cannot return. Behind her and before her lies a terrifying void. She has betrayed her father and has "no father's house for a haven" (442); Jason has left her, exiled, without a "harbor from ruin" (279). On the other side of this yawning abyss lies the fantasy of Athens's unconditional paradise, a prelapsarian garden that she can reach through flight into her fiery chariot of rage and archetypal inflation and that can raise her above this chasm of trauma and loss. Especially, this sanctuary offers her immunity from "otherness," from the random, arbitrary nature of what lies outside the self.

Medea's struggle may be understood as the attempt to deprive Jason of the power over her self: in Pucci's terms, she attempts to "retrieve her lost self from the violence of the other" (1980, p. 46). Jason has become an idealized, omnipotent figure whose separateness has become so immense and unbridgeable that he continues to exert a tyranny over her self that carries with it a fear of violation and ruthless appropriation. Medea tries to reverse the trauma of Jason's betrayal and restore her lost self from Jason in a similarly ruthless way (identification with the aggressor). From an archetypal perspective, we see that Medea begins to struggle with Jason as if he were a daemon who is determining her fate and shifting her center of gravity toward his.

Unable to endure her suffering — which she mistakes for humiliation — Medea's psyche begins to split into an "innocent victim" who has been betrayed by Jason and a "persecuting, avenging murderess" capable of destroying self and other to obtain revenge.[11] Her struggle between power and helplessness *within* the relationship with Jason is now mirrored and transferred to the inner landscape where she attempts to work through this split internally. She experiences the "victim" side of herself as at the mercy not only of Jason but of her own "heart" which appears to have its own autonomous personality and ruthless will. She asks for pity from this aggressor in her psyche as she contemplates the murder of her children:

> Do not, o my heart, you must not do these things!
> Poor heart, let them go, have pity upon the children. (1056-7)

Yet another aspect of Medea, fleeing humiliation and the pain of her traumatic abandonment, gains ascendency one line later as she begins a full-scale identification with the aggressor and plots the murder of Jason's bride:

> No, by Hell's avenging furies it shall not be—
> This shall never be, that I should suffer my children
> To be the prey of my enemies' insolence
> Every way is fixed. The bride will not escape. (1059-1062)

As Medea's *fantasy* of murdering her own children as revenge for Jason's betrayal moves into *enactment*, interior and exterior converge; imaginal space, needed to support the realm of what Winnicott (1965) calls illusion, is then annihilated.

Medea's victim–persecutor split is symbolic of a pattern we see clinically in the internal world and interpersonal relationships of the patient who has introjected an early history of violence. In the inner world, this split is amplified by the archetypal layer of the psyche, and its psychic effects are often experienced as truly demonic. This dynamic may appear, in Fairbairn's language, as a split between an "internal saboteur" who destroys psychic energy and a "libidinal ego" who is punished for its desires but remains addictively bound to its persecutor (1981). This "persecutor" always remains beyond the control of the "victim" self but retains a powerful hold on the personality because it is also a highly needed, desirable, and seductive figure (Fairbairn's exciting and rejecting object) who entices with promises and the elusive hope of merger with a grand, idealized other—precisely the qualities that the person who suffers from an internal persecutory world

---

[11]For a full examination of Medea's vacillation between the split of a "victim" and a "persecutor," see her speech in *The Medea* (1021-1080).

can't grasp. This sadomasochistic inner relationship may then be projected or lived out in relationship, where the partner who carries the "persecutor" pole of the split is experienced as all powerful, and the "victim" self is felt as lost or empty.

Medea experiences this depleted "victim" self through Jason's shattering of the marriage vows: "Oh, how I wish / That lightning would split my head open. / Oh, what use have I now for life?" (144–145). Jason's breaking of the promise contributes to the complex problem of Medea's revenge, since she is indeed "a soul bitten into with wrong" (110). Rescued by Medea in the underworld of his night sea journey, Jason, the solar hero, abandons her when he has emerged over the horizon of extraverted life again (his marriage to the king's daughter) and the demons of his process of interiority have been silenced. Like Creon, he now wants her dark, feminine force exiled from "the boundaries of my land" (276).

If Jason has violated Medea's integrity through his betrayal of the marriage vows, he has also broken a covenant with the gods, offending the divine order—Themis, "the goddess of promises," and Zeus, "the keeper of oaths" (169–170). As Medea cries out to him at the end of the play: "What heavenly power lends an ear / To a breaker of oaths, a deceiver?" (1391–1392). The divine–human connection has been shattered as well. The ego-Self axis, in Edinger's terms, has been damaged and will remain unrepaired without an adequate and deeply committed working through. As Edinger suggests:

> Whenever one experiences an unbearable alienation
> and despair, it is followed by violence. The violence
> can take either an external or an internal form. In
> extreme forms this means either murder or suicide.
> The crucial point is that at the root of violence of any
> form lies the experience of alienation—a rejection
> too severe to be endured. (1972, p. 44)

Edinger's formulation of the cycle of ego-Self identity (1972, p. 41) is useful here in understanding the way the rejecting experience that follows such an inflation (the erotic bond between Jason and Medea) can lead to permanent alienation from the Self if it is not healed through acceptance by the other, a problem we meet in the transference-countertransference agonies. In Medea's relationship with Jason, this injury is never negotiated, and their failure of mutuality—of recognition of the other's separateness—results in an ever-descending negative spiral of sadomasochistic, submission-domination dynamics and a disintegrating state of self-splitting.[12]

However, if this destruction can be *imagined* rather than *enacted*, an experience of psychic integration is possible, as Winnicott has formulated (1971, pp. 86–94). The crucial factor is that the realm of illusion holds this paradox only if the other survives the attack *in actuality*. There can then be a distinction between the object who is destroyed, *in fantasy*, and the other—often the analyst—who survives the attack without retaliation or collapse and can then be related to as over against the self. Medea's inability to suffer her loss internally without resorting to a self-and-other destructive enactment describes her own failure of interiority. Jason retains the position of the all-encompassing object of her psyche and remains the "sun" around which she revolves—like the abandoned father she tried to leave behind. With this discussion of Medea's split world, we have a foundation from which to explore her failure to reclaim her creative and spiritual self through her disobedience to her father's world.

## Disobedience, Sacrifice, and Regression

> Flow backward to your sources, sacred rivers,
> And let the world's great order be reversed. (410–411)

Disobedience, if it is to be a transformative and creative act, must involve a genuine sacrifice in order to be rendered holy (the word *sacrifice* shares the same root as *sacred*.) Disobedience requires the courage or will to let go of containment in an old order, to allow the structure of the present world to dissolve or disassemble in order for a new psychic universe to be constructed. This demands, at certain essential moments, that we "disobey" the prevailing order, leaving behind our fantasy of a paradisal realm, for a leap—without the fiery chariot of the Sun to carry us—into a psychic abyss where there are no certainties.

If Jung describes neurosis as a substitution for legitimate suffering (1937, par. 129), perhaps we can understand Medea's revenge and archetypal sanctuary as a substitution for legitimate *sacrifice*. Medea, by remaining in her magic circle of the sun and seeking a premeditated refuge with Aegeus in Athens, attempts to transcend the terror of sacrifice. She wants to sever herself from the world of the father and yet seek sanctuary there:

---

[12]For descriptions of Jason and Medea's sadomasochism, see *The Medea* (465–575 and 1323–1404).

> For this man, Aegeus, has been like a harbor to me
> In all my plans just where I was most distressed.
> To him I can fasten the cable of my safety (768–770)

Medea stares into the abyss but does not possess "the unshakeability of faith in the full recognition of the impossibility" and will not leap into the "absurd" in Kierkegaard's terms (1983, pp. 46, 48). Without a genuine sacrifice, her disobedience cannot "be made sacred," and Medea is able to deceive herself that the murder of her children is a "sacrifice" (1054). The escalating chaos of *The Medea* resembles what Jung has referred to as the "unmitigated catastrophe" of *"unwilling* sacrifice":

> The mind shies away, but life wants to flow down
> into the depths. Fate itself seems to preserve us from
> this, because each of us has a tendency to become an
> immovable pillar of the past. Nevertheless, the
> daemon throws us down, makes us traitors to . . . the
> selves we thought we were. That is an unmitigated
> catastrophe, because it is an unwilling sacrifice.
> Things go very differently when the sacrifice is a vol-
> untary one. Then it is no longer an overthrow, a
> "transvaluation of values", the destruction of all that
> we held sacred, but transformation and conserva-
> tion. (1952, par. 553)

For Jung, a dual movement of regression and sacrifice is necessary for psychic integration to occur: a backward flow of libido into the archetypal realm of the unconscious and, when the regression has been deep enough, a forward movement of psychic energy accomplished through sacrifice.

> What actually happens in these incest and womb fan-
> tasies is that the libido immerses itself in the uncon-
> scious, thereby provoking infantile reactions, affects,
> opinions and attitudes from the personal sphere, but
> at the same time activating collective images (arche-
> types) which have a compensatory and curative
> meaning such as has always pertained to the myth.
> (1952, par. 655)

The libido, then, according to Jung, regresses in order to contact the cura-
tive energy of the archetypal core of the complex. This activation of transformative energy from within the psyche cannot occur in a split-off state
that seeks sanctuary at the expense of reality but can only come through an

*adequate experience of regression that is followed by sacrifice.*[13] In fact, for Jung, although sacrifice and regression must be in relationship, "the sacrifice is the very reverse of regression — it is a successful canalization of libido into the symbolic equivalent" (1952, par. 398).

Eliade, as well, sees a relationship between sacrifice and a return to origins. For Eliade, sacrifice suspends profane time and has as its end the need "to restore the primordial unity, that which existed before the creation" (1971, p. 78). We are reminded here of Balint's "benign regression" which institutes a "new beginning" of psychic life (1979) or Winnicott's "regression to dependence" (1965, p. 253) which provides a new foundation from which the personality can take shape.

Medea longs to return to a prelapsarian garden, to get behind "created time" — the time of the wound of Jason's betrayal. Medea's impulse to restore a pretraumatic world that abolishes her painful history with Jason, although misinterpreted, carries the hope of healing: the psyche needs to return to a time before creation, before a "fall" into suffering, in order to "gather the trauma under omnipotent control" in Winnicott's language. Only by returning to the origin can the psyche come forth with its healing, regenerative capacity.

However, her regression occurs through a defensive annihilation of history and a disobedience unaccompanied by the sacrifice of her rage and archetypal illusions. She seeks sanctuary, in the chariot of the Sun and the paradise of Athens, where, enclosed in an illusory space, she can be free of the tyranny of Jason's otherness and her insufferable pain. Without a process of "re-membering" her trauma, she cannot return to her own origins, and without a sacrifice, she cannot move forward into "a new beginning."

This problem manifests for the analyst who struggles in the consulting room to maintain this *archetypal dimension of regression* — the necessity of getting back to a time before the wound — without obliterating memory of the injury and its attendant affects. Medea's flight into her chariot is consistent with what we see clinically as well, when patients attempt to protect themselves from intolerable suffering through the creation of a sustaining, archetypal world that functions to fill in the terrible psychic

---

[13]The clinical problem of regression is a controversial one and well beyond the scope of this paper. My own viewpoint, following Jung's formulation, is that it is necessary to insure that *the regression has been adequate enough before the patient makes a sacrifice* of those needs that have been denied, repressed, skipped over, or punished in earlier development. If the analyst cannot allow the regression and forces the patient to "sacrifice" too quickly, the same psychological pattern that created early wounding may be repeated.

chasms created by violation and trauma.[14] For Medea, Helius's power becomes her defense of self-sufficiency and mastery, rather than a gift of her own creative, self-sustaining fire. Her disobedience does not transform her inner world or begin a new world but is an attempt to keep herself omnipotent and unassailed by fate — to keep the other from ever violating her again.

## Seizing the Golden Fleece

> No, it would be no easy thing to take the fleece with-
> out permission of Aeetes, guarded as it is from every
> side by such a serpent, a deathless and unsleeping
> beast. (Apollonius, p. 106)

*The Medea* reveals a psychic and interpersonal universe in which the solar fire has gone out of control. Medea soars in her fiery chariot, cut off from the reality of her destructiveness; Jason abandons Medea and his children for the prestige in the royal kingdom. His violent betrayal has activated Medea's equally violent rage. Instead of the Sun's creative energy or the fire of love, a "fearful stream of all-devouring fire" (1187) issues forth. Paradox and suffering are not held and disunity takes hold. The world has polarized into opposites and the universe is inhabited by splitting energies which tear apart self from other. A chasm is created between man and woman, masculine and feminine, solar and lunar.[15] The feminine exists in its devouring, vengeful aspect (Medea destroys her children), the masculine has become ruthless, burning, and scorching (Jason's abandonment of Medea).

Only the chorus is left to call upon the life-giving capacity of the Sun to prevent Medea's murderous act:

> far shining
> Ray of the Sun, look down, look down upon

[14]Ferenczi, in his clinical diary (1988) develops this idea of the splitting of the psyche as a result of trauma and the emergence of a guardian spirit who holds the fragments of the psyche and attempts to heal it. See also Savitz (1990b, 1991) and Kalsched (1991) for the relationship between trauma, splitting, and the archetypal.

[15]Although, in most mythologies, the solar realm is considered "masculine" and the lunar "feminine," I am describing a *symbolic* system here rather than a literal or reified description of the experiences of men and women.

This poor lost woman, look, before she raises
The hand of murder against her flesh and blood.
Yours was the golden birth from which
She sprang, and now I fear divine
Blood may be shed by men.
O heavenly light, hold back her hand,
Check her, and drive from out the house
The bloody Fury raised by fiends of Hell. (1251–1260).

Medea, however, calls on the Sun's spirit for revenge: "You will never touch
me with your hand" she cries to Jason in triumph after she has murdered her
children and flies above him in her dragon-drawn chariot of the Sun: "Such
a chariot has Helius, my father's father, given me to defend me from my
enemies" (1320–1323). Free from her personal father, Medea now has an
unmediated archetypal relationship to her Grandfather Helius—the Great
Father. She begins to experience the direct burning by the sun's rays as
symbolized by the fiery chariot, the poisoned dress and diadem, her passionate love and fury. These images place us in the realm of the archetype of
the Spiritual Father as described by Edinger (in Ulanov 1971, pp. 61–62).

The qualities of the solar world—her passion, creativity, and
spirit—which are her birthright as Helius's granddaughter remain unintegrated with Hecate's feminine, lunar underworld, and, refusing to suffer
the collision of opposites, she forsakes the potential of a solar–lunar *coniunctio* (Helius–Hecate).[16] Instead, in Medea's unchecked aggression we see
a parody of true relatedness to the internal and interpersonal masculine,
solar other.

Clinically, we are aware that behind the psychic bondage to the
father are often buried the daughter's deep spiritual desires, which are
obscured and blocked when the father uses his daughter's psychic depth to
bridge to his own interiority, particularly if there is an inadequate soul
connection to his wife (Medea as priestess in Hecate's temple in her father's
dark world). This bond can be especially compelling when the mother is
unable to promote the daughter's spiritual or creative development from a
feminine ground (in *The Medea*, the mother is conspicuously absent) and
the father remains the only key to life in the outer world and to the growth
of a creative and spiritual self. The woman searching for a connection to her
creative life through such a bond with her father will remain, like Glauke
and Creon, in a deadly embrace, a "wedding with the dead below" (985)
unless she shatters her containment in her father's world through an act of

---

[16]Medea refers to Hecate as her "mistress" and "partner" and says that
Hecate "dwells in the recesses of my hearth" (384–385, 395–398).

disobedience and an appropriate sacrifice of her "privileged" role to her father.

*The Medea* gives us various images of the entangled father-daughter relationship: Medea's betrayal of her father, her murder of Pelius through his daughters, and the image of Glauke and Creon — the dead bodies entwined of father and daughter, burned in the fiery poison of Helius's golden dress and diadem. This *coniunctio* does not lead to new life but to an ungenerative death in which the old order is not rejuvenated, a new universe does not emerge, and the daughter cannot claim her psychic depth for herself. Symbolically, then, the father retains the Golden Fleece.

Aeetes, as Kerenyi describes, is the dark child of the Sun, "a king of the Underworld, the Hades side of his father" (1979, p. 12). As such, he may represent the darkness of the Sun in the underworld during the night sea journey — a time of creative introversion and suffering when the hero or heroine struggles within the belly of the monster (Jung 1952, par. 307–313). It is the sun's brilliance turned inward, to cauterize and purify what needs to be transformed. Without this stage, the creative solar fires burn out of control.

Aeetes is also the jealous keeper of the Golden Fleece, and here we find ourselves facing an inherent paradox: the Golden Fleece can never be possessed, yet we must attempt to seize its brilliant solar power for ourselves if our lives are not to remain in potential only. Without desire for the Fleece, we will be facsimiles of ourselves, inhabiting a provisional, shadowy existence on the borders of embodied life. Every act of creation — including the creation of a depth of personality — requires an act of disobedience that brings us into the ground and interiority of our own longings and creativity. The dragon of our creative life is eternally awake although, like Jason and Medea, we may believe that we can lull its power to sleep, momentarily, and seize the Golden Fleece. To possess the Fleece would be an act of inflation in Jungian language, a destructive identification rather than relationship to the archetypal. Yet, it is perhaps essential that the psyche know these ecstatic moments of Eros and heroic gesture so that we can endure the suffering and sacrifice that must follow (and that Jason and Medea attempt to avoid) as our relationship to the archetypal — or to the beloved other — is transformed and grounded.

This motif of the Golden Fleece has particular importance, clinically, when "unclaimed" areas of the patient's psychic experience are activated in the space between patient and analyst without yet having taken root in the person's interior world. These unclaimed but powerful affects often arise in the transference-countertransference field with a compelling numinosity, and as with the Golden Fleece, the patient and analyst may be tempted to seize the solar brilliance that has fired the analytic space — to enact the love or fury that fuels the transformation process and ultimately begins to scorch with its archetypal heat. This may include the emergence of erotic feelings or the origins of the person's creative self, as well as other fiery feelings of anger, jealousy, or the terror of abandonment. The analyst's "violence" — his or her exploitation, betrayal, appropriation, or denial of these affects — may cause the person to experience a sense of a violently dismembered or lost self, eclipsed by both the fire of the unmediated archetypal energy and by the analyst's own seizing of the Golden Fleece.[17]

Patient and analyst, living out such an energy together, may engage in an act of "disobedience" that, like Medea, they refuse to complete with an appropriate sacrifice. The potential for this fiery, creative energy to be psychically grounded is burnt up, and the patient may cope with this loss of trust and containment through denial of the analyst's aggression which may manifest as self-blame or self-destructiveness (Medea murdering her own children), as retaliatory murderous assault on the analyst (Jason and Medea's sadomasochism), or as a schizoid dissociation from either the affects generated or from the entire therapeutic dialogue (Medea's withdrawal into her fiery chariot). The analyst (caught in an archetypal identification) becomes the jealous keeper of the Golden Fleece, a substitute for the person's own direct relationship to the Self.[18] The patient, perceiving the therapist as the source of the archetypal energy, may get stuck in a non-transformative power struggle with the analyst, attempting to reclaim the connection to the creative fire of the Self that has come to exist in the transference-countertransference field. Although this may repeat the wounding of earlier relationships, its occurrence in the analysis is often more painful because of its acute presentness and the fact that the analyst has violated the healing archetype. The person's own connection to the healing capacity of the Self cannot occur, the persecutory internal imago cannot be transformed, and a state of perennial disrepair seizes the psyche and inhabits the analytic space.

If Medea forsakes the realm of the imaginal for that of destructive enactment or flights of archetypal fantasy, Euripides leaves it to us, as the spectators of tragedy, to recover and preserve that realm through the experience of tragic theater itself. Tragedy, as Vernant suggests, "opened up a new space in Greek culture, the space of the imaginary" (Vernant and Vidal-Naquet 1988, p. 187). The multiple meanings that are necessarily lost on the protagonists *within* the drama become available to the spectator who is

---

[17]It is essential that the analyst keep alive these feelings generated in the transference-countertransference field and important that these affects be "held" and "contained" without being seized by the analyst for his or her own exploitation.

[18]I am using the upper case "S" in the word *Self* to refer to the supraordinate guiding and organizing principle of the psyche as defined by Jung.

asked to suffer what Medea suffers and yet more. As the imaginal world closes down its possibilities for Medea, we are asked to hold the tensions, ambiguities, and paradoxes that belong to the genre of tragedy. As Vernant writes:

> the tragic message gets across to him only provided he makes the discovery that words, values, men themselves, are ambiguous, that the universe is one of conflict, only if he relinquishes his earlier convictions, accepts a problematic vision of the world and, through the dramatic spectacle, himself acquires a tragic consciousness (1988, p.43).

The establishment of a "tragic consciousness" — an imaginal realm capable of holding opposites and multiple meanings in order to be able, in Medea's words, "to suffer what should be wept for bitterly" (111–112) — is the work of the analytic "theatrical space" as well. Analysis, like Greek tragedy, lies, in Vernant's words "in that border zone where human actions are hinged together with the divine powers" (Vernant and Vidal-Naquet 1988, p. 47). Here in the analytic border zone of what Jungians refer to as the merger of archetypal and personal, or what Winnicott calls the potential space between reality and illusion, in the interminglings of human, divine, and demonic that infuse the energy of the transference, we, too, encounter the solar brilliance of the Golden Fleece that, paradoxically, we must hold but cannot possess.[19] Although Euripides' dark world has revealed the destructiveness of that longing, it leaves the spectator of tragedy — as well as analyst and patient — to imagine another possibility, a creative act of disobedience with a necessary sacrifice.

# References

Apollonius of Rhodes. 1971. *The Voyage of Argo.* E. V. Rieu, trans. London: Penguin Books.

Aristotle. 1987. *Poetics.* R. Janko, trans. Indianapolis: Hackett Publishing Co.

Balint, M. 1979. *The Basic Fault.* New York: Brunner Mazel.

Benjamin, J. 1988. *The Bonds of Love.* New York: Pantheon Books.

Edinger, E. 1972. *Ego and Archetype.* New York: Penguin Books.

Eliade, M. 1971. *The Myth of the Eternal Return.* Princeton, N.J.: Princeton University Press.

[19]For paradox in analysis, see Savitz (1986, 1990a, and 1991).

Euripides. 1955. *The Medea*. R. Warner, trans. Chicago: University of Chicago Press.

Fairbairn, W. R. 1981. *Psychoanalytic Studies of the Personality*. London: Routledge and Kegan Paul.

Ferenczi, S. 1988. *The Clinical Diary of Sandor Ferenczi*. J. Dupont, tr. Cambridge, Mass.: Harvard University Press.

Jung, C. G. 1952. *Symbols of Transformation. CW*, vol. 5. Princeton, N.J.: Princeton University Press.

_____. 1937. Psychology and religion. In *CW* 11: 3–104. Princeton, N.J.: Princeton University Press, 1958.

Kalsched, D. 1991. The limits of desire and the desire for limits in psychoanalytic theory and practice. Paper given at Fordham University.

Kerenyi, K. 1979. *Goddesses of Sun and Moon*. M. Stein, trans. Dallas: Spring Publications.

Kierkegaard, S. 1983. *Fear and Trembling*. Hong and Hong, trans. Princeton, N.J.: Princeton University Press.

Otto, R. 1958. *The Idea of the Holy*. J. Harvey, trans. New York: Oxford University Press.

Ovid. *Metamorphoses*. R. Humphries, trans. Indiana: Indiana University Press, 1972.

Pomeroy, S. 1975. *Goddesses, Whores, Wives, and Slaves: Women in Classical Antiquity*. New York: Schocken Books.

Pucci, P. 1980. *The Violence of Pity in Euripides' Medea*. Ithaca, N.Y.: Cornell University Press.

Savitz, C. 1986. Healing and wounding: The collision of the sacred and the profane in narcissism. *Journal of Analytical Psychology* 31,4:319–340.

_____. 1990a. The burning cauldron: Transference as paradox. *Journal of Analytical Psychology* 35,1:41–58.

_____. 1990. The double death: The loss of the analyst in the analytic hour. *Journal of Analytical Psychology* 35,3:241–260.

_____. 1991. Immersions in ambiguity: The labyrinth and the analytic process. *Journal of Analytical Psychology* 36,4.

Ulanov, A. 1971. *The Feminine in Jungian Psychology and in Christian Theology*. Evanston, Ill.: Northwestern University Press.

Vernant, J. and Vidal-Naquet. 1988. *Myth and Tragedy in Ancient Greece*. J. Lloyd, trans. New York: Zone Books.

Winkler, J., and Zeitlin, F., eds. 1990. *Nothing to Do with Dionysos?* Princeton, N.J.: Princeton University Press.

Winnicott, D. W. 1965. *The Maturational Processes and the Facilitating Environment*. New York: International Universities Press.

_____. 1971. *Playing and Reality*. New York: Tavistock Publications.

# SOME ARCHETYPAL FOUNDATIONS OF SELF-SPITE IN THE WELSH *MABINOGION*

## Sylvia Brinton Perera

**D**isobedience takes many forms—resistance to outer authority or to the internalized voice of the containing collective, the superego. But it can also, and most painfully be a resistance to the individual Self, to its gifts and guidance.[1] In each case, the rebel seeks to assert or preserve some threatened integrity. The disobedience is ultimately a sign of active life energy. Its positive value is less readily apparent, however, when the individual seems to be silently spiting her Self, opposing the unfolding of her own development.

A medieval Welsh story from *The Mabinogion* presents one mythic paradigm for the psychological pattern underlying such inner disobedience to one's own gifts and nature. "Math, Son of Mathonwy" (Jones and Jones 1949, pp. 55–75; Ford 1977, pp. 91–109) is a tale of the rising Celtic, patrifocal aristocracy as it was reshaped by later Christian writers. In it, the authority and nurturant, initiatory, and transformative powers of the female in the old religion are envied and usurped, causing the goddess Aranrhod to retaliate. Repudiating the ones who would shame and coopt her powers or try to make her use them for their own purposes, Aranrhod verbally asserts her authority to empower her son but then refuses to do so.

---

[1]Self is a Jungian term that refers to a superordinate ordering and directive center of both the conscious and unconscious aspects of the individual psyche. See Whitmont 1969, chapter 14.

## The Story

In north Wales in ancient times the king, whose name was Math, had to follow custom and hold his feet in a maiden's lap unless he was at war. One of his sister's sons lusted after the footholder. The other nephew, Gwydion, brought about a war with the province of South Wales to get Math out of the castle, thus creating the opportunity for his brother to rape the royal footholder. After the king of the south was killed in combat by a combination of Gwydion's magic and swordsmanship, Math returned home, discovered his nephew's trickeries, and bemoaned his dishonor. He married the raped footholder to "redress" the wrong done. He also punished his nephews. After they had served their sentence and were restored to favor, Math sought advice from Gwydion about finding another maiden on which to rest the fortunes of his realm. Gwydion proposes his sister, Aranrhod. She is told to step over Math's druid wand to test her virginity. This causes her to give birth prematurely to twins, probably fathered by Gwydion himself. Aranrhod immediately retires to her castle, abandoning her maternal duties as birth mother, nurturer, namer and initiator into life's roles and relationships. One twin swims into the sea and the other is raised by Gwydion.

Later Gwydion pursues Aranrhod to give the boy a name so he will not remain a "still nameless nonentity" (Rees and Rees 1961, p. 242). Aranrhod speaks and is silent. She swears the lad will never get a name except from her, and she refuses to give him one. Nonetheless, she, too, is tricked by the magus. Gwydion and the boy return to her court in the guise of two shoemakers with illusory leather made from seaweed.[2] They lure her to their boat to fit her with golden shoes. As she goes aboard, the boy casts at a wren alighting on the ship and hits it in the leg. Aranrhod exclaims, "Faith . . . with a deft hand has the fair one hit it." Gwydion claims those words, *Lleu Llaw Gyffes* ("Light" or "Fair One of the Deft Hand"), as the name for her son. In anger, Aranrhod then swears that her son will never bear weapons unless she arms him, and that she will never do. When Lleu is older, however, Gwydion tricks her once more. He and Lleu visit her castle disguised as bards. During the night, he magically musters an invading armada, and Aranrhod rushes in to arm the disguised youth to help defend her castle. When this ruse is unmasked, Aranrhod swears a third vengeful destiny on her son: he shall not have a wife of a "race that is now on earth." Spurred to further magical craftsmanship in response to this dictum that must be respected, Math and Gwydion create a beautiful woman out of

---

[2]In Gaul, the three Lugoves, a triadic form of Lleu, were patrons of shoemaking (Bromwich 1969, p. 177).

three kinds of flowers. They name her Blodeuedd ("Flowers") and marry her to Lleu.

The final episode of the tale recounts Lleu's betrayal by his newly created wife, who becomes as deceptive as her male creators.[3] Blodeuedd soon finds a lover and plots to kill Lleu. But he is invincible unless he meets his death in one particular way. Blodeuedd lures the secret of his vulnerability out of him. He reveals: "I cannot be slain within a house, nor can I outside. I cannot be slain on horseback, nor can I a-foot." He can die only when standing on the edge of a bathtub and a goat's back under a thatched frame beside a river and by means of the cast of the sacred spear, which in the older traditions was Lleu's own emblem and tool. Like the wren on the boat that he hit to gain his own name, he must be hit to undo his human form. Blodeuedd's lover makes the required killing spear, which can be crafted only on Sundays during mass.[4] Then she prepares the place on which Lleu must stand to be smitten. At the fated time at year's end, Lleu is struck and flies away in the shape of a wounded eagle. Gwydion finds him, at last, ridden with decay in the top of an oak and magically sings spells to lure down the royal bird. With his wand, he then restores Lleu to human form. When Lleu is healed, he kills his wife's lover exactly as he was speared, and Gwydion turns "Flowers" (*Blodeuedd*) into "Owl" (*Blodeuwedd*), a fearsome creature of the night.[5]

## Commentary

Aranrhod was originally the Great Goddess and divine mother of the gods and peoples of North Wales (Markale 1975, pp. 127–132). In this medieval tale, she is shorn of her majesty, although the translations of her name — "Silver mound" (Gruffydd, 1928, p. 189) and "Silver wheel" (Ross 1967, p. 227) — suggest her former status. The word *Aran* survives in the name of several mountains and islands in what is now the United Kingdom and in Breton and Gallic proper and place names (Bromwich, 1961, p. 277–278)

[3]While this is a common folktale motif, there may be some allusion to Delilah here, since Old Testament parallels were not uncommonly woven into medieval tales in the scriptoria (see McCone 1990, chapter 3).

[4]Like the smith god, Gofannon, who killed Lleu's twin, this lover, Gronw, is also a crafter of metals. He accomplishes his task during sacred time but by defiling its current Christian definition.

[5]Blodeuwedd also means flower face in Welsh. This play on similar words is part of the word magic of the Celtic bardic/seers, and the correspondences can shape their tales (Markale 1978, pp. 72–74).

suggesting that Aranrhod was once identified as an earth, sky, water, and mountain deity. Her castle, Caer Aranrhod, was considered to be a rock in the sea, one mile out from the prehistoric mound of Dinas Dinlle (near Caernarvon). Visible only at low tide, her island realm seemed to rise into human ken and disappear like the remains of other Celtic sunken cities (Markale 1975, chapter 3). These realms represented the powers and mores of a pagan supernatural world lost to consciousness except at certain times when mortals might gain access to them.[6] Their loss was often ascribed to otherworld folk, who took vengeance when the pace and process of their ancient habitations were disturbed (Rhys 1901, chapter 7). The repetition of the motif of angry retaliation against the later derogating culture in other tales of sunken islands helps to confirm our reading of Aranrhod's spite.

Aranrhod, like other pre-Celtic goddesses, rules over the whole of nature. She is one of the many supreme Spirit Women Beings said to live on primal islands (cf. Allen 1986, pp. 13–18). Her sea-washed castle lies in a transitional area between and including the realms of water and earth. Like other ancient goddesses, she is the mother of twins. In this story, her golden-haired son jumped into the western ocean and swam away after his birth, receiving the name Dylan Eil Ton ("Sea, Son of Wave"). The other, Lleu, known throughout Celtic lands as Lugh, Lug, or Lugoves (Bromwich 1961, p. 421), has been identified with the god of lightning, craftsmanship, and battle skills. Caesar called him the Gallic Mercury (*De Bello Gallico*, VI, 17).

In the traditional Welsh Triads, Aranrhod is named one of the "Three Fair Maidens of the Island of Britain" (Bromwich 1961, p. 198). She is a "chief beauty" (Welsh: *gwenriein*) who represents the spiritual matrix that generates and contains polarizations within its balanced order. Thus she appears between night and day, sea and land, as the ruler of the borderline area including and mediating both. Her castle is sometimes identified with the Corona Borealis (Rhys 1901, p. 645), suggesting she was considered the deity of the silver wheel of constellations around the northern pole star. Here, she represents the deity as the Great Round of revolving cosmic time and natural process, the mysterious pleroma containing All, within an ordered, stillness-centered cycle. Aranrhod is also described as "famous for beauty beyond the dawn of fine weather" (Bromwich 1961, p. 277). This image again connects her to an aesthetic that celebrates times and spaces in which the complementaries are contained, confounded, and sacredly bridged —just as they are in cosmic

---

[6]Islands and cities rising from the water is a fairly common motif in dreams, where it suggests that previously unavailable material is rising into consciousness for exploration by the waking dreamer.

processes. Thus, she represents the beauty of patterned order behind nature's apparent chaos. Celtic culture intuitively knew and honored that pattern, which we are beginning to discern with the help of advanced mathematics and technology (Gleick 1987).

In the Welsh Triads and the Mabinogion, Aranrhod is described as a daughter of Don, the Welsh equivalent of Danu or Anu, the pre-Celtic Mother of the Gods worshipped as the force manifest in the earth and various rivers across Europe. In Triad 35, she is called a daughter or sister of Beli, the ancestor deity from whom the ruling classes of early Wales believed themselves descended (Bromwich 1961, pp. 76, 282). By implication, she was such a divine ancestress figure herself.

It was as such a powerful and majestic divinity that she refused to name and arm her son, forcing Gwydion to circumvent her power through trickery. Into the fifteenth century, the bardic tradition still named her with phrases more commonly used to describe the Virgin Mother of Christ. (cf. Berger 1985). She was praised as the "chaste, white-armed wise one . . . Aranrhod, like the snow" and described as the beloved footholder of king Math (Gruffydd 1928, p. 193, quoting the bard, Lewis Mon). The footholder, much like the goddess of sovereignty in Irish myth (Rees and Rees 1961, pp. 73–76; Markale 1975, p. 132), symbolizes the divine matrix on which the kingdom (personified by the king) and its customs and well-being rested. In historical Welsh courts, the footholder or footstool (*troediawc*) was a royal official who attended the king and had special privileges, including that of granting merciful freedom to those condemned by the king (Markale 1975, p. 131).

The rape of the sacred footholder by the king's lustful and ambitious nephews establishes the initial crisis in the narrative. It also shows us that the early gynocentric culture of Wales, to which King Math still submits in the story, is being rudely forced and nearly overpowered by a more androcentric dynasty. Pre-Celtic societies across Europe worshiped an ever-virgin goddess as the primal force of creation, destruction, and renewal. Known by various names in different localities, which like the tribes themselves were often named after her, she was also called the Mother of the local gods. Later, in western Celtic lands, she became the symbol of the principle of sovereignty supporting the temporary rule that magically and actually ensured the well-being of tribal lands, herds, humans, and crops. She was virgin regardless of her physical chastity because she "reflects the virginity of nature with its brilliance and wildness, with its guiltless purity and its strangeness" (Gimbutas 1982, p. 199) and because she represents spiritual integrity and self-renewal. She chose the most virile and skilled partners for her consorts and allowed the kings to rule only as long as the kingdom thrived (Rees and Rees 1961, pp. 74–76). The nephews of King Math, on the other hand, represent the culture of a newly arrived warrior aristocracy and its more patrifocal, royal, and druidic rulers.[7] The story is thus set "at the cross-roads of two types of civilisation" (Markale 1975, p. 132). Aranrhod herself gestates what will live on in the patrifocal world that she abandons. The narrator thus grants the new culture a potent validating ancestress.

In the world of old Celtic myths, the burgeoning patrifocal development never completely supplanted the original Welsh and Irish customs. The medieval scribes, however, did their best to assert the masculine biases of the Roman church into Celtic lands. Thus, the writer of "Math, Son of Mathonwy" assures us that marriage is adequate redress for the raped woman and that any other physically chaste female will do for a footholder.[8] In the tale, Aranrhod is called by her brother, Gwydion, to submit to their uncle Math's chastity test. It is an insult to the old order to demand sexual virginity of the goddess. That she agrees to the ordeal is the fulcrum upon which the rest of the tale hangs. From her perspective, we may wonder why she would submit to stepping over Math's druid wand, thus aborting her twins.[9] The rape of the footholder represents the dishonor of the older culture in which the goddess stands in her own authority. Aranrhod is made to enter this tale already passive, polite, and numb, very much like any human rape and incest victim. But Celtic goddesses were representations of wild and passionate sexuality, forever virgin in the sense

[7]There is an individual psychological correlate to this process. Just as traditional Celtic culture kept young children at home with mother or wet nurse and then sent them (at age five or seven) into fosterage for education, so the bond to matrix was supplanted by the bond to peers and the skills and mores necessary to serve the warrior aristocratic society at large. We maintain this developmental watershed in our understanding of psychological development when we stress the oedipal phase of the masculinized ego as the intensification, prohibition, and rupture of the child's desire for mother by the beginnings of libidinous identification and investment with the aggressor-father.

[8]The term used to describe Aranrhod when she appears before the king is *morwyn*. This originally meant "free young girl, outside all male constraints, namely woman defined according to the criteria of a gynaecocratic society" and is connected with *morgan* the mysterious fairy of the sea. For Gwydion, Math, and the writer, however, *morwyn* connoted only physical virginity (Markale 1975, p. 130).

[9]We have similar questions about other Celtic goddesses, such as Branwen and Macha, who also seem to acquiesce in their own downfalls. They seemingly went too "gent[ly] into that good night" and did not rage and disobey until they had capitulated to the beloved enemy and had then no revenge except to give a curse on dying or make a grief-filled suicide (cf. Condren 1989, pp. 28–36).

that Esther Harding has clarified (1971, chapter 9). Incest among the immortals was never a crime but rather the hotbed of special offspring. We can see the narrator caught between two radically different cultures, concepts of virginity, and perspectives on the archetypal female.

We know from clinical examples that one problem in Aranrhod's willing submission to those who would use her for their own needs lies in her bond of love and loyalty to her destroyer. Aranrhod has a hidden bond with the brother who impregnated her, just as the Irish nature and mare goddess, Macha, is bonded to her own lover, the man whose twins she chose to bear as she raced to her death (Kinsella 1969, pp. 6–8). Aranrhod's brother becomes the magus of the new dynasty, which seeks to overthrow the old religion. He is also considered the father of her son. Perhaps Aranrhod and Macha, like all primal divinities, may be seen as offering themselves to make the necessary foundation sacrifice for the new culture. Perhaps they, in their omniscience, agreed to submit to the ordeals of the new culture and withdraw in order to make space for their offspring—the twins who represent the polarities of the new consciousness. If we take the goddess's powers seriously, we cannot simply say she was a dominated victim. The acts of the Irish divinities, Macha Lethderg and Morrigan, like the Greek Artemis and Demeter, belie such a simplistic view. Such powers cannot die. But like Aranrhod in this tale and many other goddesses, they can go away. They can withdraw into unconsciousness and function as an eruptive impediment or spur to development from outside of human ken even as the succeeding culture struggles to coopt, combat, and repress their powers.[10]

Such a view of the withdrawal of the archetypal feminine does not exonerate the derogation of the female perpetrated in the name of patrifocal cultures, but it fits the psychology of heroic, male ego development in the West—the psychology to which the scribe aspired. And it fits the traditions borne out in many mythologies in which the primary divinities (considered the all-encompassing One or pleroma) are broken up to be accessible to consciousness in the incarnate world. The original wholeness deintegrates to support differentiation and rational consciousness with its boundaried polarizations. We are now discovering the limits and dangers of such consciousness and returning to honor the levels of being, process, and attunement within the whole that the goddess symbolizes, but this tale comes from

[10]The analogy is related to the ways in which a child's consciousness of being, with its concomitant self-perceptions of integrity and adequacy, withdraw into unconsciousness when she or he is forced to overadapt to collective performance, doing standards. Winnicott has written most poignantly about this (1971, pp. 79–82).

the beginnings of the deintegration phase. It tells us that the Great Round produces twins and challenges the trickster magus to show his powers.

After Aranrhod's twins are aborted, she withdraws to her castle in hurt pride and anger, which the scribe characterizes as passive shame. In vengeance for the insults to her and the sudden wresting of her procreative power, the goddess retaliates. She abandons her newborn sons to their uncle/father. One swims into the sea and is later killed by another uncle, the god of smithcraft. In this motif, flowing life is destroyed by skilled performance. While still a fetus, the other child is claimed by Gwydion and closed in a chest at the foot of the bed until it cries out and is delivered from the chest. Gwydion is depicted as the boy's savior and midwife. He rears the infant in what is probably the first incubator recorded in literature. Here, vulnerable life is saved by skilled performance. The future of both children is thus determined not by the organic processes of being, but by the intervention of skillful doing.

Earlier in the story, Gwydion tricked the neighboring king, Pryderi, to claim his herd of domestic pigs, animals long associated with kingship and the goddess. These pigs were valued gifts from Pryderi's stag god initiator in the underworld. Gwydion offered a trade of horses and hunting array (animals associated with the patrifocal aristocracy), which he had created by magical illusion. The discovery of the ruse and robbery caused the war that called Math from his castle, creating the opportunity for his nephews to rape the footholder. In this incident, Gwydion is depicted as a trickster and thief just as he is when he calls Aranrhod to the druid wand that robs the goddess of her full term or when he steals name and arms for the boy. We might see Gwydion one-sidedly as a paradigm of the womb-envier who serves as instigator of the modern, male-dominated practice of medicine and the science of obstetrics. He is also the magus and trickster who ushers in a new array of cultural skills and technology to supplant or speed the organic processes of nature.

In this tale, Aranrhod is represented as so negative and withholding that the reader is persuaded that a new cultural ethos and harbinger are needed. Later commentators have even seen the goddess as merely a "hostile mother" (Rees and Rees 1961, p. 242). Thus, Aranrhod's spiteful disobedience to her sacred maternal role is used to condone her overthrow. Her disobedience to the call of her own maternity is used to corroborate and support her aggressors. Against her authority and the customs of the old religion, Gwydion asserts his newborn, trickster magic with righteousness — like the parent or the tyrant who assumes the child's incapacity or the citizen's disobedience gives leave for authoritarian control.

The story of Gwydion's rearing of Aranrhod's son establishes the primacy of the father as caretaker. Again, the text reveals the overturning of the mores of ancient Welsh culture in which male children inherited name and property from their mothers.[11] In such a matrifocal society, the mother's brother was a primary guardian of her children. Gwydion, son of the goddess Don and brother and husband of Aranrhod, slides between two forms of culture. He serves his own uncle, Math, to install the masculine succession, but he slips into his role through his relationship to the goddess. He is both maternal uncle and incestuous father of Aranrhod's son, the king-to-be, Lleu. He both obeys the goddess and tricks her. With his trickery, he creates new forms of masculinity. With his incubator womb and ideal flower woman, he creates new forms of femininity.

In Welsh custom and mythology, the ways of the matrifocal world were never fully supplanted. Sons, including Gwydion himself, were named after and/or by their mothers. This is psychologically valid. Just as Aranrhod names her son on the basis of her objective experience of him, so any mother's empathic perception of her child first names and defines the new life as continuous with herself and her vision. Thus, the truth-seeing mother grants a blessing of definition that will continue to hold the child when he or she separates from the early relational matrix. Such definition conveys identity, affirmation, and integrity. Its distortion or its lack is a blight on further development. In psychology, we call such naming "mirroring." To refuse or distort this blessing is felt as a sadistic spiting of the primal bond.

Gwydion, as father and mentor, provides care and education for Aranrhod's son, but he still recognizes the initiatory powers of the mother goddess. When the lad is four, Gwydion takes him to Caer Aranrhod for a name. Then, like a shaming adversary, he demands from Aranrhod what it is hers by matrifocal custom to give. The goddess is still enraged by her brother's usurping power. She asserts herself by refusing him and withholding her son's name. She states and disobeys her own matrifocal custom, swearing "on [the child] a destiny that he shall not get a name until he get it from me" (Jones and Jones 1949, p. 64). She even disowns the boy, calling him Gwydion's. Her refusal gives value to the masculine by creating a new line of succession through the father. Because her refusal keeps the child separate from what was still acknowledged as a necessary-for-life atonement with the maternal matrix of being, it must be repaired. Gwydion does not ignore the old customs and their psychological validity. In spite of his derogation of the goddess, he must still obey her and work out the destiny

[11]In Welsh culture this custom persisted until the end of the nineteenth century. History and tale attest to the rites of matrilineal succession as well. In parts of the British Isles, royal rule passed to the queen's daughter and her consort, who ruled after the old queen had died even if the old king survived her.

she has set upon her son. He uses magic, disguise, and trickery to con the goddess into giving the boy his initiations—his name, his tools of strength, and his bride. Aranrhod is made to seem the simple dupe of strategies used by the burgeoning masculine power and performance drive that represents the mythologicalization of early tricksterlike ego development. And when she finally fulfills her maternal role, her acts are made to seem the result of her vanity and insecurity.

In a final insult to Aranrhod, who disappears from the story while Blodeuedd takes her place, Gwydion and his magus uncle use their skillful means to create a bride for the young Lleu. Two men like gods give birth through magic to something beyond nature—a new kind of mother, daughter, beloved. It is a remarkable achievement that may refer to the subsequent flowering of mental consciousness, which also reimagined the natural world and created new ideals and service.[12] This flower bride represents the male's ultimate capacity to usurp the generativity of the female and to control her spirit. With their manipulations, they create a masculine ideal of woman out of flowers. They imagine her beautiful, passive, and without shadow. But while "Flowers" represents to wishful consciousness merely some aspects of the archetypal feminine, this seemingly ideal bride, who is not of "any race on earth," does not lose her connection to the underlying pattern of the ancient goddess. Rather, we can see her becoming a radically polarized version of Aranrhod, who represents the prepolarized whole.

Because Blodeuedd has been created by men to match their masculine ideal, she has a correspondingly contemptible but potent shadow. When Lleu leaves her to visit his uncle, she reverts (in ways the church fathers loved to execrate) to what was repressed from consciousness in the new ideal—unfettered sexual passion and ancient pagan ways. She betrays the husband for whom she was made with a royal huntsman lover she invites in. Then she overthrows the new customs of her creators and chooses her own new king according to the old mores.[13] The couple spend a year plotting Lleu's destruction. "Flowers" is as manipulative as her creators, but she is wily in the service of the emotionality women came to carry for men. "Under pretence of loving care," she drew out of Lleu the complicated

[12]The theme of the birth of male offspring through two males, one of whom takes the female shape, runs through the curious episode of Gwydion's punishment. While this may refer to initiatory rites, this later birth also images a primitive level of nonphysical creativity of the upper phallus and a Christianization of homoerotic practices like those which took place among the *fianna* (societies of youths in Ireland).

[13]Markale (1975) has written of the refusal of Celtic "flower maidens" to capitulate to patrifocal domination (see chapter 6 and pp. 32–33).

scenario by which he could meet his death. This required creating a sacred, liminal dimension, one that lies athwart and beyond the concretely particular opposites that make up the ordinary world. For Lleu is a son of his mother and her prepolarized matrix. When the spear pierces Lleu, who is standing in the prescribed place where he can be killed, he flies away in the shape of a wounded eagle. His transformation implies that the unfoldment of the masculine spirit causes and carries its own wound because of its need to polarize. With unconscious mental tricks, it tricks itself, ignores the body's passion and must leave the passionate lovers to each other's delights and kingdoms.

Gwydion seeks "his nephew" by following a sow, reminding us of his earlier theft of these animals, which were considered guides to the otherworld. Gwydion finds the maggot-ridden eagle, restores Lleu's human form, and heals the wasted man. Again, the actions taken by the supernatural flower woman against her confinement in masculine ideals and powers create the opportunity for Gwydion to assert his magician's might. Against the female's power to destroy, this magus asserts his will and skill over death's transformation. Thereby he seems to claim all the power over life, death, and regeneration once held by the goddess. He is made to seem fully a god.

Gwydion retaliates to coalesce his triumph against Blodeuedd, the once-flower woman. In words that are reminiscent of Yahweh's to the serpent, he says:

> I will not slay thee. I will do to thee that which is
> worse . . . I will let thee go in the form of a bird. And
> because of the dishonor thou hast done to Lleu Llaw
> Gyffes thou art never to dare show thy face in the
> light of day, and that through fear of all birds; and
> that there be enmity between thee and all birds, and
> that it be their nature to mob and molest thee wher-
> ever they may find thee; and that thou shalt not lose
> thy name, but that thou be for ever called Blo-
> deuwedd ("Owl," also "Flower-Face"). (Jones and
> Jones 1949, pp. 73–74.)

With this, he commits the flower wife he had created as a sunny ideal to the darkness of the unconscious and to identification with her own shadow as a threatening raptor of the night. The owl was another ancient symbol of the goddess. Here Gwydion, repudiating the power and wisdom of the underworld, can only curse the darkness and the female spirit. He dismembers the full range of archetypal female powers once held by Aranrhod and renders most of its components negative. He radicalizes her disobedience into adversarial combat. He darkens her wide powers and splits them from consciousness. He tries to minimize what remains, making Blodeuwedd the helpless victim of day-flying birds, which represent the mental dimension that is unfolding in patriarchal culture. Thus, the goddess becomes a symbol of death and the dangerous forces of the unconscious and is dismissed by the mind. Her original pattern of wholeness is bifurcated. The archetypal matrix of life and being is seen as a one-sided threat against which the "good" and magically powerful father as the exemplar of patrifocal culture has proven that he can readily exert himself.

This tale reflects the patriarchy's distortion of the feminine pattern of wholeness and its nurturant and transformative support of human development. The goddess is reduced to a naive simpleton and vengeful adversary, disobedient to her own original roles and potencies. Yet she still holds and withholds her potency. Each of the developmental initiations which were customarily given by the mother become obstacles that the masculine mind and power must wrest from her. Embroiled in honor, shame, and competitive power motives, the goddess spites herself, her son, and the life process. She withdraws her power and presence from her own cycle and its process of development and must be tricked to grant what she had hitherto freely claimed and donated through initiations. In "Flowers," she becomes a trickster herself and again rebels against the new culture. However, "Owl-Face" must carry all the negative projection of that archetype as well. Thus Gwydion, the arch trickster, seems to serve life, while "Owl-Face," the dark feminine, carries off the cruelty and predatory powers of trickery as she is made to flee into the night. On this split the story ends and much of Western culture set its foundation.

## Clinical Relevance

From a clinical perspective, Aranrhod's myth describes a pattern of behavior and development that we now see in its extreme forms as pathology. It represents a dislocation of organic development from the matrix of Self and being that occurs mainly during two phases. One is in infancy when the child's sense of validation is made conditional upon active doing and claiming control over body, self, and objects. The child is made to feel that love is conditional only on adequate performance. Feeling thus intrinsically abandoned, the child precociously develops a false self and suffers a distortion of true ego development, one which must rely heavily on what feels like the powers of illusion and trickery. Like the figure of Gwydion and the patrifocal culture he represents, the child feels magical and powerful. Like the figure of Lleu, however, the child also feels that her or his existence and emotional vitality are unsupported because they are cut off from the maternal matrix. But unlike this Welsh story, Western culture has rarely perceived the need for an adequately mediated return to the mother for the blessings required for thriving in life. With the recent restoration of value to the archetypal feminine and the growth of therapies that honor the mother-child bond, this primary necessity is again being brought to consciousness and facilitated.

A less well documented phase of dislocation from the Self and a more conscious disobedience to its call may occur in adolescence. This problem is found most often in gifted women (and men) who have had to turn against the development of their own talents and body to safeguard themselves as they enter marriage or male-dominated educational and vocational activities. Invariably the clients I have treated have had problems within their parental context that have created fault lines in their basic structure. But they have nonetheless managed to make for themselves a noncompetitive, creative life in which to form and contain libido, one that is safely separate (sometimes secret) from family and society. With a shift toward the needs for dependent intimacy in partnership and overt exploitation of their gifts by career and often narcissistic partners, they tend to split off from the flow of libido and turn against their talents in an effort to avoid what they perceive as their misuse in an alien mode. They then make an effort to live, like Blodeuwedd, in a false self persona that matches the cultural ideal.

Like Aranrhod, who shares a hidden bond with her rapist brother, the young adult caught in either phase of this pattern is inevitably closely related to the robber or rapist. This figure is often the primary caretaker on whom the child originally found the Self projected. Or it may be the beloved partner carrying similar positive projections in late adolescence. In both cases the partner betrays the projection of the Self and acts the robber and rapist, becoming caught like Gwydion in power dynamics. Thus, the young adult is eventually torn between dependency on and loyalty to that betraying other and loyalty to her or his individual Self and its gifts and calling.[14]

When the personal caretaking partner figure is envious or possessive and no other adequate-enough figures have been available to carry the child's Self projection, it will be left to therapy to uncover the integrity hidden under Self disobedience in its passive-aggressive and Self spiteful manifestations. Until recently, our modern culture lacked adequate images

---

[14]That this pattern of self-spite is clinically more common in women may be the result of the greater importance of relational issues in female development and the unfortunate propensity of many mothers in the patriarchy to envy and/or curtail their daughter's development beyond what they achieved themselves.

on which to project the female Self.[15] This creates severe difficulties in honoring the female Self, which often gets projected instead onto woefully inadequate humans. Mothers have been asked to carry the full weight of archetypal burdens, which is an impossible task for humans to bear. Without an alternative and because of fear and need for support, the client has often felt it equally impossible to assert herself actively against those on whom the Self has been projected. Thus the girl and woman tends to reverse her aggression and spite her own unfolding. Such mixed assertion has all the ambivalence of Aranrhod's withdrawal. Because the prepolarized matrix of being is lost to consciousness, the woman tends to fall in with the perception of radical polarization held by the cultural canon and strives for the flowery ego ideal while hiding her own dark wisdom and power. She thus identifies herself as negative within the cultural perspective and tends to have a positive shadow.

One example of this pattern, which can occur in both women and men, unfolded in the case of a musician who abandoned her potential career and her personal love of music as soon as she was safely out of her parental house and could forego her defensive compliance with the extrinsic motivation she felt from her parents. In therapy, she expressed this withholding as a passive-aggressive defense of her integrity:

> I will not be used, so I cannot play. It has always
> given my father too much clutchy joy that I am his
> talented one. . . . He needed to rob my talent to feel
> good, but I cannot produce for that. I would rather
> be autistic and silent than feed the demonic greed and
> envy in him . . . But the trouble is, I can't play any-
> more at all. I've lost touch with the me who could
> create because it got so full of refusal, it all got too
> loaded and . . . blighted.

Like many abused and narcissistically used children, she had refused to thrive in order to protect the supreme value with which she felt most identified. In therapy, she realized she could not even listen to music without extreme discomfort because it reminded her of her "blighted" love for her instrument and her ability to play it freely. Like Aranrhod, she did not even want to approach her potential creativity. Instead, she had tried to deny, disown, and destroy it. She had taken up a career in advertising. Function-

---

[15]A similar problem occurs with the human father and the projection of the masculine Self, since the chthonic element has been missing in the culture or relegated to the devil.

ing poorly as a "super-woman," she had developed chronic stomach pains and came into analysis to deal with omnipresent fear and resentment of her husband on whom she projected her own tendency to self-deprivation. After a time, she saw that she had lived "off [her] center" and in disobedience to her own deepest calling. She intuited the steps she needed to make to begin to fulfill it. But she had also introjected the thieving parent and used its manipulations and strength in a reversal to prevent herself from dangerously "living her bliss." For her, the thief/rapist functioned intrapsychically as guardian/parental complex to rob and dominate her own talents so they could not be usurped by the destructive envy of her father and father complex.

Invariably, the women caught in disobedience to the Self in order to safeguard it feel themselves to be split—like Blodeu(w)edd. The ideal they strive to embody to appear valuable to the demanding collective and/or to their beloved and to conceal their true core can only be a persona or false self. Their true reality comes to feels negative and frightening to themselves, for it, like the cursed owl, must flee from its attackers. These attackers represent internalized parts of their own ideation, which identify with the aggressor and which can easily get projected onto all relationship partners.

In therapy, healing can sometimes restore the woman to her true resonance with the original pattern of wholeness represented by Aranrhod. (The pattern for men may be somewhat different, but it still involves reconnecting to the individual pattern of wholeness.) Such healing proceeds very much along the lines of Gwydion's fostering and restoration of his son. It recapitulates the various phases but in a reverse sequence. In a new creative process that leads back to lost origins, the wounded and festering analysand slowly moves from the top of the oak or out of the night where she has taken refuge from attack to bond with the therapist as surrogate caretaker. Restored to human connection, she must then be refostered in the container of therapy, learn new skills, and create/discover the name and style truly descriptive of her identity. Finally atoned with the prepolarized images of archetypal female through the archetypal transference to the therapist and through potent dream images of divinely powerful Self figures, which like the "silver wheel" represent and mirror back her individual wholeness, she can separate from the containment of psychoanalysis.[16]

[16]These phases are similar to the sequence Harold Searles (1961, chapter 18) describes of chronic schizophrenics: out of contact, ambivalent symbiosis, therapeutic symbiosis, and resolution of symbiosis. They apply equally to most long-term psychotherapeutic and psychoanalytic interactions.

# Conclusion

The tale of Aranrhod and Blodeuedd/Blodeuwedd provides us with a model of disobedience which operates in modern analysands. When the figure on whom the image of the Self is projected betrays the projection, these analysands react like Aranrhod. They withdraw and spite themselves to curtail the natural blossoming of their potential. They disobey their unique, Self-determined pattern of individuation just as the goddess disobeyed her own authority and process. Aranrhod's story represents a radical shift toward a new culture that was the creation of figures beloved by her but envious and inimical to her customs. Many modern analysands are faced with similar conflicts as a result of the hypertrophy of what Gwydion's culture and consciousness has brought us. This causes in them a split between the guidance of the individual's inner Self and the defenses of the developing psyche attempting to incarnate this Self within an inimical context. In such cases the beckoning individuation pattern must be hidden, withheld, and even resisted to protect its gifts and talents from rape, robbery, and misuse by powerful and envious others to whom the individual is still bonded and loyal. Individuals may find healing through a reconnection to the original wholeness of the psyche represented in the image of the all-containing "silver wheel."

# References

Allen, Paula Gunn. 1986. *The Sacred Hoop: recovering the Feminine in American Indian Traditions.* Boston: Beacon Press.

Berger, Pamela. 1985. *The Goddess Obscured: Transformation of the Grain Protectress to Saint.* Boston: Beacon Press.

Bromwich, Rachel. 1961. *Trioedd Ynys Prydein: The Welsh Triads.* Cardiff: University of Wales Press.

Condren, Mary. 1989. *The Serpent and the Goddess: Women, Religion and Power in Celtic Ireland.* New York: Harper and Row.

Ford, Patrick. 1977. *The Mabinogi and Other Medieval Welsh Tales.* Berkeley, Calif.: University of California Press.

Gimbutas, Marija. 1982. *The Goddesses and Gods of Old Europe 6500–3500 B.C.: Myths and Cult Images.* Berkeley, Calif.: University of California Press.

Gleick, James. 1987. *Chaos: Making a New Science.* New York: Viking.

Gruffydd, W. J. 1928. *Math vab Mathonwy.* Cardiff: University of Wales Press.

Harding, M. Esther. 1971. *Women's Mysteries, Ancient and Modern: A Psychological Interpretation of the Feminine Principle as Portrayed in Myth, Story and Dream.* New York: Harper Colophon Books.

Jones, Thomas, and Jones, Gwyn. 1949. *The Mabinogion,* rev. ed. London: Everyman's Library.

Kinsella, Thomas, trans. 1969. *The Tain: Translated from the Irish Epic Tain Bo Cuailnge*. London: Oxford University Press.

Markale, Jean. 1978. *Celtic Civilization*. London: Gordon and Cremonesi.

_____. 1975. *Women of the Celts*. London: Gordon and Cremonesi.

McCone, Kim. 1990. *Pagan Past and Christian Present*. An Sagart: Maynooth University Press.

Rees, Alwyn, and Rees, Brinley. 1961. *Celtic Heritage: Ancient Tradition in Ireland and Wales*, London: Thames and Hudson.

Rhys, John. 1901. *Celtic Folklore, Welsh and Manx*, London: Oxford University Press.

Ross, Anne. 1967. *Pagan Celtic Britain*. New York: Columbia University Press.

Searles, Harold. 1961. *Collected Papers*. New York: International Universities Press.

Whitmont. 1969. *The Symbolic Quest: Basic Concepts of Analytical Psychology*. New York, G.P.Putnam's Sons.

Winnicott, D. W. 1971. *Playing and Reality*. New York: Basic Books.

# SUCHIEH

## THE UNTAMED SHREW OF
## *HSING-SHIH YIN-YUAN*

### Fan Pen Chen

**A** rebel of the patriarchal Confucian society to which she belongs, the protagonist, Suchieh, in the momentous eighteenth-century novel *Hsing-shih Yin-yuan* (*Marriage Destinies to Admonish the World*), is probably the worst shrew ever portrayed in Chinese literature.[1] Doomed to be matched to a spiteful mate, the girl's subsequent hatred for her husband, her ruthless treatment of him, as well as her rejection of Confucian values, have made her one of the most fascinating characters in realistic Chinese fiction. Hers is a condemned female voice within a male-dominated society.

Depicted as a willful beauty, Suchieh is so full of wrath and so defiant of accepted social constraints that her actions verge upon insanity. She is referred to as a madwoman, a tigress, the seed of misfortune, the root of calamity, etc., by the narrator and other characters in the novel. Even the author himself seems to find it hard to comprehend the raison d'être of such a woman. He can only explain her madness through the traditional karmic literary framework. She is the reincarnation of a she-fox spirit whom her husband had killed in his previous life. Therefore, she is a terrible shrew in order to avenge the wrong perpetrated during her previous existence.

The reasons for her behavior are readily visible without having to resort to the karmic explanation. Her personal history, the influence of her mother in particular, provide adequate explanation for her behavior and freedom of thought. Her madness can be seen as a form of rebellion against the patriarchal society in which she resides. The subversive nature of the character poses such a threat to the traditional Chinese society that she must be continuously punished and used by the author for didactic purposes. Viewed from a social or male perspective, Suchieh is most contemptible. Yet the novel is also so faithful mimetically — it includes all the motives for her behavior and her thoughts — that a modern reader can, in fact, identify

---

[1]Consisting of almost a million character-words in one hundred chapters, *Hsing-shih Yin-yuan* was one of the longest traditional Chinese novels and was written by Hsi-chou Sheng, a pseudonym meaning "man of Western Chou."

with her and see the madwoman as a strong female determined to reject the authority of the patriarchal power structure.

In introducing the worst shrew in Chinese literature, I intend to examine the factors which inform her behavior from a feminine perspective. The punishments Suchieh receives reflect the price one must pay for deviance and defiance in the traditional society. Ironically, for someone who is supposedly avenging a karmic wrong, she suffers more than the original culprit, Ti Hsi-ch'en.

Suchieh begins her career as a shrew the moment she marries into the Ti family. The night before her wedding, she dreams that her heart is ripped out and replaced by an evil one to serve better the purpose of vengeance. She shocks everyone during her wedding by bawling out the master of ceremony (44:572).[2] She then locks the husband out of the bridal chamber three nights in a row, much to the distress of the bridegroom and the parents of both families. He finally uses trickery to consummate the marriage (45).

Soon after the wedding, they get into a quarrel which turns into a fight. Her husband, Ti Hsi-ch'en, grabs hold of a whip which she immediately snatches from him. She then pushes him onto the floor with one hand, sits on his head, and gives him a full beating (48:615), seizing his power and lording over him both figuratively and literally. When she receives a similar beating from her hot-tempered mother-in-law, she sets their house on fire.

Verbal and physical abuse of her husband and total defiance of parental authority are common staples of Suchieh's repertoire. Her unseemly behavior is not limited to verbal abuse: she claws, slaps, clubs, and bites.

Her methods of interrogation and torture are at once ingenious and invidious. The first time she interrogates Ti Hsi-ch'en, she ties him to her bed and stabs him with two large needles (52:656). The second time, she jabs him with an iron tong, creating innumerable grapelike bruises (59:744). The third time, she burns holes in brush pens with iron chopsticks for picking up coal and strings them together to press his fingers (63:784).

Her determination to subdue the husband and use him to vent her suppressed emotions is reflected in extreme irascibility and cruelty. After suffering a great humiliation, she bites a piece of flesh almost completely off from his arm, causing him to roll on the ground in pain (73:901). Other methods to her "madness" include sponsoring a Buddhist ritual for the deceased for her living husband (74:914–915) and using him to feed the mosquitoes in her room (75:917).

[2]The numbers in parenthesis refer to the chapter and page numbers of the edition cited in the references.

When he escapes to the capital and becomes free of her both physically and emotionally (he takes another wife), her anger seems to turn into a frenzied hatred. She dresses up a pet monkey in Ti's clothes and clobbers it as if it were the husband (76:937). She tries to use voodoo to murder him (76:938–939) and sues him for rebellion (89:1087–1088).

She is responsible for the paralysis of both her mother-in-law and her own father, and for the deaths of all her parents-in-law and parents. When her father-in-law takes in a concubine, she tries to castrate him to prevent the birth of another heir (56:707). Her ultimate display of disrespect for tradition and filial piety, however, is the use of the reverse sides of the portraits of her deceased in-laws as wallpaper for a shed (76:936).

The success Suchieh achieves as a terrible shrew is due not only to her preposterous actions but also to her sharp tongue. Her tirades, though merciless, are truthful but demonstrate total disregard for property and authority. Even when her own father chides her for fiercely beating a maid who is implicated in some missing food, she retorts,

> "A married daughter is a piece of property sold. This is none of your business! It's only a maid and now you've taken her away anyway! If you hadn't sat stuck on your butt drooling for food, there wouldn't have been any chicken to miss and any of this trouble!" (48:614)

She so craves freedom—the ability to leave the inner apartments and visit the sights—that she considers the secluded life of women at an official residence to be imprisonment and would rather die than be cooped up. When she fails to persuade Ti's cousin and his family to let her out of their luxurious residence in Peking, she attempts suicide so that "at least her ghost would be able to roam" (77:951–952).

She fears neither death nor divorce (73:901). Indeed, Suchieh's disregard for both divine retribution and bad reputation enables her to elude the grip of Confucian ethics. She once yells at Ti, "If you hope to use this to discredit me, you are dreaming! I, Old Su, have no fear of defamation, and I have no desires for having any commemorative steles built for me!" (66:822).

The modern reader may appreciate Suchieh's need for freedom and her rejection of Confucian values, her unconventional way of thinking and her defiance of the patriarchal authority. But her inversion of conjugal and familial hierarchies makes her a misfit in her society. The Confucian world order is based on hierarchy. Ministers must obey their rulers, wives must obey their husbands, children must obey their parents, servants must obey their masters—each person has his or her place socially and its observation is considered necessary to maintain order and stability in traditional China.

Anyone who flouts this hierarchal order is not only considered a deviant but deemed punishable. The punishments Suchieh receives for her defiance increase in severity with time and seem to be commensurate with the atrocities she perpetrates, yet she is so consumed by anger and hatred that she is forever undaunted in her pursuit of revenge.

After Mrs. Ti's death, a sister-in-law of the deceased gives Suchieh such a sound beating that her arms swell like vats (60:748–749). To force her to repent, her congenital fear of falcons (she is, after all, a fox in her previous life) is used to scare her out of her wits and does restrain her temporarily (63:786–788). She gets beaten up and stripped naked by a bunch of hoodlums during a temple festivity, which she attends against all advice (73:900). The monkey she ill-treats eventually breaks loose and gouges out one of her eyes and her nose (76:937).

As she becomes an object of contempt, the whole world, except for her birth mother, seems to conspire to cheat and deceive her.[3] Even a blind man manages to trick money out of her by pretending to perform voodoo on Ti (76:938–939). When she chases after Ti to his new residence and family in Peking, she misses him, is sent away, and ends up trapped with his relatives, where she would have been kept forever if she hadn't tried to commit suicide (77:945–952).

When she chases after Ti again to Szechuan, she is abandoned by her servant half way (86). She eventually returns home after much suffering, sues Ti for rebellion but is easily disproven, and has all her fingers smashed by order of the presiding magistrate (89:1092). When she tries to exact revenge on her neighbors who bore witness against her, she is again badly hurt by an Amazonian neighbor (89:1095–1096). She finally reaches Ti's residence at Ch'eng-tu, Szechuan, with a group of pilgrims. But she barely exhibits her wrath before Ti's new wife gives her a sound beating, with the aid of the maids, and subdues her (95:1155–1161). She almost kills Ti several times, but he eventually receives aid from a monk and causes her to fall ill, become half paralyzed, and die.

According to the karmic explanation, her shrewishness is preordained in order for her to exact revenge for a past crime. One wonders, however, whether all the sufferings she has to endure in the process of avenging herself are worthwhile, and whether it is fair that she should become more victimized than the original sinner who finally leads a peaceful life until the ripe age of eighty-seven. The novelist's karmic explanation of Suchieh's shrewishness and "irrational" behavior seems to have flaws.

Many modern critics have tried to analyze Suchieh from various

---

[3]This birth mother, a concubine, is different from her formal mother, the main wife of her father.

angles beyond the karmic explanation. Andrew Plaks deems her plagued by recidivism — habitual relapse into crime or antisocial behavior; he calls her a pathological case (1985, pp. 559, 579). He seems to agree with the other characters' assessment of her as a psychological deviant.

Some critics have gone beyond identifying her psychological deviance to suggesting factors which inform Suchieh's shrewish character. Her innate personality and the influence of those around her are the main determinants. Her low-born, ignorant birth mother and her father's murderous brother have been noted as the sources of her "bad blood" (Chu 1978, p. 131). Her lack of formal education (common among girls), the bad influence of this birth mother, Lungshih, and the spitefulness of Suchieh's husband have also been offered as reasons for her behavior (Hu 1935, pp. 381–383).[4] Yenna Wu suggests that the husband's fear and the weakness and tolerance of most of the people around her encourage her shrewishness (1986, p. 149).

Of the above, I feel that Suchieh's willy-nilly marriage to a contemptible mate and maternal influence play the most significant roles in shaping her deviant propensities. Ti Hsi-ch'en's character and his relationship with Suchieh require a more elaborate exposition than have been done previously. Suchieh's shrewishness is, in part, the result of the traditional conjugal system in which the ties between families override the compatibility of individuals. I consider maternal influence as an understatement for the complexity of the relationship between this mother and daughter. I would like to discuss this on a different plane to show that Suchieh acts as an "avenging angel" for her oppressed mother and that her defiance of authority echoes the desires of all such powerless victims of society.

The relationship between Ti and Suchieh never had the benefit of a romantic beginning or even blissful ignorance. Suchieh grows up with full knowledge of the stupidity and mischievousness of her betrothed. From the beginning, Suchieh has felt an intense dislike for Ti. Even as a child, she tells her mother, "I don't know why, but I feel angry whenever I see him. I can't stand the sight of him" (25:339). It could be because her brothers attend the same tutorial classes as Ti and most likely take pleasure informing and teasing her about the behavior of her fiancé.

Rarely is there a more distracted mind than Ti's for studying. After having wasted four years at a local school, his furious mother convinces his father to hire a tutor for the twelve-year-old as well as for a nephew of hers and Suchieh's brothers. During their first class,

---

[4]Hsu also deems Ti Hsi-ch'en a weakling deserving of the harsh treatment from Suchieh (1931, p. 458).

> All the others easily had their readings cor-
> rected and returned to their seats, Ti Hsi-ch'en alone
> could not recognize a single word . . . Having no
> other recourse, the tutor divided the four or five lines
> of the text into two sections and taught each section
> twenty to thirty times — but it was still like playing
> harp to an ox. (33:434)

Blockheaded as he is when it comes to studying, Ti is, however, most mischievous. He is basically an immature teenager who exhibits unacceptable behavior, generates some laughs, but begets no respect.

Suchieh, on the other hand, is not only a ravishing beauty but also more intelligent than her husband (56:710).[5] She is also fully aware of the fact that her brother wrote the answers for Ti when he took the preliminary civil service examinations. When she tries to confiscate her sister-in-law's dowry, she screams at Ti in the midst of an extended tirade, "Even before I married you, my brother had given you a bachelor's degree. Here you are wearing a head-scarf,[6] clothed in a blue gown and walking around full of airs. Shouldn't you think a little? Where did all these honors come from?" (56:710). Thus Suchieh's rebelliousness and cruelty seem reactions to her fate. She accepts the marriage arrangement but the buried rancor erupts through other means.

In my attempt at unraveling many of the enigmas surrounding Suchieh's behavior, I found her affinity with her birth mother, Lungshih, particularly revealing. Lungshih, a low-born concubine, who always sees eye to eye with Suchieh's point of view, is blamed for misleading the daughter (48:617) and has gotten kicked (48:617) and slapped by her professor husband (56:704) on two occasions on account of speaking on behalf of Suchieh. Suchieh is much more powerful than this mother of hers, and she carries herself quite differently. But their mentalities are so akin to each other that an analysis of Lungshih sheds light on many of Suchieh's anomalies. Suchieh's greed, laziness, love for freedom and diversions, disregard for authority, and rejection of social hierarchies all seem to be manifestations of her mother's dark desires. By possessing the power that Lungshih has always envied and abusing it with a vengeance, Suchieh can be seen as the mother's doomed emotional surrogate.

An ignorant and uncultured woman who serves as cook and maid

---

[5]Although unschooled, she understands the ribald, unorthodox nuptial songs at her wedding better than Ti.

[6]A sign of honor, permissible only to scholars who had passed the examinations.

to the family, Lungshih is taken in as a concubine (the legal wife has been childless). She gives birth to three sons and a daughter, but her status is still essentially that of a slave. As both a woman and a slave, she ranks among the lowest socially, a fact of which she is keenly aware and resentful.

When Lungshi fails to rally any support for a ludicrous plan to avenge a beating received by Suchieh, she wails,

> "If I were a proper wife, even my fart would have
> been considered fragrant." (60:752)

When she cannot get the main wife, Hsueh T'ai-t'ai, to go visit Suchieh and volunteers to go herself, Hsueh T'ai-t'ai says,

> "A concubine visiting the in-laws? If you don't mind
> being slighted by them, go right ahead. I'm not going
> to stop you."
> Lungshih mumbles, "So what about it? Do
> main wives have horns on their heads and scales
> down their bellies?" (63:787)

She is even slighted by the sensible and kind Mr. Ti because of her impudent attitude and behavior and her low position. When she tries to argue with him, he says, "It's dark. Do go home. You don't count!" (73:904).

Lungshih's frustrations are best expressed in the following tirade. When she fails to get her sons to perform an unreasonable request, she utters the agony of many concubines:

> "Oh my god! Why am I so unlucky? When my man
> was around, I was under his control. When he died,
> the main wife is like a leech on the leg. I . . . waited
> until the main wife is dead. But now I end up in my
> sons' hands and still can't have my way!" (68:849)

She seems to delight in Suchieh's defiance of that which she is incapable of fighting, the patriarchal culture. In encouraging Suchieh in deviant behavior, however, she is, in fact, pushing the girl toward annihilation. The line between protecting and spoiling her child and using her daughter as a release for her own suppressed rancor is so fine that the relationship between the two transcends simple maternal influence. Its significance lies in the engendering and perpetuation of abnormal behavior in an oppressive environment and the harm that a tormented mother can bring to her beloved child. Lungshih is so anxious to have her daughter do what she cannot do herself that she fails to see the injuries that such behavior would lead Suchieh into.

The most dangerous concept that Lungshih seems to have ingrained in Suchieh is the rejection of the hierarchal system and its authority. When Suchieh demands that she be treated as an equal by her father-in-law in the following tirade after her temple trip debacle, she is espousing an unacceptable mode of thinking.

> "As for the husband, when his wife goes afar to visit a temple, if he's at all human, shouldn't he have followed her? If he had followed me yesterday, would the hooligans have dared to do a thing? No, he didn't go with his wife so that he could entertain his father's guests at the tomb![7] That old father-in-law of mine is also totally senseless. Did he have to entertain on this particular day? Since you knew that your daughter-in-law was going to the temple, what's wrong with entertaining on another day?" (74:907)

Suchieh's disregard for social hierarchies and her general lack of status consciousness are also manifested in her comfortable close association with the low-class members of the ostracized women's religious group (56:705) and her willingness to be disguised as a maid in order to visit an imperial temple at the capital (78:958–959).

Suchieh's story without the karmic, retributive element is a tragic tale of a strong female forced into marrying someone she detests; she abuses the power she possesses and has to suffer for her defiance of the accepted norm. Influenced by her birth mother not to submit to the strictures of their patriarchal society, to reject the role of self-abnegation deemed rational for women, she becomes a madwoman. Her story is that of a woman who rebels against patriarchal domination so vehemently that she loses sight of her own humanity. Defiance and deviance are the only means available to Suchieh to release her pent-up anger and attain freedom and equality, but the price that such a woman must pay in traditional China is insanity, physical and psychological torment, and death.

---

[7]Mr. Ti had recently built a tomb for himself and was celebrating its completion with a banquet that day.

# References

Chu Yen-ching. 1978. Hsing-shih yin-yuan yen-chiu. M.A. thesis. Taiwan National University.

Hsi-chou Sheng. 1986. *Hsing-shih yin-yuan*. Taipei: Lien-ching ch'u-pan shih-yeh kung-ssu.

Hsu Chih-mo. 1931. Hsing-shih yin-yuan hsu. *Hsu Chih-mo ch'uan-chi*. Taipei: Chuan-chi wen-hsueh ch'u-pan-she 6:439–458 (rpt. 1967); and the above edition of *Hsing-shih yin-yuan*: 1225–1237.

Hu Shih. 1935. Hsing-shih yin-yuan chuan k'ao-cheng. *Hu Shih lun-hsueh chin-chu*, vol. 1. Shanghai: Shangwu yin-shu-kuan 1:333–402.

Plaks, A. 1985. After the fall: *Hsing-shih yin-yuan chuan* and the seventeenth-century novel. *Harvard Journal of Asiatic Studies* 45:543–580.

Wang, Chi-chen. 1984. Marriage as retribution. *Chinese Middlebrow Fiction from the Ch'ing and Early Republican Eras*, Liu Ts'un-yan, ed. Hong Kong: The Chinese University of Hong Kong Press.

Wu, Yenna. 1986. Marriage destinies to awaken the world: A literary study of "Xingshi Yinyuan Zhuan." Ph.D. diss. Harvard University.

# VIRGINIA WOOLF

## THE TRAGEDY OF UNCONSCIOUS DISOBEDIENCE

### Jane White-Lewis

**A** disobedient act includes three important ingredients. First, one must be able to recognize the presumed injustice, to identify the problem, to know who the enemy is. Second, some sense of agency seems essential—a good enough, strong enough ego to have the courage to confront, speak out, and suffer through the consequences of disobedience. Third, having access to one's anger seems necessary in both knowing what one is angry about and having the psychic fuel to do something about it. If the disobedient act is to lead to increased consciousness and to the psychological development of the individual, some awareness of the meaning of the experience seems essential. Related to the Latin words *oboedīre* (to listen to) and *audīre* (to hear), "disobedience" includes the meaning of not listening, not hearing. If the experience of disobedience involves not listening and not hearing the dictates of one's own inner authority or voice, the result can be tragic.

In 1929, Virginia Woolf wrote *A Room of One's Own*, a spirited discussion of difficulties facing women writers and a strong indictment of patriarchal attitudes and institutions. Although Woolf's work was written more than sixty years ago, the energy and freshness of her prose give the book a contemporary feeling; it is easy for the female reader to identify with Woolf's concerns and her impassioned responses to "Oxbridge." Woolf presents herself as a woman who not only recognizes the injustice of a patriarchal system, but has the strength and courage to speak out against it. A current of mocking irreverence and potential disobedience runs throughout the book.

Reading *A Room of One's Own*, one senses that Virginia Woolf could clearly identify injustice experienced by women, was consciously indignant, and had the strength and confidence to speak out. By writing, publishing, and speaking publicly, this enormously gifted writer was disobedient; she challenged the conventional expection of woman's silence. One might expect that Woolf's fiction would be filled with lively, competent, effective women daring to be disobedient; that she would embrace feminist causes; that she would effect change and be changed by the process. Instead, Woolf tended to create conventional, proper, obedient female characters; feminist figures in her novels are rather shabby, pathetic, and foolish. Woolf did not want to be identified as a feminist; the feminist movement "repelled her aesthetically" (Batchelor 1971, p. 173). Little development is seen in her female characters; little psychological development is evident in her own life. Experiencing depression periodically throughout her life, Woolf committed suicide by drowning in 1941 at the age of 59.

What happened to that confident, outspoken voice in *A Room of One's Own*? In Woolf's essays, novels, letters, and diaries, we can find clues. In the essay "Professions for Women" (1931), for example, Woolf mentions two obstacles preventing women writers from expressing themselves: the "Angel in the House" phenomenon and the difficulty of speaking truthfully about passions and body because of the "extreme conventionality of the other sex" (1931 p. 62). The "Angel in the House" was the ideal Victorian woman. Chaste, sympathetic, charming, unselfish, selfless, obedient—she had no mind or wish of her own. Always supportive and uncritical of the men in her life, she served as a looking glass "reflecting the figure of man at twice its natural size" (1929, p. 35). Woolf claims to have "killed" the "Angel," but admits that "the second [obstacle], telling the truth about my own experiences as a body, I do not think I solved. I doubt that any woman has solved it yet" (1931, p. 62). What Woolf does not seem to recognize is that she has not, in fact, dealt with the "Angel" and that the two issues are closely intertwined. Obviously, she is still caught in the "Angel" mentality when she worries "what men will say of a woman who speaks the truth about her passions" (ibid.). Furthermore, it seems to me, the "Angel" cannot be killed until a woman can fully know and own her passions.

Filled with autobiographical material, Woolf's novels work and rework a variety of themes, including the "Angel" and "Body" motifs. Mrs. Ramsey, in *To the Lighthouse* (1927), is, for instance, a typical "Angel." Modeled after an idealized image of Woolf's mother Julia Stephen, Mrs. Ramsey is pictured as loving, gentle, generous of spirit, but with "scarcely a shell of herself left for her to know herself by; all was so lavished and spent" (1927, p. 38). Worshipped by all, she gives, sweetens, and renews the lives of those around her. She reassures her demanding, petulant, self-pitying husband while submitting to his tyranny. Mrs. Ramsey cannot, of course, openly express annoyance; "Angels" do not get angry. Her only revenge is to refuse to say she loves him.

Similarly, Julia Stephen could not protest. Surrendering herself to the countless demands of her family as well as the sick, poor, and needy, Julia "wore herself out" (Woolf 1976a, p. 133) and, like Mrs. Ramsey, died at an early age. Given her husband's attitude—"woman was then (though gilt with an angelic surface) the slave" (1976a, p. 145)—surely she must have resented her situation. Like Mrs. Ramsey, her only form of disobedience was to withhold love.

With a mother in Victorian bondage as a role model, Woolf inevitably found the expression of anger problematic. In *A Room of One's Own*,

Woolf referred to anger as "the black snake" (1929, p. 32). She was contemptuous of strong affect in others and, undoubtedly, her reluctance to identify with the feminists was related to their public and passionate expression of hostility. A similar attitude shaped her literary criticism: anger should not "tamper" with the "integrity" of a novel. Woolf criticizes Charlotte Brontë for writing "foolishly," "in a rage where she should write calmly" (1929, p. 73). Whereas Woolf praises Jane Austen who, like Shakespeare, wrote "without hate, without bitterness, without fear, without protest, without preaching" (1929, p. 71), she complains of Brontë's "buried suffering smouldering beneath her passion" and objects to the "indignation" which deforms and twists her novels (1929, p. 72). Woolf's argument does not seem very convincing; her comments seem odd and more a reflection of her own psychological issues than her literary perception and sensibility. She seems unaware that the impassioned passages she quotes from *Jane Eyre* have a vitality and emotional truth that enliven the novel, just as her own sarcasm, indignation, and heat effectively engage the reader of her essay. Probably Woolf's denunciation of Brontë's passion rings false because of her own inability to connect more consciously with her deeper layers of rage.

A variation on the "Angel" theme appears in *Mrs. Dalloway* (1925). Concerned with the interaction between the "Angel" and "body" motifs, Woolf powerfully portrays the high psychological and emotional cost of playing the role of the chaste "Angel." Having chosen a respectable, safe, and comfortable life, the charming Clarissa Dalloway seems to enjoy her socially enviable existence as she busies herself with the preparations for her party.

Although memories from the past tug at her throughout the day, she seems strangely unaware of the marked contrast between the richness and vibrancy of these recollections and the superficiality of her present situation. Beneath Mrs. Dalloway and her perfect wife/hostess persona lives Clarissa, a woman who is emotionally unnourished, isolated and disconnected from her daughter, her husband, her self. The interactions between Clarissa and her daughter Elizabeth are painfully awkward and are contaminated by Clarissa's spoiling envy of Elizabeth's relationship with Miss Kilman. Feeling Clarissa's disapproval and emotional unavailability, Elizabeth turns to her father. A poignant passage reveals the "emptiness about the heart of life" (1925, p. 45) and the emotional and sexual inadequacy of Clarissa's "proper" marriage. "Like a nun withdrawing" Clarissa retires to her narrow bed in the attic for a midday rest.

> Lying there reading, for she slept badly, she could
> not dispel a virginity preserved through childbirth
> which clung to her like a sheet . . . She could see what
> she lacked. It was not beauty; it was not mind. It was

something central which permeated; something warm
which broke up surfaces and rippled the cold contact
of man and woman, or of women together. (1925, p.
46)

In marked contrast to the controlled and presentable Mrs. Dalloway, the troubled Septimus Warren Smith thrashes around in his turbulent
craziness. Seeking psychiatric help for his war-related distress, Septimus is
subjected to inept and insensitive psychiatric treatment. Neither Dr. Holmes
nor Sir William Bradshaw can hear or imaginally see his profound torment.
Neither is interested in listening to his truth or in finding meaning in his
images and puns. Desperate, Septimus commits suicide by throwing himself
from a window. In the midst of her dinner party, Clarissa receives the news
of his death. Although the two characters never actually meet, a moment of
identification reveals both the depth of Clarissa's despair and of her connection to Septimus: "She felt somehow very like him—the young man who
had killed himself. She felt glad that he had done it" (1925, p. 283). Clarissa's superficial persona can be seen as a "cover" or defense against her own
Septimus pathology, her own potentially disruptive unconscious contents.
Both Clarissa and Septimus are cut off from their psychological truth;
anger lies deep in their shadows.

Biographical material as well as Woolf's diaries and letters, which
have been published since her death, reveal that both Clarissa and Septimus
are representations of Virginia Woolf. Clarissa Dalloway, fretting about the
details and success of her party, is familiar to the reader of Woolf's diaries.
Surprisingly unreflective, the diaries are filled with the details of her social
life and written in a style that she might attribute to her "tea-table training"
(1976a, p. 150). For example, less than three weeks before her suicide,
Woolf wrote in her diary, "No, I intend no introspection. I mark Henry
James's sentence: Observe perpetually. Observe the oncome of age. Observe
greed. Observe my own despondency. By means it becomes serviceable"
(March 8, 1941). Like Clarissa, she did not or could not probe for meaning
in her experiences. And like Clarissa, she was desperately lonely in her
nonsexual, nonintimate marriage to Leonard Woolf.

Undoubtedly Septimus Smith represents Woolf's tortured self.
Surely it is no coincidence that Virginia, the seventh child in the bizarre
Stephen household, chose the name "Septimus" for this soul-aching character. Dr. Holmes and Sir William Bradshaw are drawn straight from her
experience; she, too, suffered disastrous psychiatric treatment (Trombley
1982, Poole 1990). Reading Leonard Woolf's unperceptive and myopic
account of Virginia's ordeal, one is chilled by his lack of awareness of his
own unconsciously hurtful involvement in her struggles. In *Beginning
Again*, Leonard Woolf wrote:

The point is that her insanity was in her premises, in her beliefs. She believed, for instance, that she was not ill, that her symptoms were due to her own "faults"; she believed that she was hearing voices when the voices were her own imaginings; she heard the birds outside her window talking Greek; she believed that the doctors and nurses were in conspiracy against her. These beliefs were insane because they were in fact contradicted by reality. (1963, pp. 163–164)

Although Virginia insisted that she was not insane and that her symptoms were due to her own "faults," apparently no one bothered to inquire what she meant by "faults." Nor was any effort made to understand the unconscious contents that were surfacing. No one asked what the voices were saying or what her associations were to the birds speaking Greek. As DeSalvo and Poole have demonstrated, Woolf's "imaginings" and the images that pervade her novels are filled with meaning and reveal her inner struggles and unresolved complexes (DeSalvo 1989, Poole 1990). With unexamined preconceptions, Woolf's caretakers—like those of Septimus— assumed she was "insane" and did not listen to her. If she complained that the doctors and nurses were in conspiracy against her, she was labeled "paranoid"—when, in fact, Leonard was consulting with her caretakers and making decisions about her treatment plans without her knowledge. If she insisted that she was not "ill" or if she protested against the "drastic regime" of enforced rest and feeding, such assertions and disobedient behavior were additional proof to Leonard and her "medical specialists" of her "madness." One can imagine that the situation was crazy-making for Virginia, and one can speculate that unconsciously Leonard Woolf defined his wife as sick and fragile, as the "patient," to disguise his own pathology. Such a violation must have produced in Virginia a profound rage.

Tragically, Woolf, like Septimus, never found a therapist who could hear her pain, who could find meaning in her "imaginings" and understand her "madness" (in both senses of the word). By 1939, the lack of a therapeutic container was especially unfortunate considering the increasing external and internal stresses: the death of her beloved nephew Julian Bell in the Spanish Civil War, the beginning of World War Two and a threatened German invasion, an emotional and physical separation from both her sister Vanessa and her close friend and ex-lover Vita Sackville-West, and the growing fear of her diminishing ability to write. In this troubled context, Woolf began the unsettling process of reexamining her childhood experiences and of writing her autobiography, her "auto-analysis," "A Sketch of the Past" (1976a). In this work she found the courage to speak more openly about her "experiences as a body." Although she had spoken almost twenty years earlier of her half-brother George Duckworth as the "lover" of the Stephen sisters (1976b, p. 177), in "A Sketch of the Past," Woolf revealed having been sexually molested at about six or seven by her other half-brother, Gerald Duckworth. With this memory came the strong feelings associated with the event as well as an awareness that this sexual abuse contributed to her life-long intense shame, insecurity, and fear of her own body (1976b, p. 69).

Also at this time, Woolf met Freud and started reading his works. With her new interest in psychodynamics and with an appreciation of "ambivalence" (1976a, p. 108), Woolf reexamined her parental relationships. The portrait of her father that emerges in her autobiography is considerably more complex than the one drawn a decade earlier in *To the Lighthouse,* where he appears as Mr. Ramsey. Woolf describes Leslie Stephen as the "tyrant father—the exacting, the violent, the histrionic, the demonstrative, the self-centered, the self pitying, the deaf, the appealing, the alternately loved and hated father" (1976a, p. 116). She speaks of his "honesty, his unworldliness, his lovableness, his perfect sincerity . . . his attractiveness" (1976a, p. 110). Woolf reveals her emotional involvement with him—not only her frustration and rage at him but also her love for him, her identification with him, and her desire to please him (1976a, pp. 110–111).

Likewise, Woolf's picture of her mother in "A Sketch of the Past" goes beyond the idealized Mrs. Ramsey/Julia figure in *To the Lighthouse.* A Victorian matron appears—sometimes severe, depressed, and unavailable. She must have been a "general presence," Woolf writes: "Can I remember ever being alone with her for more than a few minutes? Someone was always interrupting . . . She had not time, nor strength, to concentrate, except for a moment if one were ill or in some child's crisis, upon me, or upon anyone—unless it were Adrian. Him she cherished separately; she called him 'My Joy' " (1976a, p. 83). Woolf recalls the scene when she was only thirteen and her mother lay dying: "And there is my last sight of her; she was dying; I came to kiss her and as I crept out of the room she said: 'Hold yourself straight, my little Goat' " (1976a, p. 84). In this more balanced account of Julia, Woolf reveals some awareness of the complexity of her mother, but the underlying rage which so often accompanies such emotional and physical abandonment is buried under a nostalgic, aching sadness and longing.

Some understanding of Woolf's history and her deep unresolved abandonment issues help us make sense of her marriage to Leonard. He provided a perfect hook for her projections; he was the devoted, but emotionally unavailable, caregiver like her mother. And just as she had idealized her mother, so Woolf defended against her true feelings toward Leonard. Although at some level she must have felt intense rage about his treatment of her "madness," his insufferably controlling behavior, his refusal to allow her to bear children—she wrote in her suicide note:

> You have given me the greatest possible happiness.
> You have been in every way all that anyone could be.
> I don't think two people could have been happier till
> this terrible disease came . . . What I want to say is I
> owe all the happiness of my life to you. You have
> been entirely patient with me and incredibly good . . .
> I don't think two people could have been happier
> than we have been. (L. Woolf 1968, pp. 93–94)

Insecure with a fragile sense of self, Woolf as woman/wife could not fully access her true feeling and remained silent; but as a writer she could speak out in her fiction, even if not consciously aware of doing so. During this period when Woolf was revealing in her autobiography the incest and pathology of the Stephen household, she was writing her last novel, *Pointz Hall*, later to be published as *Between the Acts* (1941). Reflecting her life, the work is permeated with the almost unbearable tensions of conflictual relationships, of threatening war and destruction, of images and allusions of incest and anger.[1] Leaska speaks of the "extraordinary tonal and metaphoric congruencies" (Woolf 1983, p. 9) between her autobiography and *Pointz Hall*. He adds:

> She began to siphon into her novel emotions which
> seemed to have no other outlet. It is perhaps for this
> reason that so many of the ideas and events of daily
> life became part of the novel before they were permit-
> ted the time necessary to undergo the mysterious
> alchemy of aesthetic transformation. (Woolf 1983, p.
> 4)

As Woolf wrote and rewrote the novel—toning it down and erasing autobiographical details— she must have been aware of the rawness of her fiction and its connections to her own life. In the published version of the novel, Woolf has eliminated or modified passages of openly expressed anger that appear in earlier drafts, in *Pointz Hall*. The revisions point

---

[1]Based on details in *Pointz Hall/Between the Acts*, Alma Halbert Bond makes a strong case for Leonard's infidelity during this period as well as throughout the marriage (1989, pp. 164–168). Given Woolf's psychological and emotional state, such unfaithfulness would have been devastating—and enraging.

directly to areas of conflict and demonstrate Woolf's struggles to contain her anger.

Woolf was reluctant to publish the novel she referred to as "completely worthless" (1980, p. 456) and kept insisting on more revisions. Was she uncomfortable with the book because she revealed too much to her reader and to her self? Or because her anger "tampered" with the "integrity" of the novel? In any case, a central image of the book is unsettling, angry. On the way to the barn in search of Mrs. Manresa "between the acts," Giles comes across a "snake in the grass."

> There, couched in the grass, curled in an olive green ring, was a snake. Dead? No, choked with a toad in its mouth. The snake was unable to swallow; the toad was unable to die. A spasm made the ribs contract; blood oozed. It was birth the wrong way round—a montrous inversion. So, raising his foot, he stamped on them. The mass crushed and slithered. The white canvas on his tennis shoes was bloodstained and sticky. (1941, p. 99)

Woolf's association of snake with anger and of this particular scene with Leonard[2] coupled with age-old associations of snake with killing and/or curing underscore the centrality of this intense affect in Woolf's psychology.

In *Between the Acts*, Miss LaTrobe—who as the author of the village play is a voice for Woolf the writer—produces her pageant based on the history of England. In an attempt to convey her "message," she unsettles the audience with mirrors held up by the actors, and she forces the spectators to see themselves as they really are. But her effort is a failure. Hurt, alone, feeling misunderstood, repressing her anger—she slinks off to the local pub to drown her despair in alcohol.

Even before *Between the Acts* was published, Virginia Woolf—frightened, despairing, and feeling utterly alone—drowned herself in the River Ouse. Emotionally damaged and not consciously aware of her core issues and her own murderous rage, Woolf could not listen to her own truth and act on it. The sense of agency that had enabled Woolf to write and

[2] "'There couched in the grass . . . was a snake' VW recorded in her diary (September 4, 1935) that she and Leonard saw a snake swallowing a toad in the garden at Rodmell. She continues with a description of her dreaming of men committing suicide by means of water" (M. A. Leaska in Woolf 1983, p. 218).

publish was turned against her self. Tragically, she committed a profoundly hostile and unconsciously disobedient act.

# References

Batchelor, J. B. 1971. Feminism in Virginia Woolf. In *Virginia Woolf: A Collection of Critical Essays*, C. Sprague, ed. Englewood Cliffs, N.J.: Prentice-Hall, pp. 169–179.

Bond, A. H. 1989. *Who Killed Virginia Woolf: A Psychobiography*. New York: Human Sciences Press.

DeSalvo, L. 1989. *Virginia Woolf: The Impact of Childhood Sexual Abuse on Her Life and Work*. New York: Ballantine.

Poole, R. 1990. *The Unknown Virginia Woolf*. Atlantic Highlands, N.J.: Humanities Press International.

Trombley, S. 1982. *All That Summer She Was Mad: Virginia Woolf—Female Victim of Male Medicine*. New York: Continuum.

Woolf, L. 1963. *Beginning Again*. New York: Harcourt Brace Jovanovich.

_____. 1968. *The Journey Not the Arrival Matters*. New York: Harcourt Brace Jovanovich.

Woolf, V. 1925. *Mrs. Dalloway*. New York: Harcourt Brace Jovanovich.

_____. 1927. *To the Lighthouse*. New York: Harcourt Brace Jovanovich.

_____. 1929. *A Room of One's Own*. New York: Harcourt Brace Jovanovich.

_____. 1931. Professions for Women. In *Women and Writing*, M. Barrett, ed. New York: Harcourt Brace Jovanovich, pp. 57–63.

_____. 1941. *Between the Acts*. New York: Harcourt Brace Jovanovich.

_____. 1976a. A sketch of the past. In *Moments of Being*, J. Schulkind, ed. New York: Harcourt Brace Jovanovich, pp. 64–159.

_____. 1976b. 22 Hyde Park Gate. In *Moments of Being*, J. Schulkind, ed. New York: Harcourt Brace Jovanovich, pp. 164–177.

_____. 1980. *The Letters of Virginia Woolf*, vol. 6. New York: Harcourt Brace Jovanovich.

_____. 1983. *Pointz Hall*, M. A. Leaska, ed. New York: University Publications.

_____. 1984. *The Diary of Virginia Woolf*, vol. 5. New York: Harcourt Brace Jovanovich.

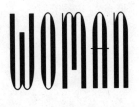

# WOMAN

## *of*

# POWER

—

*Whose Hero Is She, Anyway?*

# Princess of Resolution

## THE EMERGENCE OF AL-AMIRA DHAT AL-HIMMA, A MEDIEVAL ARAB WARRIOR WOMAN

### Wen-chin Ouyang

*Zeus had gotten Metis the Titaness with child and fearing an oracle that it would be a boy child who would depose him, he enticed Metis and swallowed her. But the child continued to grow inside Zeus and eventually he had such terrible headaches that he summoned Hephaistos, the smith, to cleave open his skull with an axe. With a wild battle cry, out leapt Athena, fully armed.*

Hesiod, *Theogony*, 887–902

Since her leap from her father's head, the goddess Athena has rivaled-without threatening-men in leadership. "She is the rescuer from every danger and peril, the advisor for every tight spot, and the highest wisdom. The people's chiefs and leaders as well as the whole people itself, are advised by her; she presides over local, tribal and national gatherings" (Kerenyi 1951, pp. 8–9). Athena, one of the feminine archetypes, is often considered a symbol of intellectual and social creativity, operating on masculine principles. Al-Amira Dhat al-Himma — a fictitious Arab folk heroine — reminds one of Athena in many ways; she was a warrior and wise leader, but in contrast to Athena, she was viewed as a complete woman.[1]

---

[1]Dhat al-Himma does not represent in the Arabic folk tradition the archetype that Athena represents in Greek mythology. Hesoid and Kerenyi's descriptions of Athena, however, conveniently sum up the persona of Dhat al-Himma.

Al-Amira Dhat al-Himma (Princess of Resolution) is the only heroine celebrated in the Arabic folk tradition as the hero of an epic cycle, in
*Sirat al-Amira Dhat al-Himma* (henceforth *Al-sira*)—the longest extant
prose epic cycle in Arabic, running to about seven thousand printed pages.[2]
Arabic folk narrative in general and the epic cycles in particular may be
considered, among other things, the popular rendition of the history of
Arab-Islamic civilization through the history of a specific tribe (Ibrahim
1971, pp. 120–121). That epic cycles may be considered alternative historical narratives finds support in the fact that the term *sira* is used to designate
the narratives—both popular and official—dealing with the life of the
Prophet Muhammad and his companions. *Al-sira* itself documents and
interprets the events of a specific period in Islamic history, namely, the
period extending from the time of the Umayyad 'Abd al-Malik b. Marwan
(ruled 685–705) to the time of the 'Abbasid al-Mu'tasim (ruled 833–842)
through the military adventures of the tribe of Banu Kilab and their participation in the Islamic inroads into the Byzantine Empire.

More important, *Al-sira* records the process of coming to terms
with the radical changes in Arab society initiated by the rise of Islam in the
seventh century. *Al-sira*, like ancient myths and legends, constitutes a conscious manifestation of the collective unconscious (Neumann, 1954, p. vii),
wherein a new system was evolving which would make sense of the manifestation of moral and social values that were coming to govern the human
enterprise. The radical changes imposed on a society with longstanding
values inevitably caused a rebellion in the collective unconscious. Yet inherent in the act of rebellion is also the act of coming to terms with reality. *Al-
sira* is an example of this paradox.

*Sirat Al-Amira Dhat al-Himma* covers the three aspects of the
major transformation in Arab society: the shift from prepatriarchy to patri-

---

[2]"Princess of Resolution" is an idiomatic translation and does not fully
convey the full significance of the term *amira*. The word *amira* (m: *amir*)
functions as an intensive (emphatic) form of the active participle derived
from the roots *a-m-r*, meaning command. *Amir* thus conveys that the
person of the title is a commander, not only a prince.

Reference to more than ten epic cycles in Arabic folk tradition may
be found in classical Arabic sources, but only ten are known to have
survived in texts at the present, with the word *sira* preceding the title of
each. These epic cycles are *Antara b. Shaddad, Dhat al-Himma, Futuh
al-Yaman, al-Hilaliyya, al-Zahir Baybars, Sayf b. Dhi Yazan, Hamza al-
Bahlawan, Firuzshah, Ahmad al-Danaf* and *Ali al-Zaybaq*. As their titles
indicate, the heroes celebrated by these epic cycles are all men except *Dhat
al-Himma,* the lead character of which is a woman.

Quotes from *Sirat al-Amira Dhat al-Himma* throughout this paper
will be based on the text published in 1980.

archy; the emergence of Islam as an all-encompassing system governing the religious, legal, moral, and social values; and the emergence of the Umayyads first and the 'Abbasids second as the political authority of the newly defined Arab nation. These radical changes—requiring rapid psychological adjustments—created chaos in the lives of the people witnessing them and, above all, anxiety in their hearts. The journey of Dhat al-Himma represents the journey of the Arab collective unconscious as it comes to terms with these changes.

At the outset, two interrelated problems come to mind. First, can one identify the precise moment in which human civilization was transformed from prepatriarchy into patriarchy? It is generally recognized that such a transformation was a long process that occurred over several thousand years. Scholars of ancient myths have found evidence to support the notion that there was a period of prepatriarchy, although no one has been able to point to a precise period in which the transformation took place. This observation applies to the development of Arab-Islamic civilization as well. Second, how accurately can the extant "text" of *Al-sira* reflect this transformation, given the fact that it is impossible to identify an "authentic text," in this case because *Al-sira* belongs to a primarily oral tradition and did not possess a "text" until the twentieth century. My contention is, however, that within the structure of the narrative of *Al-sira*, there is evidence of this transformation. In fact, *Al-sira* provides us with a fairly precise timetable of this transformation. Although characteristics of patriarchy were already detectable at the time of the rise of Islam (and here I refer to evidence found in *Sirat 'Antara* which appeared before *Al-sira*), according to *Al-sira,* patriarchy became the dominant structure in the Arab society at the beginning of the eighth century; specifically during the reign of 'Abd al-Malik b. Marwan (ruled 685–705). The transformation from prepatriarchy to patriarchy is revealed in the narrative's depiction of its female characters, their fates, and their position in society.

Although the core content of *Al-sira* is the "heroic" exploits—arranged in chronological order—of Dhat al-Himma and her son 'Abd al-Wahhab in Byzantium in the ninth century, it contains a long prologue—the events of which are also arranged chronologically—in which the genesis of Dhat al-Himma is related. Dhat al-Himma belongs to Banu Kilab, a prominent tribe well known among the Arabs from as early as pre-Islamic times. Among the characters, whether those who bear direct relations to Dhat al-Himma or those who interacted with them, two among several female characters are significant: Qattalat al-Shuj'an (Slayer of Courageous Men) and

Layla bt. ʿAttaf.[3] My choice of these two characters is determined by my understanding from the context of the narrative that they are the two most important female figures prior to the appearance of Dhat al-Himma; considerable space and attention were devoted to them. The difference between the portrayals of these women—especially in view of the order of their appearance—carries the implication that the values associated with the status of women in society, be they moral or social, had undergone major changes resulting in the subordination of the feminine by the masculine. The beginning of *Al-sira* is symbolic of the beginning of the process of transformation. The epic cycle begins with recounting the events that led to the birth of the patriarch of Banu Kilab, Junduba, the great grandfather of Dhat al-Himma. Junduba, the narrative tells us, was born during a raid of an enemy tribe on his own. During the chaos of the raid, his father was killed. His mother, al-Rabab, then nine months pregnant, collected some of her valuables and fled with the help of a "trusted" slave. When they reached the desert, the slave, seduced by her beauty, attempted to rape her immediately after she had given birth. Having failed, he drew his sword, slew her, ran away with her valuables, and abandoned the newly born infant to die (*Al-sira,* 10–14). Junduba, however, was found, adopted, and raised by a prince, and in time he became the leader of Banu Kilab. The birth of the patriarch, represented by Junduba, in this instance seems to be at the expense of the abrupt and violent death of the matriarch, represented by al-Rabab. The plights of the two female characters who appeared after al-Rabab represent yet another stage of the process of suppressing the feminine. Without this background, the rebellion of Dhat al-Himma would not have been significant.

Qattalat al-Shujʿan, a warrior woman, appears fairly early in the narrative. She represents the perfect woman of the Arab heroic age: beautiful, desirable, gallant, and courageous all at the same time. She was the first wife of Junduba. The circumstances of their matrimony are noteworthy. During one of his raids, Junduba came upon a veiled knight (*faris mulaththam*) challenging him to a duel. A battle ensued, Junduba defeated the knight and yanked off the veil (*litham*).[4] Suddenly "a face shining like a full moon" was revealed to him. He took one look at her "beauty and grace," heard her "eloquence," and instantly fell in love. Upon his inquiry of her identity, she related to him her story in "eloquent" verse. Qattalat al-Shujʿan, daughter of a famous Arab warrior from the tribe of Banu Bakr,

---

[3]Other female characters of similar traits exist in *Al-sira*. For the purpose of this paper, however, I will focus on these two examples.

[4]*Litham* is a veil worn by both men and women and functions like a mask to conceal the identity of the wearer.

was brought up as a warrior. Her surpassing beauty and courage made her a desirable mate for many prominent Arab warriors. However, she intended to accept no one but he who was her superior, he who could defeat her in a duel. When suitors clamored for her hand, Qattalat al-Shuj'an, fearing that her father might marry her off to any of them, left the tribal abode with a handful of warriors and took up residence in the desert, where they supported themselves by raiding passing caravans. Now that she was defeated by Junduba, she urged him to seek her father's permission to marry her.

> You captured me and then released me,
> You are my equal, so fulfill my desires.
> Ask for my hand and win me over quickly,
> For I accept you, may peace be upon you. (*Al-sira*, pp. 29–31)

Her forthrightness reveals that the feminine maintained its influence up to this point, for although the narrative is explicit in conveying that Junduba fell in love with Qattalat al-Shuj'an, there is no indication that the idea of marriage crossed his mind. It was Qattalat al-Shuj'an who proposed that he go to her father, led him to their tribal abode, and announced the news to the tribe (32–34). After their marriage, they shared many adventures together.

Their equal partnership ended abruptly, however, and with no warning or structurally justifiable reason; Qattalat al-Shuj'an was killed suddenly. Because of its unexpectedness, the death of Qattalat al-Shuj'an must be examined and interpreted in the light of the broader context of change that was taking place in the emerging new society and consequently in the psyche; for the removal of Qattalat al-Shuj'an — one feminine type — paved the way for the emergence of Layla bt. 'Attaf — a new feminine type. The particulars of the events that led to the killing of Qattalat al-Shuj'an are therefore pertinent.

On one of their adventures, the narrative relates, Junduba and Qattalat al-Shuj'an encountered the would-be Umayyad caliph Hisham b. 'Abd al-Malik b. Marwan. The latter, having fallen in love with Qattalat al-Shuj'an, approached her and proposed an indecent liaison. With his proposition rejected, Hisham — unable to sustain his anger — ambushed Junduba and Qattalat al-Shuj'an, captured Qattalat al-Shuj'an while Junduba was busy fighting, and carried her off to Damascus. When Hisham's various attempts at seducing her failed, he ordered her killed and buried at night. The manner in which Qattalat al-Shuj'an was captured and subsequently killed is significant; whereas earlier in the narrative she was celebrated as a warrior woman constantly on horseback, we learn that she was captured in her camel litter (*hawdhaj*), completely unable to fend for herself (p. 47). Junduba, on the other hand, although tearful and indignant, did nothing.

Rather, he found solace in the arms of another woman, Husna, who was known for her beauty alone (p. 49).

The new feminine type, a glimpse of which may already be seen in Husna, emerged under the shadow of the violence of Qattalat al-Shuj῾an's death. In fact, the emergence of the new feminine type exemplified by Layla bt. ῾Attaf, niece of Junduba and his son al-Sahsah's wife-to-be, could not have been possible without it. Qattalat al-Shuj῾an and Layla bt. ῾Attaf constitute opposite types of femininity. The rise of Layla into prominence in the narrative indicates that the values that shaped and informed the view toward Qattalat al-Shuj῾an were radically altered. The characteristics of a perfect woman as exemplified by Qattalat alShuj῾an — beauty, bravery, and eloquence, and her equality with man in the male–female relationship — were no longer valid by the time Layla appeared. With the emergence of Layla as the model of womanhood in the narrative, a new set of rules governing the relationship between man and woman was also emerging.

In contrast with Qattalat al-Shuj῾an, Layla represented the patriarchal concept of womanhood: she was beautiful but passive and weak, and her relationship with both her father and her cousin al-Sahsah form the basic understanding of the patriarchal male-dominated male–female relationship. The newfound womanhood was enforced by concepts which manifest themselves in social institutions designed to safeguard the domination of patriarchal authority over the feminine. These institutions appear for the first time in this epic cycle in relation to Layla, institutions against which Dhat al-Himma would rebel. These institutions, highlighting the weakness of the female character, underscored the segregation of the sexes — with the idea that woman was the source of dishonor, the domination of the male in male–female relationships, and the reduction of the status of women to that of property.

Unlike her predecessor, Qattalat al-Shuj῾an, Layla's character was completely lacking in resolution; she exhibited neither aspiration nor ability to control her destiny. Whereas Qattalat al-Shuj῾an chose the man she married, Layla expressed no opinion — not to mention will — on her two marriages, first to Hurayth and second to al-Sahsah. In the first instance, she was forced to marry al-Hurayth by her father when the latter heard a rumor of al-Sahsah's death. In the second instance, she was literally rescued from the claws of al-Hurayth and thrown into the arms of al-Sahsah. Despite her love for al-Sahsah, she did not pursue her union with him actively but waited for him to accomplish the task, while she shed many bitter tears during the long wait. Her passivity was even more pronounced when al-Sahsah married another woman; she did nothing but weep. Layla's weakness was not an innate quality but a by-product of a society in which segregation between the sexes, i.e., isolation of women from society, had become the norm. Layla was deprived of access to the outside world and, therefore, deprived of freedom, which in essence meant power to act.

Segregation was a justified social institution, the narrative explicitly states, because women were potential threats to the code of honor. Accordingly, when al-Sahsah turned twelve, his cousin Layla was segregated from him, and for communication, they relied on go-betweens, or secret visits by al-Sahsah to Layla at night when it became necessary (pp. 103, 110, 113). Despite the narrative's emphasis on the chastity of both characters (p. 111), the revelation of these secret visits placed her life—not his—in immediate jeopardy. Her father, under the pretext of preserving his honor, actually pulled out his sword to kill her, only to be dissuaded by his wife, who convinced him that killing Layla would create an even graver scandal in the community.

Honor, in this case, resembles a commodity, the possession of which is desirable and the loss of which is shameful. The transference of honor to a physical entity, women in this case, had further ramifications on the attitude toward women in real life; it shaped the view and dictated patterns of behavior toward women. Women, who represent honor, were thus treated like material property that men guarded jealously. Layla was the victim of this complicated notion of honor, which was manifest on two interrelated levels: that which operated according to the view of the relation between honor and woman (i.e., women as potential threat to honor), and that which functioned on the basis of the relationship between honor and property, leading to a reductive treatment of women; in this case, Layla was considered not more than a valuable piece of property. The tension between Layla's father and al-Sahsah was prompted by their mutal desire to possess Layla. The former's wrath against the latter is otherwise inexplicable, for the young lovers, the narrative tells us, were observant of the honor code. But because Layla was also considered a piece of property, her father's anger and jealousy become understandable; by falling in love with her first cousin, who customarily had the right to marry her, her father was at risk of losing her to his nephew. His anger subsided only when the value of Layla might be redeemed: in exchange for his life when al-Sahsah saved him from being killed; or for a handsome dowry when he agreed to marry Layla off first to al-Hurayth and later to al-Sahsah.

Reducing the status of women to that of property dictated disparity in the male–female relationship. In contrast to the equal relationship between Junduba and Qattalat al-Shuj'an, the relationship between al-Sahsah and Layla was marked by inequality. Layla's passivity toward the men in her life is noted throughout the narrative, but highlighted when, "in awe of him," she refrained from asking al-Sahsah to help her father despite the urgency of the latter's predicament (p. 238), and when she quietly swallowed her humiliation as al-Sahsah took up a second wife, an act that Qattalat al-Shuj'an would not have tolerated.

Layla's relationship with the men in her life—her father and husband—represents the typical male–female relationship in patriarchy.

Within the larger context of the narrative—especially in view of the relationship between Junduba and Qattalat al-Shuj'an—it tells the story of the increasing domination of the masculine over its feminine counterpart. The imbalance caused by such an abrupt shift of power inevitably led to a rebellion of the feminine, a rebellion designed to counter-balance the masculine domination and, paradoxically, to heal the wounds inflicted by this imbalance. The rebellion of Dhat al-Himma must be viewed against the background of her great-grandmother's oppressed existence.[5]

Dhat al-Himma was a born rebel. Although the narrative provides no explicit explanation for her rebellion, a closer examination of the larger context may provide us with some clues. Dhat al-Himma was the great-granddaughter of al-Sahsah from his second wife, Umama. Al-Sahsah's two wives, Layla and Umama, bore him one son each: Zalim (the oppressor) and Mazlum (the oppressed), who shared the control over and wealth of Banu Kilab tribe. The binary oppositions represented by these two brothers may be interpreted to indicate the subordination of the feminine by the masculine, for Mazlum is the progenitor of Dhat al-Himma, whereas Zalim's progeny is al-Harith.

It was under the circumstances of the rule of these two brothers that Dhat al-Himma was born. Like Athena, she was destined for greatness before she was born. Al-sira actually begins after five hundred pages of narrative, for on this page the birth of Dhat al-Himma is recorded. The mention of her birth is accompanied by a prophecy: Dhat al-Himma, pure, righteous, free, and wise, would be the warrior (mujahida) who would defend the shari'a (Islamic law) (p. 500).

The circumstances surrounding her birth are of special interest to the thesis of this paper; they set the stage for the appearance of the hero—in this case the heroine—and constitute the necessary context within which the appearance of the hero would be significant. Dhat al-Himma was born during the time that Zalim and Mazlum were competing for the rule of the house of Kilab. Since they were unable to settle the issue by the sword, they reached an accord: whichever of their wives, who were both pregnant, gave birth to a boy, that father would gain the right to rule. Subsequently, a male infant, al-Harith, was born to Zalim and a female infant, Dhat al-Himma, to Mazlum. Some suggested to Mazlum that he kill his daughter, but Su'da, a slave woman, advised against it. She instead proposed that she tell Zalim that a male infant was born but that he died at birth, and that she bring her

---

[5]Strictly speaking, Layla is not Dhat al-Himma's great-grandmother, for Dhat al-Himma is the granddaughter of al-Sahsah's second wife. However, the fate of Dhat al-Himma's great-grandmother does not differ from that of Layla's.

up as her own. Mazlum agreed to this proposition and the birth of Dhat al-Himma was concealed, which act enabled Mazlum to continue to share the leadership of Banu Kilab with his brother. The concealment of her identity was only the first step in Dhat al-Himma's hero's journey toward self-discovery. Shortly after her birth, she was captured together with Su'da and Marzuq, son of Su'da, by the raiding Banu Tayy, and she grew up in exile, not knowing her own lineage.

Dhat al-Himma's evolution as a hero involved the discovery of both her inner and outer self. The first was completed by her redemption from slavery, and the second by reconciliation with her father. Redemption further required two steps: acquiring the skills needed to do so, in this case martial arts, and actually doing so. For the first step, we learn from the narrative that she took up martial arts at a tender age, and that she was already undefeatable when she was seven (p. 507). As for the second, the actual act of redemption, it was initiated by an act of killing. In repelling the sexual advances of a certain prominent knight, Dhat al-Himma killed Qarih b. Qabus al-Ta'i. Subsequently, his brothers came to al-Harith, her master, demanding revenge or ransom. Although al-Harith paid the ransom to avoid bloodshed, he was outraged at the prospect of being poor and was tempted to punish Dhat al-Himma by killing her. She then offered to take a few warriors and raid other tribes in order to make up for his loss, which she did; she consequently came to be known as Dhat al-Himma. The process in which Dhat al-Himma acquired her name is symbolic of the process of the discovery of her inner self. The narrative makes a reference to the fact that she was known as Dahiya bt. Tayy (death engendered by Tayy) — not a very flattering reflection on her character — when she killed Qarih. However, when she successfully proved her abilities and redeemed herself, the narrative tells us, she came to be known as Dhat al-Himma (she who possesses resolution) — an entirely positive designation.

The process of her reconciliation with her father — the discovery of her outer self — was characterized by danger and surprise. She continuously, although unknowingly, raided her father's properties, which led to their confrontation. After a long and hard duel, she captured her father, chained him, and imprisoned him. While she was preparing to execute him in public, Su'da, Dhat al-Himma's milk mother (wet nurse), caught a glimpse of Mazlum by chance and was able to intervene in time to prevent a tragedy.[6] Dhat al-Himma's reconciliation with her father marked a turning point in

---

[6]In Islam and Arab customs, a milk mother could be anyone who has fed a child her milk. Her relationship to the infant is like that of the mother's, and the relationship of her own children to the infant is like that of siblings. In the case of Dhat al-Himma, Su'da was her milk mother, and

her career as a hero. Reconciliation meant regaining her status as a member of the "free" nobility and provided her actions with legitimacy. Without it, the rebellion of Dhat al-Himma could not have been as easily accepted, for her rebellion was poignantly from within.

The life of Dhat al-Himma is characterized by her rebellion against both the traditional and the newly established moral and social codes. During their captivity, Suʿda, in order to ensure their survival, was willing to do anything her captors requested, even letting Dhat al-Himma serve them as a slave. Dhat al-Himma, at a tender age of no more than seven, vehemently refused. She said (addressing Suʿda): "Be silent, Suʿda! By the covenant of protection of the noble Arabs, and the right of Him who raised the seven heavens, and Him who will resurrect the dead from their graves, I will kill myself by my own hands, for I am neither a slave nor a servant" (p. 506). She was accordingly left alone.

Dhat al-Himma's rebellion extended to encompass all those which form the core of masculine power in patriarchy: the tripartite structure of authority represented by father, husband, and son, a structure that is manifest in the patriarchal moral and social codes as well. Dhat al-Himma's rebellion against her father, husband, and son is tied in with her rebellion against the patriarchal social structure at large, making her rebellion a complex issue.

Dhat al-Himma's relationship with her father, Mazlum, is similar to but at the same time different from Athena's relationship to Zeus. Like Athena, she was first forsaken by her father, but in this case the reason was shame and humiliation (p. 505). After their confrontation, like Athena and Zeus, they ruled together, but the relationship between them was such that she was the leader and he the led. In short, she usurped his authority.

Dhat al-Himma's relationship with al-Harith—her cousin by blood and husband by law—is perhaps the most complex of Dhat al-Himma's relationships with men. In the narrative, we are told that al-Harith was in every way Dhat al-Himma's equal but was repeatedly rejected by her. Her rejections stemmed not from her dislike or disapproval, but from her objection to marriage in general. To her, she was created for a greater cause. She said (addressing her father): "By God, Father, I have no need for a husband. I was created for war not for men. Only my sword, my armor and arms will sleep with me . . . By God, if you force me, I will leave your camp"

hence her son, Marzuq, was her milk brother. By law and custom, Dhat al-Himma and Marzuq were sister and brother and were not allowed to marry, i.e., to have sex. This notion becomes significant when Dhat al-Himma is later accused of committing adultery with Marzuq; in this case, she is accused of commiting two offenses, adultery and incest.

(p. 532). Al-Harith, failing to understand her aspirations and unable to accept her rejection, forced himself upon her. He first manipulated his connection with the caliph, the supreme authority of the Muslim community, and had a marriage contract concluded in the absence of Dhat al-Himma under the supervision of the caliph himself. He then had her drugged and consummated the marriage while she was unconscious. When she came to and realized what had happened, she wanted to kill him, only to be prevented by her father (p. 592). However, she was able to sever all her ties with him, although turning him into her arch enemy, and take away the son they conceived that night. Al-Harith and Dhat al-Himma represent the binary oppositions formed by the masculine and feminine — yang and yin — components of the collective unconscious at a stage of confrontation. Al-Harith, an equal of Dhat al-Himma in every sense, represents the domineering masculine power, while the latter represents the indomitable feminine power. Their confrontation and separation symbolizes the splitting of the feminine from the masculine, a wound that necessarily requires healing.

Dhat al-Himma further defied the third component of the male authority represented by her male son, 'Abd al-Wahhab — a celebrated hero in his own right. In this relationship she remained the authority figure throughout the narrative but was not completely unchallenged.[7] However, when her authority was asserted, she usually came out on top. This is most apparent when 'Abd al-Wahhab attempted to marry against her wishes. To solve their differences, they resorted to a duel, out of which Dhat al-Himma emerged triumphant (Ibrahim 1971, pp. 86–87).

Implicit in her rebellion against the normal male authority figures was Dhat al-Himma's rebellion against the social and moral codes instituted by patriarchy, especially the code of honor, which women were expected to abide by without questioning, since the time of Layla. This was not the case with Dhat al-Himma. When 'Abd al-Wahhab was born, he resembled neither his father nor mother, for while both were light-skinned, 'Abd al-Wahhab was dark. The women who attended the birth, fearing a scandal, advised that 'Abd al-Wahhab be killed. Dhat al-Himma rejected the option and chose instead to conceal the identity of 'Abd alWahhab. When the identity of 'Abd al-Wahhab was discovered, both Zalim and al-Harith accused her of committing adultery with her milk brother Marzuq, and al-Harith demanded that she be punished. While her father weakened, Dhat al-Himma — believing firmly that the truth would eventually triumph —

---

[7]Dhat al-Himma's relationship with 'Abd al-Wahhab is more complex than that of the struggle of power between the masculine and the feminine; it deals with the mother–son relationship as well. However, this issue is beyond the scope of this paper.

refused to yield. Instead, she embarked on a journey to Mecca in search of a genealogist (*shaykh al-qafa*) to determine the true parantage of 'Abd al-Wahhab.[8] In public — and under the intense scrutiny of society — she nevertheless successfully redeemed herself. With this episode behind her, she was able to join the troops of the 'Abbasid Caliph and command an army that was responsible for the Arab-Islamic conquests in Byzantium and the security of the borders.

Dhat al-Himma's defiance of the dominant patriarchy, as manifest in the tripartite structure of male authority and its supporting social and moral codes, tells an incredible story of the feminine power in the psyche. During her trial as a hero, she experienced many betrayals by the men in her life. Her father forsook her at birth, and when her reputation was at stake, he was the first to entertain doubts about her integrity (pp. 599–600, 615). Her milk brother, Marzuq, administered the drug that enabled her rejected husband to rape her (p. 590). Her uncle instigated her husband to demand her punishment, and in the fury of confrontation, he pulled out his sword, attacked her, and inflicted serious wounds upon her (p. 598). Most important, her husband continuously violated her (pp. 598, 599). Against all odds, Dhat al-Himma survived, not only intact as a person but triumphantly to become a hero. She went on to become the supreme leader of Banu Kilab and assured their survival in the volatile climate during the transfer of political authority from the Umayyads to the 'Abbasids.

The emergence of the rebellious Dhat al-Himma as a hero is thus significant; through her heroic acts she embodies the collective unconscious on her journey of self-discovery and self-identity. Paradoxically, Dhat al-Himma represents the healing power of the great mother. When Banu Kilab, supporters of the Umayyads, contemplated opposing the 'Abbasids by force, Dhat al-Himma dissuaded them and prevented their dissension. She united them and successfully brought under the command of the 'Abbasids, leading them to conquests into Byzantium under the flag of Islam. The narrative conveys to us that Dhat al-Himma embodies all the virtues of a good Muslim woman: she devoted her life to the cause of Islam, both on a personal level and a national level; in private, she was devout, and in public, she raised her sword in defense of Islam. This is no coincidence, for Dhat al-Himma symbolizes the compensatory power of the feminine archetype, which enabled the collective unconscious to come to terms with the aforementioned radical changes, including Islam. Once Islam was accepted by the collective unconscious, other issues automatically fell into

[8]A genealogist was a specialist known in pre-Islamic Arabia who determined the genealogy of a person by examining physical traits.

place; cooperation with any political authority as long as it ruled in the name of Islam, be it the Umayyads or the 'Abbasids, became acceptable.

The main events in *Al-sira* occurred during the reign of al-Mu'tasim. This means that the bulk of the story was perhaps composed and told during and after his time. This will place the timeframe of this epic cycle between the end of the ninth century and beginning of the tenth century. This is precisely the period during which Islam established its identity as a civilization.

# References

Hesoid. *Theogony*. In *Hesoid and Theogony*. Dorothy Wender, trans. London: Penguin, 1973.

Ibrahim, Nabila. 1971. *Sirat al-Amira Dhat al-Himma, Dirasa Mugarana*. Cairo: Dar al-Kitab al- 'Arabi li al-Nashr wa al-Tiba'a.

Kerenyi, Carl. 1951. *The Gods of the Greeks*. New York: Thames and Hudson, 1979.

Neumann, Erich 1954. *The Gods of the Greeks*. New York: Thames and Hudson, 1979.

'Ali b. Musa al-Maqanibi, et al., eds. 1980. *Sirat al-Amira Dhat al-Himma*. Beirut: al-Maktaba al-Thaqatiyya.

# FROM COATLICUE TO DOÑA LUZ

## MITOTES IN CHICANA LITERATURE

## Tey Diana Rebolledo

The word for myth in Spanish is *mito*, therefore, *mitote* could be translated as a big or large myth. The word *mitote* itself means riot, uproar, disturbance, or disobedience. The subject of this paper is both myth *and* uproar or disobedience, insofar as Chicana writers use and create mythology to subvert traditional literary discourse and to establish powerful female figures who are able to control their destinies, often against traditional or patriarchal hegemony, as well as to empower women. The archetypes that Chicana writers utilize, or create, in their writings are based on several traditions: the pre-Columbian Mexican tradition; the historical tradition of La Malinche; the Catholic tradition as seen specifically in the Virgin of Guadalupe, the Mexican mestiza virgin; and the folk traditions of La Llorona and the *curandera/bruja*. These images are central to Chicana literature and have undergone various transformations. They are also figures that epitomize the evolutions of the Chicana writers themselves.

Roman Catholicism, with its emphasis on the personal intervention of the Virgin Mary and its cult of *Marianismo* or Mariology (that is, that to emulate the Virgin, one should emulate her characteristics of faith, self-abnegation, motherhood, purity, and passivity), has heavily influenced Hispanic women who look to the intervention of the Virgin in their daily lives. In Mexico, the Virgin of Guadalupe, the first mestiza virgin, with her miraculous appearance to Juan Diego in the early colonial period, is an important symbol. The introduction of the Virgin in an area known to be the sacred worshiping place of an important pre-Columbian Nahuatl goddess, Tonantzín, facilitated the native Mexicans' acceptance of this "Indian" madonna. Moreover, the Virgin of Guadalupe represents the merging of European and Indian culture since she is, in some senses, a transformation or "rebirth" of the native goddesses. Tonantzín is, interestingly enough, an aspect of the great Nahuatl goddess Coatlicue.

> Coatlicue was the strangest goddess of pre-Spanish America. . . . The metaphysical conceptions of death and resurrection which came together in her as the "filtheater" belong to the oldest ideas of mankind . . .

> a temple was erected for her as Tonanzin [sic] (our
> mother), on the site of which there stands today the
> church of the "Virgen de Guadalupe," the patron
> saint of the Mexican Indians. (Anton 1973, p. 58)

Because there is a significant connection between the European, albeit Indianized, madonna and the female Nahuatl deities, we shall discuss the main characteristics of these various deities to see where they differ and where they might coincide. And we will see what aspects of all these important cultural images contemporary Chicana writers define for themselves as significant.

Coatlicue is an extremely complex goddess of many aspects and is considered to be probably the most ancient of the deities (Anton 1973, p. 58). She incorporates aspects of goddess and monster and was threatening as well as beneficent. Another Nahuatl goddess, Tlazolteotl, is the goddess of filth and, as such, is linked to that aspect of Coatlicue. Filth, in the Aztec world as in the Christian world, was symbolic of sin. Tlazolteotl has four phases, related to the four phases of the moon, and in one of these phases, the third, she had the power to cleanse or "forgive" all sin and was thought to be connected with witchcraft.

Thus, significant aspects of the characteristics of Coatlicue (incorporating those of Tonantzín/Tlazolteotl) included the following: goddess of love and of sin, she created and devoured life; as personification of awesome natural forces, she was the monster who devoured the sun at night and brought it to life in the morning. An ageless goddess, she represented beginning and end and was at the same time threatening and beneficent. Coatlicue represents, therefore, all aspects of a dual nature and is a cyclical figure.

The characteristics of *any* of the Catholic Virgins, whatever her aspect may be, would include the following: she was the symbol of purity and freedom from all sin; her central role was as mother of Christ and, therefore, of all Christians; and she had dignity as Queen of Heaven and Earth. She was the helper of the sick, comforter of the afflicted, mother of good counsel, and Queen of Peace. She is also intercessor and "mediatrix" before God, her own son, on behalf of her human children, thus it is mostly *through* her and not *to* her that Catholics pray. The Virgin of Guadalupe, then, is a unilateral figure because she represents only the positive, good, beneficent side of nature, and not the duality.

What becomes clear upon examining these characteristics, is that in the merging of Tonantzín (Coatlicue) and the Virgin of Guadalupe, those characteristics of the Nahuatl deity not acceptable to the Church were dropped: they were considered inappropriate to the virtuous symbolism of a Catholic virgin, mother of God. It was necessary to negate the powerful characteristics of Tonantzín (Coatlicue) in her attributes of judging, creating, and destroying. She was independent, wrathful, competent; her power to create and destroy was autonomous, as was that of most of the Nahuatl deities; it was not a power emanating from a central male figure.

For Chicano culture, the Virgin of Guadalupe represents certain values considered positive for women: unselfish giving, intercession between earth and spirit, and the ideal qualities of motherhood. She is the higher being who can be appealed to on a very personal level. In the intimate relationship the culture has with its saints, there are stories of individuals putting the image of the Virgin in a corner or "punishing" her in some way if she does not perform properly. Many women feel she has much more power that the "official" ascendancy given to her by the Church. For one thing, she is seen as having a mother's hold over her son—that it is not just through him that she derives her power, but that from the respect he has for her, she only has to look at him for him to obey her commands. In her images in Chicano culture she stands alone (without her son), and in her dress she wears the ancient symbols of Tonantzín. The Virgin is the patron saint of the Chicanos and the visual image of contemporary popular culture (as seen in lowrider manifestations). Her image was central to the 1960s strike marches from the grape fields of California to Sacramento when the United Farm Workers walked with two banners, the red and black thunderbird symbol of the UFWA and that of the Virgin of Guadalupe.

Notwithstanding the Virgin's strong image in popular culture, sometimes she is represented in a problematic manner by many Chicana writers, and even—ironically at times—as a symbol of failure. The Virgin is seen often as not active enough, a somewhat passive figure created by the patriarchy, an image giving them mixed messages: how can one be a mother and a virgin, too? How could "Mary 'get around' Jesus to do anything and still be the sweet, gentle handmaid of the Lord?" (Ohanneson 1980, p. 42). She is also often seen as the image of the unattainable. She has failed to intercede politically for her people in the United States; she is powerless—like a traditionally submissive "madrecita mexicana"—and she advocates acceptance and endurance, not action.

If the existing images of the Virgin of Guadalupe, because of their negative connotations, cannot be held out entirely as a progressive image for Chicana writers, how can a strong image, so important to the culture in general, be redeemed as a mythology for contemporary women to live by? Part of the solution has been a circuitous route working around the positive but passive figure of Mary, back to the strengths and power seen in the Nahuatl deities. The writers attempt to incorporate the power and control of these goddesses to the goodness of the Virgin, thereby creating a third, more acceptable cultural heroine: the *curandera* (the healer). The literary route that leads to the mythic image of *curandera* evolves, moreover, through a number of heroines, each of whom contribute particular characteristics, amplifying the wide spectrum of cultural heroines available as literary images.

A directly oppositional figure to that of the Virgin Mary is the Eve/ Lilith figure. If the Virgin is seen as representing the spiritual and positive aspects of women, Eve/Lilith is not only seen as the seductress, temptress of man's flesh and sexuality, but also as incorporating all the power that lies behind passion, energy, and desire (as well as knowledge) (Stevens 1973, pp. 90–101). In Mexican as well as Chicano culture, Eve has been incorporated into the Malinche/La Llorona figure. La Malinche/Malintzín/Doña Marina is the Nahuatl woman of noble birth who was sold into slavery by her family. When she was fourteen, she was given away again, among twenty other women, to Hernán Cortés when he arrived in Mexico. Because she had the ability to speak both Nahuatl and Maya, and because Cortés had in his retinue a Spaniard, Geronimo de Aguilar, who had been shipwrecked on the Yucatan coast and who spoke Spanish and Maya, she was, from the beginning placed in a central role as translator. From there she became Cortés's mistress. Her name became identified with that of the conqueror, and by the twentieth century in Mexico, the word *Malinche* or *Malinchista* became synonymous with a person who betrays her or his country. The historical figure, Malinche, went on to have a child by Cortés, and when Cortés was ordered to bring his Spanish wife to the new world, Malinche was married off to one of his soldiers, don Juan de Jaramillo. Her child by Cortés was sent to Spain to be educated, and Malinche died in relative obscurity at a young age.

The image of *La Llorona*, the weeping woman, brought together both Indian and Spanish folklore and legend. In both cultures, there were prevalent images of women who either had their children murdered, or who murdered or abandoned their children and could not rest thereafter. The lamenting spirit of these women continued to roam forever, appearing to those who rode or walked deserted roads, particularly at crossroads. La Llorona was connected both to Spanish medieval notions of ánimas en pena, spirits in purgatory expiating their sins, and to the Medea myth. She was also closely identified with pre-Columbian Aztec cultural heroines such as *Mocihuaquetzque*, valiant women who died in childbirth. They were the only Aztec women to achieve afterlife in the place of the heroes. These women were venerated by Aztec warriors, who believed that carrying the third finger of the women's left hand into battle would protect them. It was also believed they had supernatural powers and *brujos*, witchdoctors, would try to obtain their hair or their left arms to be used in rites of magic. When they had achieved their afterlife, they were known as *cihuapipiltin* or night ghosts, who lay in wait at crossroads, wished epilepsy on children, and incited men to lewdness. They were also vaguely connected to attributes of Coatlicue, who also at times roamed the crossroads.

The mysterious forces combined in La Llorona, life-giving and death-taking (also, it should be remembered, forces attributed to Tonantzín/Coatlicue) made her the scapegoat of the cause of children's drowning in the Hispanic United States, since she was associated with rivers and ditches as well as crossroads. The images and mythology about La Llorona and La Malinche coalesce in folklore until in many areas in the Southwest they are one and the same woman. In general, the image is a negative one, tied up in a vague way with sexuality and the death or loss of children: the negative mother image. For La Malinche, sexuality is connected to her liaison with Cortés and the subsequent perceived betrayal of her people; in the case of La Llorona, she often appears to young men who are roaming about at night, who believe she is a young girl or beautiful young woman and, as they approach her (with sexual intent in mind), she appears to them as a hag or as death personified. The Chicana writer's response to La Malinche/La Llorona is varied and complex. However, one thing is certain: in their writing, these two figures are almost never confused: the identities of the two remain clear and defined. The relationship of Chicana writers to La Malinche is one which has undergone constant examination and reevaluation since the Chicano Renaissance. The points of identification for these writers seem to arise from the following:

1) La Malinche personifies the Indian women taken by the Spanish conquistador/conqueror — (raped, if you will, by her historical and cultural circumstances). La Malinche herself was the victim of both her family circumstances and historical circumstances. Chicana writers find it difficult to place the symbolic blame of history on a woman who was a victim and not an instigator.

2) La Malinche also stands for the conquest of the Indian race by the European white race, which holds the power and considers itself superior intellectually, socially, culturally. Thus the Indian roots of Chicana culture were for a long time denied as the Mexican-American attempted to assimilate into the dominant culture. The resuscitation of La Malinche as part of the process of *mestizaje* brings her also into the forefront as the symbolic mother of a new race. Recognition of La Malinche as a complex figure with both positive and negative aspects would imply, therefore, integration of these Indian roots.

3) Part of Malinche's historical importance has been her ability to translate for Cortés — thus giving him

knowledge and power over the Indian tribes. History tells us that La Malinche *chose* to aid Cortés, saving his life on more than one occasion. Chicana writers identify with the act of interpretation as they shift consciously from one language to another, from one culture to another. In the power structure, they always have to take into consideration their relation to the dominant culture. Thus, the writer's identification with the act of translation or interpretation and of culture shifting is closely aligned with the figure of La Malinche.

4) Because Malinche was used as an object of sexual desire, she is often portrayed as a whore, standing for the stereotyping of a "lower" culture's (the Indian) sexuality. Lesbian Chicana writers are sometimes portrayed as "Malinches." Cherríe Moraga, for example, equates the limitation of autonomy of the Chicana, part of the "sexual legacy" of the myth of Malintzín, as that of any Chicana who defies tradition (particularly sexual tradition) and is therefore seen as a traitor or a lesbian.

5) Many Chicana writers think of La Malinche as a woman who had and made choices — rather than as the woman so often portrayed as the passive victim of rape and conquest. Because she possessed the power of language and political intuition/knowledge, they see La Malinche as a woman who deliberately chose to be a survivor — a woman who, with a clairvoyant sense, cast her lot with the Spaniards in order to ensure survival of the race — a woman who lives on in every Chicana today. It was often because of her diplomacy and intelligence that a more total annihilation of the Indian tribes of Mexico did not occur. And it is, in her capacity as intercessor and helper, that La Malinche takes on the attributes of the Virgin Mary.

To illustrate the incorporation of La Malinche into contemporary Chicana literature, let us examine two short narrative pieces on La Malinche which are incorporated into recent novels. The first narrative is "The Discourse of La Malinche" in *Puppet* (1985) by Margarita Cota-Cárdenas, the second is a dream sequence found in *Paletitas de Guayaba* (1991) by Erlinda Gonzales-Berry.

In "The Discourse of La Malinche," Margarita Cota-Cárdenas stretches the "dialogue" across history, weaving the speech act of La Malinche into the speech of a teacher at a university, Miss Lencha. La Malinche and Miss Lencha are closely identified by the linguistic word play implicit in their names, as well as symbolically. The structure of the dialogue captures the confusion, ambiguity, and conflicting opinions Chicanos feel about the nature of La Malinche. Closely identified with La Malinche in her traditionally defined aspect of traitor is Chicana feminism. During the early days of the Chicano Renaissance, it was decided at some level that in order to make headway, the group—by means of collective activity—needed to appear unified on all fronts. The women participated, and wanted to participate, equally with the men in the *Movimiento*. Often, however, they found themselves staying home and taking care of the children or in the kitchen in the traditional role of nurturer, preparing food and coffee while the men plotted revolution.

The women who were concerned with women's issues or who dissented in opinion from the males were considered to be traitors, *Malinchistas*. It has taken some time for women's concerns and women's writing to be accepted as legitimate concerns for all Chicanos. Thus, part of the ideological praxis of "The Discourse of La Malinche" is that the maligning of women by old myths, values, and attitudes needs to be re-thought. Cota-Cárdenas, therefore, not only attempts to bring the myth of La Malinche into some realm of personal perspective, but she also provides La Malinche with a personal dialogue by way of explanation of her role in history. Furthermore, she examines the role of the conquistadors in their military as well as religious function, linking them to anyone who imposes an ideology on others, thus linking them also to those Mexican Americans who try to limit other Chicanos (and Chicanas) by forcing a single vision of what being Chicano should be through cultural stigma. The question of the merchandising of ideology is brought into the forefront from the beginning, as La Malinche seeks to distinguish how labels begin.

> Are you Malinche a malinche? Who are you (who am
> I Malinche)? seller or buyer? sold or bought and at
> what price? What is it to be what so many shout say
> sold-out malinchi who is who are we/we what? at
> what price without having been there naming putting
> labels tags what who have bought sold malinchismo
> what other -ismos invented shouted with hate react-
> ing striking like vipers like snakes THEIR EYES like
> snakes what who what. (Cota-Cárdenas 1985, p. 85)

For Cota-Cárdenas, La Malinche is caught between two cultures, a woman caught in the crisis of identity, of her beliefs. The Chicano is also caught between two cultural systems; and the Chicana is then caught between those two and, additionally, between gender differences in Chicano culture. Thus La Malinche become the formative symbol for all Chicanas caught "between two systems in a conflictive state" (ibid.). The only way to survive is to practice a subversive disobedience.

La Malinche has been "labeled" by others from an early age, a labeling that has continued in her historical legacy to the present. Cota-Cárdenas uses humor to underscore this reality.

> Using the latest terminology and it's so useful nowadays, I'm going to tell you about my formative years: at the age of five, more or less, I left off being the favorite eldest daughter of my tribe, when some very immediate relatives sold me, to some more distant buddies, who bought me . . . at what price? I don't know, I only remember that I went kicking that I wanted my mama that why had my papa abandoned me yes yes I went yelling loud too why why and they said tie her up she's too forward too flighty she thinks she's a princess thinks she's her father's daughter thinks she's hot stuff that's it doesn't know her place a real threat to the tribe take her away haul her off she's a menace to our cause that's it only learned to say crazy things to say accuse with HER EYES and they didn't want then troublemakers in their country.
> (Ibid., p. 86)

These labels, specific here to La Malinche, are, of course, the very labels culture uses to restrict and limit women's activity, socially as well as intellectually. The personal vindication of Malinche's version/subversion sets up the dialogue with the patriarchal version (history, myth). The "message" La Malinche brings us is that one must take great care in accepting passively all that is told us by the culture. This action must, of necessity, be disobedience. In the dialogue, Miss Lencha suffers from a paranoia born of centuries of oppression—from a long-silenced sense of oneself—from lack of freedom to express openly what it is to be a woman in a culture that has held up as a role model that "goodness" and nurturing acceptance of the Virgin. The paranoia is expressed in these terms: "You keep being afraid of you don't know what of SOMEONE who wants you to shut up for you not to ask questions not to challenge no to NOOOOOOOOOOOOO and the insomnia with puppet and other signs of the barrio about which you had never through before or much and now that there's no time left" (ibid., p. 89). The acceptance of cultural norms, now critically viewed and questioned, introduces into the writer a sense of outrage at allowing herself and other women to be silenced: "(and this rage started to enter you suppurating and you began to write poetry at all hours and you strike out at everything now)" (ibid., p. 90).

Erlinda Gonzales-Berry, in her novel *Paletitas de Guayaba*, also uses the Malinche prototype to develop cultural ideas about assimilation/ translation. For Gonzales-Berry, La Malinche, who appears to the young heroine Mari (a symbol for Marina) in a dream, is once again a teacher. Mari is a young Chicana traveling by train to Mexico City to study. In an atmosphere rich with sensual descriptions, Mari dreams she is propelled into a capital where the canals of ancient times still reach into the heart of the city. There she meets "La Señora" (a term of respect for La Malinche) who tells her, "How beautiful you are . . . I knew all along that my sin would produce a beautiful and strong race" (Gonzales-Berry 1991, p. 73). Marina takes Mari through a historical discourse prior to the destruction of the great city of Tenochtitlan. She predicts the end of their race as they know it, the Spaniards' lust for power and Aztec leadership's weakness being contributing factors. She also acknowledges that the Spaniards are undergoing a period when their own empire is disintegrating, and the New World will be their salvation. She tells Mari, "We women, we are strong, Mari; our strength comes from the silence imposed upon us by social and legal hands that gag our mouths" (ibid., p. 77). Marina continues by noting she is at the crossroads of a treacherous dilemma. She decided to join Cortés in order to alter the destiny of her people, who otherwise would be on the road to annihilation.

> I use the power of my voice and I offer it to Cortés thus becoming his tongue and his pimp. Yes, the necessary link between his world and ours. My goal is to help him fulfill his imperial designs through discourse and through compromise. I see this as the only means of salvation for our race, for that is what most obsesses me at this critical moment. (Ibid., p. 77)

In her feminist revision of history, Marina, as the voice, expresses her understanding of how women, as oppressed in her time as in the present, finally overcome their silence to speak:

> Look, women in this society, just as they will be in yours, are mere objects, are furniture, are the property, first of their fathers and, later of their husbands. The only honor that is granted to them is sacrifice, but only if they are virgins. Great honor!

> . . . We are relegated to the world of shadow and of
> silence; but that silence gives rise to the word which
> wallows in our own bile becoming rancor and rage,
> but also song; and that word joins another and
> another to become a long and strong chain which
> envelops and strangles us. . . Can you imagine, Mari,
> if each chain of words of every woman of the world
> were to unite, the power that we could generate?
> (Ibid., p. 76)

Most important is the transformation of La Malinche from a silent
figure to one who presents her own dialogue with myth and history. The
rich and complex figure of Marina/Malintzín/La Malinche gives Chicana
writers much area to explore.

Although equally complex for Chicana writers, the figure of La
Llorona is quite different. She approximates in popular folklore all those
ancient Nahuatl deities who had life-giving and life-destroying abilities. La
Llorona is often the "boogie man" of Chicano culture. The haunting of
young children encompasses bad memories of childhood and is, at times,
connected to family violence. As Cordelia Candelaria notes, in "Go 'Way
from My Window, La Llorona":

> You've hounded me beyond belief, scaring
> My childhood away from me, spooking
> My sleep to reels and reels of horror shows. . .
> Married forever in sickness and in sickness
> Til death parts them in sickness
> And in loudness
> at midnight, in beatings and blood
> And weeping children and everyone big
> Drunk and endings of kisses happily forever
> Sickness, befitting the passionate prelude.
> Go!
> follow your babies llorando
> Into the rolling water del rio
> Let them stare you clear-eyed into Hell.
> (Candelaria 1984, p.164)

La Llorona is also symbolic of Chicano culture whose children are
lost because of their assimilation into the dominant culture or because of
violence, prejudice, poverty, neglect, and abuse. La Llorona suffers—she
has lost her children, perhaps through no fault of her own, but she is
condemned to wander endlessly, reminding us constantly of our mortality
and obligations. While La Llorona represents ambiguity, guilt and loss and

inspires fear of the unknown, she is nevertheless part of us—a dark part with which we need to come to terms. Gloria Anzaldúa, in "My Black Angelos," connects La Llorona with "la bruja con las uñas largas," linking her with fearful creatures such as Medusa (wild masses of hair) and evil witches, as fear of this unknown creature "drenches" the lyric speaker:

> she picks the meat stuck between my teeth
> with her snake tongue
> sucks the smoked lint from my lungs
> with her long black nails
> plucks lice from my hair.
> aiiiii aiiiii aiiiiii
> She crawls into my spine
> her eyes opening and closing,
> shining under my skin in the dark
> whirling my bones twirling
> till they're hollow reeds.
> (Anzaldúa 1987, p. 184)

In this poem, La Llorona stalks the speaker, infuses herself into her as finally La Llorona and speaker become one. She will continue to stalk us and to haunt us until we come to terms with her.

More recently Sandra Cisneros, in "Woman Hollering Creek," has used the underlying symbolism of La Llorona to turn the image into a source of strength for the Chicana. In this short story, Cisneros underpins the structure of the narrative with the myth of a woman heard crying at night. A young battered Mexicana wife, aided by several Chicanas who sympathize with her, manages to escape from the restrictive violent atmosphere of her home and return to her family in Mexico. At the moment of her flight, the Chicana who is driving the getaway truck opens her mouth "and let out a yell as loud as any mariachi." She explains, "Every time I cross that bridge I do that. Because of the name, you know. Woman Hollering. Pues, I holler" (Cisneros 1991, p. 55).

For Chicana writers, La Llorona also represents that mourning for lost culture, lost self. Moreover, the search for self, in terms of Nahuatl myths, has also included the redemption, the resumption of the total power held by the Nahuatl female deities—the negative as well as the positive.

Perhaps the most prominent contemporary disobedient feminist hero is the *curandera/partera/*healer who is also the *bruja/*witch. As do most complex symbols, the *curandera/bruja* encodes both positive and negative attributes—attributes judged as such by the individual writer. In general, the *curandera/partera* (curer/midwife) is the positive side—a woman whose life is devoted to healing, curing, helping—again attributes which may be connected to the Virgin Mary. The other side, the *bruja*, is more problematical for the writers, as we shall see, for the *curandera* is always also the witch: that is, she has the power to become one but she may never choose to do so. She is a figure, like that of La Llorona, who emerges from the history and traditions of multiple cultures: the enormous healing knowledge that the Arab culture had brought to Spain, medieval Spanish healing traditions, and Native American traditions of herb women, folk doctors who taught the Spanish arrivals their knowledge. The *curandera* is close to nature, possessing intuitive as well as cognitive skills; she is a powerful figure and is seen throughout Chicano writing, even in the early writers. The fact that the *curandera* has emerged as a powerful figure in the writing of both women and men demonstrates not only her enduring qualities as myth and symbol but also the close identification of the culture to this figure.

The image of the *curandera* as a "seer" is central to Chicano literature. Sandra Cisneros, in *The House on Mango St.*, has the child narrator, Esperanza, come in contract twice with *brujas/curanderas*. The first encounter is with a "witch," Elenita, who has all the trappings of her trade but who, in reality, is only an ordinary healer: she cannot "read" the heroine's future.

The second encounter with "The Three Sisters" yields better results. This time, however, the child is unable to define and decipher the "sisters" or what they tell her. The occasion of the visit is the death of Lucy and Rachael's baby sister, and Esperanza feels strange in the presence of death. The old ladies call her over, give her a stick of gum to make her feel better, and ask her name:

> Esperanza, I said . . .
> Make a wish.
> A wish?
> Yes, make a wish. What do you want?
> Anything? I said.
> Well, why not?
> I closed my eyes.
> Did you wish already.
> Yes, I said.
> Well, that's all there is to it. It'll come true.
> How do you know? I asked.
> We know. We know.
> (Cisneros 1985, p. 97)

Esperanza is given the solution to her destiny by one of the "sisters," even though it will not be until the writing of the book that she understands it. And Cisneros ends the narrative on a mysterious note, encircled by childhood rhymes of ritual and magic: "Then I didn't see them. Not once or twice or ever again" (ibid., p. 98). Of course, the "sisters" have given exactly what Esperanza needs to learn about her life; she can't erase what she knows, she can't forget who she is.

The *curandera* emerges as a powerful figure in Chicano literature because she is disobedient, a woman who has control over her own destiny as well as that of others. Her strength lies in her relationship to the earth and nature—she understands the cycles of development and destruction, thus harking both to the past and to the future. She incorporates intuition and rationality, she studies power and harnesses it, she understands human as well as animal nature, she listens, she takes an active role in her environment. However, and perhaps this is the secret of her attractiveness to the writer, she also has the capacity to fight evil with destruction. She can and does seek vengeance and revenge. She is careful to retaliate only against a particular evil doer and not in general; evil is always dealt with in the particular. The *curandera* is a witch and not a witch. She can control the other world but generally she has chosen to heal. She is both at the center and at the edge. These qualities of the *curandera* can be seen in the poem "Curandera" by Pat Mora:

> They think she lives alone
> on the edge of town in a two-room house
> where she moved when her husband died
> at thirty-five of a gunshot wound
> in the bed of another woman. The curandera
> and house have aged together to the rhythm
> of the desert.
> . . .
> Her days are slow, days of grinding
> dried snake into powder, of crushing
> wild bees to mix with white wine.
> And the townspeople come, hoping
> to be touched by her ointments,
> her hands, her prayers, her eyes.
> She listens to their stories, and she listens
> to the desert, always, to the desert.
> (Mora 1984, p. 26)

Thus, like the Virgin, the *curandera* has the capacity for intervention between earth and spirit, but as a symbol she represents more than the helping, nurturing side. She has the capacity to heal—but like the Nahuatl deities, she also has that capacity for death and destruction. And because she also has those capabilities, she becomes an incredibly powerful figure. This can be seen in "1910" by Mora.

In Mexico they bowed
their heads when she passed.
Timid villagers stepped aside
for the Judge's mother, Doña Luz,
who wore her black shawl, black
gloves whenever she left her home —
at the church, the mercado, and the plaza
in the cool evenings when she strolled
barely touching her son's wrist
with her fingertips,
who wore her black shawl, black
gloves in the carriage that took her
and her family to Juarez, border town, away
from Villa laughing at their terror when
he rode through the village shouting,
spitting dust,
who wore her black shawl, black
gloves when she crossed the Rio Grande to
El Paso, her back straight, chin high,
never watching her feet,
who wore her black shawl, black
gloves into Upton's Five and Dime,
who walked out, back straight, lips quivering,
and slowly removed her shawl and gloves,
placed them on the sidewalk with the other
shawls and shopping bags.
  "You Mexicans can't hide
  things from me," Upton would say.
  "Thieves. All thieves.
  Let me see those hands."
who wore her black shawl, black
gloves the day she walked, chin high,
never watching her feet, on the black
beams and boards; still smoking,
that had been Upton's Five and Dime.
(Mora 1984, p. 31)

In this text, we have the image of the *curandera* all dressed in black and
elevated above the store — walking (or perhaps dancing, flying) on the
beams. Doña Luz (light) is important because she has the ability to react
against evil, seen here in the form of racial prejudice. Mora skillfully juxta-
poses the mythic repetitive image of this woman and the historical placement of her leaving Mexico (the revolution and the date of the poem) with
Upton's dialogue (still a contemporary one): the shameful attitude of "you

Mexicans" as opposed to "us Anglos" and his disgraceful treatment of a respected lady. Doña Luz is able to avenge herself as well as all Mexicanos who are treated in this manner. This is the power of the *curandera/bruja* who circumvents all the passive, helpless figures of "la sufrida madrecita mexicana" and shows what a strong woman is capable of.

One of the most important powers the *curandera/bruja* has is her ability to transform. She can transform the ill into the cured, the straying husband into a faithful one. Using psychology, she can transform people's perception of a situation as well as the situation itself. Mora has written an article where she explains that, for her, writing is a ritual which transforms reality as well as one which attempts to organize and heal. Writing identifies social ills, and self-awareness often leads to a healing process. If the Chicana writer, as well as many Chicanas, feels alienated and fragmented in today's society, writing, self-awareness, and a close connection with one's culture provides a sense of rootedness, unity, and power that duplicates that of the curandera/bruja. Thus, Mora can connect writing with chanting and ritual.

The understanding of the need to accept all aspects, both obedient and disobedient, of our mythology is clearly enunciated by Gloria Anzaldúa, who calls it the "Coatlicue state." Coatlicue, in her great and strange stone representation in the Museum of Anthropology in Mexico City, is shown as a goddess with a skirt of serpents. Anzaldúa links these serpents with her own growing-up experiences with snakes—recognizing that, for her, the serpents (and Coatlicue) have special meaning. "She, the symbol of the dark sexual drive, the chthonic (underworld), the feminine, the serpentine movement of sexuality, or creativity, the basis of all energy and life" (Anzaldúa 1987, p. 35). The Coatlicue state represents deep psychic images of the contradictory. Anzaldúa states that the wound caused by the serpent should be cured by the serpent. And so the Coatlicue state is that state in which the contradictions, the dualities (or multiplicities) are lived with. In an earlier book, *This Bridge Called My Back*, the healing process is more explicitly explained.

> It makes perfect sense to me now how I resisted the act of writing, the commitment to writing. To write is to confront one's demons, look them in the face and live to write about them. Fear acts like a magnet; it draws the demons out of the closet and into the ink in our pens. . . . Writing is dangerous because we are afraid of what the writing reveals: the fears, the angers, the strengths of a woman under triple or quadruple oppression. Yet in that very act lies our survival because a woman who writes has power.

And a woman with power is feared. (Anzaldúa 1981,
p. 71)

The *curandera/bruja* figure incorporates the figure of the Virgin
with those of the pre-Columbian deities in all their attributes. The *bruja/
curandera* is also connected to the figures of Malinche and La Llorona,
thereby in a most powerful way redeeming the Nahuatl dualities and negative and positive aspects of the folk legends—fully incorporating all of the
myths as well as the *mitotes*. In poem after poem, the subversion is repeated
over and over: to become ourselves, in the fullest way possible, one must
integrate the serpents, the negative, the disobedience, and accept the power
of self-knowledge and self-expression that comes with it. It is the power that
comes from this integration of myth, legend, and history that infuses Chicana writing and the Chicana writer.

# References

Anton, F. 1973. *Women in Pre-Columbian America*. New York: Abner-Schram.

Anzaldúa, G. 1981. *This Bridge Called My Back*. C. Moraga and G. Anzaldúa,
eds. New York: Kitchen Table Press.

Anzaldúa, G. 1987. *Borderlands/La Frontera. The New Mestiza*. San Francisco:
Spinsters.

Candelaria, C. 1984. *Ojo de la Cueva*. Colorado Springs: Maize.

Cisneros, S. 1985. *The House on Mango St*. Houston: Arte Público Press.

_____. 1991. *Woman Hollering Creek and Other Stories*. New York: Random
House.

Cota-Cárdenas, M. 1985. *Puppet*. Austin: Relámpago Press Books.

Gonzales-Berry, E. 1991. *Paletitas de Guayaba*. Albuquerque: El Norte
Publications.

Mora, P. 1984. *Chants*. Houston: Arte Público Press.

Ohanneson, J. 1980. *Woman: Survivor in the Church*. Minneapolis: Winston
Press.

Stevens, E. P. 1973. "Marianismo: The other face of machismo. In *Female and
Male in Ibero America*, A. Pescatello, ed. Pittsburgh: University of
Pittsburgh Press.

# Lye Throwers and Lovely Renegades

## THE ROAD FROM BITCH TO HERO
## FOR BLACK WOMEN IN FICTION
## AND POETRY

### Jewelle Gomez

**W**hen I began work on my novel, *The Gilda Stories* (1991), I did research on the development of heroic or mythological characters in fiction. My novel is about Gilda, who escapes from slavery in 1850, and traces her life through the next several centuries. Gilda, you see, becomes a vampire. My idea was to create an independent black woman who interprets our lives through a phenomenal perspective. While the premise falls into the genre of fantasy fiction, the book itself — like all speculative fiction — is really about the human condition: loneliness, love, families, and heroism. In creating a woman figure of larger-than-life proportions, I was looking for the type of character and situation to which the burgeoning aesthetics of feminism had given birth. While speculative fiction has traditionally been dominated by male writers, the women's movement has encouraged a wealth of imaginative and expansive writing. Most of it falls into a kind of nurturer/utopian mold, while only a small portion of it is more traditionally adventure-oriented. But the poetry that has emerged from the women's liberation movement has frequently produced heroic characters or at least those who seek to adhere to a higher ideal than is expected of women.

Where do I find women heroes in a world trapped in the circuitous channels of deconstruction and the smug cynicism of demythologizing. For women, and for black women especially, this question is posed within the context of a history of oppression and the triumphs and failures that attend it. Under this oppression, the same words used to describe a male hero — aggressive, fearless, unyielding — mean "bitch" when applied to a woman. A man who takes the initiative to control his own life, resists the influence of others, and creates his own rules by which to live is applauded. But because of the restricted nature of the roles assigned to women in U.S. culture, there is little approval for a woman who exhibits the same behavior. Young girls are not expected to take to the road, test their mettle, express bravado, or any of the numerous bold options young boys are directed toward. The glory of women has been said to be in learning the rules of society, upholding them, and teaching them to their children. Deviation from those rules is cause for scandal and ostracism. A woman committed to independent action is a bitch, a woman whose frustration has left her devoid of civility and servility.

Afro-American women have lived with two contradictory perceptions: the role of woman has been both assigned and denied. Black women have been encouraged to imitate white female behavior, but at the same time media presentation — film and print — educational materials, employment opportunities, personal interactions all confirm that they could never truly attain womanhood in this culture. They can never be white. The role of "woman" becomes delimited by racial, sexual, and economic exploitation, it can not embody a full range of meaning: pure, worthy of honor, delicate, intuitive, intelligent, strong, tough, kind, etc.

Afro-American literature has contributed to this proscribed sense of who black women are in several ways, first by developing the "passing novels" of the 1920s. These works made a plea for the humanity of blacks by depicting black women of intellect and sensitivity, but their capacities seemed inextricably tied to how easily they could pass for white — in appearance and demeanor. During the period called the Harlem Renaissance, writers such as Jesse Fauset and Nella Larsen deliberately drew their female protagonists as fair-skinned, usually thoughtful, aware of all of the appropriate social behavior and frequently tortured by their need to depart from it. Later literature, fueled by the black power movement of the 1960s, created a precipitous dichotomy. In it, black women were rescued from the precarious emulation of Eurocentric manners and elevated to the pedestal of the African princess. The prime role was now to bear children for her black prince and help give birth to a new African world. The black female experience was removed from the shadow of white society and reconstructed under the shadow of black men.

Emergence from either of these shadows is frequently construed as hostility, uppity behavior, disloyalty, and a number of other descriptions that imply that black women have legitimacy only in relationship to others, either white society or black male society. It was acceptable for black nationalists in the 1960s to say that the only position for black women in the revolution was prone. Any attempt to refute that was and still is viewed as traitorous. One need only remember the recent Supreme Court confirmation hearings in the Senate. Professor Anita Hill's testimony about Judge Clarence Thomas's sexual harrassment was drowned out under his cry of "techno-lynching."

There are several writers who have attempted to shift this balance of power. Many such writers have historically been dismissed or denounced by literary critics. Zora Neale Hurston is a most graphic example of a black woman writer whose accomplishments became fully appreciated only in light of the women's movement of the 1970s. Her personal boldness and refusal to frame the lives of Afro-American women within the parameters of genteelness left her unappreciated for many years after the work she did during the Harlem Renaissance.

Gwendolyn Brooks, widely respected for her poetry, won the Pulitzer Prize in 1950 but was ignored or disparaged when her first novel, *Maud Martha*, appeared in 1953, the same year that James Baldwin's *Go Tell It on the Mountain* was published. The book's intensity and social realism was startling to some, a welcome relief to others more in tune with the actual role of women in African American society. This work returned to what Barbara Christian (1985) has described as the "complex existence of the ordinary, dark-skinned woman, who is neither an upper-class matron committed to an ideal of woman that few could attain . . . nor a downtrodden victim, totally at the mercy of a hostile society."

A number of other writers have found this "complex existence" a fertile ground for their work. For Alexis DeVeaux, a poet and playwright, the title of one of her plays, *No* and its subtitle, "A Necessary Weapon," explicates her place in the literary tradition. It is that ability to say "no" and make one's own path that is the groundwork for heroism for black women. There are some mythic figures in U.S. literature that break the molds and deliver the heroic characters that black women hunger to see in literature: Toni Morrison's Pilate in *Song of Solomon*, Alice Walker's Shug Avery in *The Color Purple*, and Audre Lorde in her "biomythography" *Zami: A New Spelling of My Name*. The world that Afro-American women characters inhabit has yet to grow large enough to accommodate their complex existence. Neither naturalistic nor fantasy writing has offered enough space where Afro-American women can be hero rather than "bitch." Yet both types of fiction, as well as poetry, offer places where women might throw off traditional expectations and plant the seeds of legend.

In the 1970s, the same movement that focused a spotlight on the work of Zora Neale Hurston, the women's movement, also generated a spurt of fantasy fiction written by women. This work was a departure from the style, which is generally dominated by men, and created a new tradition of women-centered fantasy writing. As I read and reread some of this fiction, I discovered that black women characters of heroic dimensions were almost impossible to find. Where are black women writers like Marion Zimmer Bradley, Alice Sheldon, or Joanna Russ? What is our *Wanderground*? Who is our *Woman on the Edge of Time*? Such an absence seemed impossible. America lives on icons, idealized figures who represent our intellectual and emotional fantasies. We all grew up with them, from Captain Video to Wonder Woman. Rock stars and cartoon characters provide the subconscious guide to society for almost every American regardless of race or socioeconomic status.

Could it be that black women were somehow lacking in either epic experience or mythological substance? Is that why none seem to exist in the pantheon of icons of our youth? If that were not true, why do we not have fantasy fiction writers and black women heroes? And finally, is it at all important that they exist?

That black women could be incapable of historic, heroic behavior seemed unlikely. We need only look as far as Sojourner Truth, clearly a larger-than-life figure in our history, who might have served as a model for mythic interpretation. But perhaps this history was too immediate. The exploits of the recent century and a half are familiar and might not, in our minds, lend themselves to fantasy fiction yet.

But ancient African civilization certainly yields numerous mythic figures, both real and imagined. As Runoko Rashidi points out in an essay on African goddesses (Van Sertima 1935), the advent of Islam destroyed evidence of many goddesses of early Africa but those who did survive are at least the equal of goddesses of other cultures. Many of the European goddesses have even been suspected of being patterned directly after African foremothers like Neith, worshipped in 4000 B.C. as the self-begotten mother of all who mated with the wind, or Hathor, the moon goddess and guardian of the Nile Delta. She was the giver of joy to all humankind as well as the guardian of the dead. Isis, the dominant goddess of Egypt, was worshipped even through Roman domination. Her relentless pursuit of the murderers of her husband culminates in a virgin birth of a child who ultimately avenges the husband's death. Each of these are figures who do not remain within the bounds that have, of late, surrounded the idea of womanhood. They have cast off rules and are certainly the stuff of heroic fantasy.

Historical fact is, as it has been reputed to be, at least as wild as fiction. The list of African warrior queens make the comic book Superfriends look like Yale preppies on holiday in Ft. Lauderdale. These women were not the romantic black queens idealized by the male-focused poets of the black arts movement in the 1960s. They may, indeed, have filled the above description but they also fit what Marie Linton-Umeh describes as an African woman hero: "One whose outstanding and admirable achievements are divers, and one who can be defined as having leading roles assigned to her because her superior gifts of body and mind. And who possesses a number of qualities that most members of the community lack . . . and acknowledge" (Van Sertima 1935, p. 135).

Some of the warrior queens of Africa have been immortalized by history. The queen of Ethiopia (960 B.C.), Makeda, was so mythologized that her title became synonymous with regal supremacy: the Queen of Sheba. In addition to her famed love for King Solomon, for whom she endured a legendary journey to learn his wisdom, she was also known as one of the greatest diplomats of her time. Cleopatra (87 B.C.), whose name entered history as a trademark for beauty, has been painted as a lurid pursuer of Roman bed partners when, in fact, her political and sexual alliances (aside from being fun) were made to serve Egypt. Her suicide was not a result of a broken heart but the act of an Egyptian nationalist who could not bear the loss of control of her country.

Nzingha, of what became Angola, formed alliances with the Dutch to rout the Portuguese slave traders and commanded a body of Dutch soldiers in 1646 and an army of women. She was called by her other generals, "a cunning and prudent virago so much addicted to arms that she hardly uses other excerises and so generously valiant that she never hurt a Portuguese after quarter was given and commanded all her servants and soldiers to do the same" (Van Sertima 1935, p. 129). She was a charismatic leader who regularly addressed her legions personally and prompted the desertion of thousands of slaves who were enlisted in the Portuguese army. She was named queen at the age of forty-one because she was a shrewd military strategist and charming diplomat. She and her tribe were fierce enough to form a human chain to prevent the docking of Portuguese slavers.

African history has provided the role models for an expansion of our concept of who can be a hero, but few of us have taken a cue. When this store of wealth has been exploited, it has generally been by white male writers who deracinate the history of Dahomean Amazons and turn them into Wonder Woman and Queen Hera. It is clear that the history of African women has many epic figures for those of us interested in the fantasy genre. But why have so few black women writers been intrigued by either this genre or this history? The possible reasons are numerous.

Until the broad-based civil rights movement, the middle passage and enslavement were the most significant metaphorical (and real) events in African-American history. Their far-reaching effects on society have yet to be fully explored by anyone, former slave or former slave owner. But one of the distinct legacies of that most peculiar institution was a perversion of the African-American sense of worth in our own culture and a sometimes prosaic proscription of how literature functions. We have been trapped in the metaphor of slavery and its immediate social and economic ramifications, and we are at a loss as to how to extrapolate an independent future.

Over the years, the scope of black women characters has expanded to include the now-familiar roster of mammy, sex kitten, slut, long-suffering survivor or victim, matriarch, and bitch. While the matriarchal or independent characters (Eva Peace, Nanny, Shug Avery, Pilate) have provided what might be termed heroic figures, it is, interestingly enough, the last character, the bitch, who comes closest to being mythic.

European American heroism is predicated on male dominance, usually exemplified by some deed which serves to rescue the female object of his affection as a metaphor for wresting society from the grip of evil. But for the African-American woman, this kind of romanticism is antithetical to our heroism. We have as frequently had to be the rescuer as the rescued in this society. Romantic heroism implies that women must be deferential and dependent, abdicating our responsibility to perform personally or politically mythic deeds. We must be appendages of men, complimentary and symbolic of their heroism.

And, to take it a step further, concurring with Barbara Christian's analysis in her book on black feminist criticism:

> the stereotypic qualities associated with lesbian women: self-assertiveness, strength, independence, eroticism, a fighting spirit, are the very qualities associated with us [meaning black women in general], qualities that we have often suffered for and been made to feel guilty about because they are supposedly "manly" rather than "feminine" qualities . . . . 1985, p. 200)

This type of black woman character is for me, close to mythic because, unlike the traditional female figures, even those black women who are strong survivors, the "bitch" is the center of her own world. She controls her life and will stop at little to achieve her goals. Such a character is Cleo Judson in Dorothy West's *The Living Is Easy*, originally published in 1948. In the story, Cleo, born of modest means, is majestic, disdainful, self-centered. She schemes to outwit everyone, including her husband, and wrings profits from whomever she can. She is self-preservation run amok. Yet, in spite of these extremes or maybe because of them, Cleo is one of the most compelling characters in our literary history. She is self-aware in a fanatical way. And it is the underlying knowledge of society's lack of room for her independence that turns her aspirations to bitter machinations. Cleo is barely able to contain her feelings of exclusion and disenfranchisement: "Cleo felt a sharp distaste at the surge and clangor around her that made her pause at every storefront where a man might come charging out of a doorway to brush aside any women or children who stood in the path of commerce. Here in the market was all the maleness of men. This was their world in which they moved without the command of women. . . . Curses ran lightly over their lips, wonderful expressive words that Cleo stored in the back of her head" (West 1948, p. 70)

As I read, I sit in amazement at the cleverness and ruthlessness of each deed, often hoping against hope that Cleo will repent and do something for "the greater good." Instead, she rewrites rent receipts in order to pocket $20 every time her husband pays the landlord, deliberately turns her sisters against her stepmother in a plot to persuade them to come live with her, and perpetually upbraids her daughter and her darker-skinned husband for not living up to her standards. And although she, unlike Scarlet O'Hara (another great "bitch" figure), never does "do the right thing," the character has resonance certainly worthy of her name.

Although her mythic deeds are largely negative, Cleo lives as a quintessential, larger-than-life character. Her refusal to stay within her established role as black woman necessitates her use of deviousness and callous self-interest because she can see no other way to disobey.

The acute nature of the need to break the rules of behavior in order to live as a whole person is not confined to African-Americans but will be manifest in most African women living in Eurocentric circumstances. Barbara Burford, a black women of Caribbean descent living in England, writes of this need repeatedly in her collection of short stories, *The Threshing Floor* (1989). The transition from being an ordinary black bitch to becoming a black hero is not simply a turning of a corner, it is a leap. And the first step toward that precipitous leap is the simple act of disobedience. Just as slaves learned that to live as human they had to be creatively disobeident, so, too, have black women had to reexamine their relationship to accepted behavior.

In Burford's stories, the leaps are relatively modest breaks with the subtle expectations that routinely oppress women rather than the complex strategies executed by Cleo Judson. In one story, "Pinstripe Summer," Dorothy, a mature secretary, reaches past her narrow-minded white boss and the fear of technology to embrace the advent of the computer age. At the same time, she makes a new friend of the younger black woman who comes to teach her about computers. Parallel to this awakening is Dorothy's growing obsession with a mysterious grove that she passes every day on the commuter train to work. She eventually gains personal strength because of her new confidence at work, and it inspires her to leave the train before her stop in order to explore the alien landscape of trees and brush that has beckoned to her. As she climbs through the brambles, she repeats what she calls "the dreadful repressive litanies of her upbringing": "Ladies do not wear trousers. Ladies do not ride bicycles. Ladies do not cross their legs." Dorothy remembers all the admonitions as she promises herself a pair of slacks. It is a simple act of rebellion for a black woman accustomed to trying to fit into white society. Burford's perspective, that of being black in Britain, helps her construct this powerful need to break with tradition in a way not too dissimiliar from Cleo Judson's. The differences are the period in history, Dorothy's connection to other independent women, and the options these elements offer.

Each of Burford's characters is trying to take that first step. In one story, a little girl rebels against being told she is fat and clumsy by white teachers by learning to fly. In the title story, a woman recovering from the death of her white lover learns to make a place for herself in the white village in which they'd lived. Each character must break with demands or expectations and find their own way to individuality. And, in many cases, that break must be harsh or, as with the child who learns to fly, extraordinary. Burford writes in a very naturalistic way but frequently uses fantastic or surrealistic elements to point toward the path of independence. This element, a natural part of any Afrocentric culture, gives Burford's characters the space to surpass the limitations presented them without resorting to pure trickery.

In any African-based culture, there will always be one figure with the potential for that mythic status, the conjure woman. She has been explored tangentially in African-American literature on occasion. Several stories by Alice Walker (1973) and others use the conjure woman as an otherworldly force whose magical capabilities are both fearful and awe-inspiring. But the conjure woman has not yet become a staple in the lexicon of fantasy fiction. Marie Le Veau, the leading practitioner of voudun in New Orleans and in this country, remains a mythic prototype awaiting the birth of her progeny. As a figure of such majestic disavowal of female roles, it is not unexpected that little written material is available from traditional information sources. Additionally, the figures of the conjure woman and Marie Le Veau represent a rebellion not only against their designated roles as women but also as departures from the tradition of Christianity, an uneasy position even today.

And, of course, the previously noted demand (whether explicit or implicit) that art serve politics is a further consequence of that history. The unwieldy figure of the conjure woman and discomforting reality of Marie Le Veau do not make good servants. Ironically, as we serve politics our writing is also reflecting politics. The sexism in our society is also sexism in our creative thinking.

The inability to see ourselves as the center of anything, even our own lives, has in one sense allowed black women to be the backbones of black communities, but it has also limited our perspective of the world and that of our literary critics. In the July/August 1985 issue of *The Black Scholar*, Calvin Hernton described the scurrilous attack mounted against Ntozake Shange after the production of her play, also described as a choreopoem, *For Colored Girls Who Have Considered Suicide When the Rainbow Is Enuf*. She was called man-hating, a rip-off, and a pawn of white people in the destruction of black malehood. However, what was really infuriating to her critics was not that her poems libeled black men (they did not), but that men were not central figures in them. Some critics pointed to the poem "Beau Willie Brown" (a dramatic depiction of a black man driven to madness and infanticide by poverty, lack of education, and his experiences in Vietnam) as a subversive assault on black men. In doing so, they conveniently ignored the loving portraits Shange drew of other black men, such as artists like Oliver Lake, Willie Colon, Archie Shepp, and Hector Lavoe. They also completely dismissed her touching tribute to Toussaint L'Overture, in which the little girl who narrates asserts Toussaint "waz the beginnin uv reality for me . . ." (Shange 1981, p. 27).

This poem and others show Shange's intricate weaving of black history and black family into her own liberation as a woman. The real scandal to her detractors (and to those of Alice Walker's *The Color Purple* a decade later) was that most of her poems were not really about men at all, but an exploration of female commonality. While men may have been present, the black woman's experience was the center at all times, a departure, a heroic stance, not commonly accepted in black women. And where black men do exhibit negative behavior in the poems, the response of black women is never passive or accepting, but rather angry and disappointed.

In his article, Hernton locates the real source of disturbance for the many black dissenters — a black woman writer's declaration of autonomy and refusal to adhere to the tradition of making black female feelings and concerns secondary to those of black men. He acknowledges what black women writers who participate in feminist and lesbian publishing have known all along: "The literature of contemporary black women is a dialectical composite of the unknown coming out of the known. It is an upheaval in form, style and landscape. It is the negation of the negative and it profers a vision of unfettered human possibility" (1987 p. 58).

This vision of "unfettered human possibility" is, indeed, what fantasy fiction is all about, and, by virtue of its form as well as its content, this is also true of contemporary poetry. Poetry, with its inherent epic quality and expectation of the other-than-ordinary movement and emotion, is a ready base for the leap that women need to make. To be heroic or mythic within that context, women in general, and black women specifically, need the ability to be part of the survival of a community in the manner we choose, but at the same time, keep one eye turned toward our own survival as black women. This requires a clarity about responsibility not only to the whole but to the visionary possibilities of the individual. Two pieces of fiction by black writers, Octavia Butler and Michelle Parkerson, began to open up this vision for me. These writers eschew the centuries-old idea (as Barbara Christian points out) which dictates that heroism for women consists largely of being physically beautiful and overtly compliant.

In Butler's 1979 novel, *Kindred*, the primary character, Dana (a black woman) mysteriously and literally vanishes from her modern urban home to reappear on a nineteenth-century plantation in time to save the life of the plantation owner's son, who is drowning. Repeatedly, she is drawn involuntarily into the past to save the life of the white boy, who soon becomes a man. She learns that his survival is key to the birth of an ancestor of her's, giving the rescues their dramatic glue. Dana becomes an inexplicable fixture, reappearing over the years on the plantation, providing the slaves with a magical, legendary character. Throughout the story, Dana is distinguished by her refusal to react in any traditionally prescribed way. She consistently responds to physical danger with acuity as well as strength. She uses logic and cunning, relying only on certainties, including her own intuition. She never casts others in the role of her protector.

Of course, part of Dana's strength comes from the knowledge that there is another century to which she can return when the correct conditions exist that allow her to travel in time. She is unbowed by the punitive conditions of slavery to some extent because escape awaits her more easily than the others. But her assertiveness and wisdom are part of her personality in both worlds. As if to truly challenge Dana, the author has given her several patriarchal figures to overcome: her husband, a young white writer who, in spite of his sensitivity, is perpetually naive and has no real idea of what this experience does to his wife, physically and psychologically. There is also the petulant boy who grows into a egocentric and cruel slave owner, and the boy's father who remains confounded by Dana's bewitching appearances and dangerously limited by his ignorance.

On Dana's final summoning to save the boy from a drunken accident, it is clear what sort of dissolute wastrel he has become, yet her response continues to be humane as long as he remembers her humanity. When he assaults her and attempts to rape her, she kills him with little compunction. It is not an act of cruelty but survival, cleanly done, leaving her with sadness at the taking of life but no disavowal of her right to protect herself. There is no stereotypical shrinking or shrieking, no abdication of responsibility for her own life. This is a mythic hero, traditional in her direct response to personal and social danger yet "feminine" in her refusal to disengage her emotions from the actions.

The author is admirable in her ability to avoid the idealized concepts of heroism in her writing. Dana acknowledges her emotional needs but is not paralyzed by them. The author does not create an idyllic interracial marriage or overly sympathetic husband. Dana, the hero, acts out of both the ordinary and the extraordinary.

The second story, by Michelle Parkerson, is very short, entitled "Odds and Ends, a New Amazon Fable," and appears in her collection of poetry and prose, *Waiting Rooms* (1983). Set in 2036 while a war is raging, it exists almost as a snapshot of two women warriors, Loz and Sephra, who are lovers.

In this short story, Parkerson extrapolates the future from our violent past. "The race wars of earth escalated to cosmic insurrection. Colored peoples everywhere had taken enough and took up arms" (p. 7). The warriors here are women sustaining a pitched battle against invasion and trying to maintain some semblance of personal life.

The world at war is a traditional format for creating heroic figures, although the segregation of the sexes has left women out of that picture except as nurses. Here, Loz is a "reluctant warrior" who lingers in the love of her sister warrior. After returning from a three-day pass, such love keeps her "dancing or killing, when all else fails" (p. 6). Parkerson uses her skills as a poet to make the colors of love and war vibrate for us throughout the story. She turns the familiar into mythology: the seventh sector is demarcated by Squeak's Bar-B-Q and Miss Edna's Curla Palace. And the warriors are not Rambo but women whose concern for each other is shown not just in their military responsibility but in personalized interdependence.

As described by Parkerson, Loz's lover, Sephra, is the "last in a notorious line of lye throwers and lovely renegades" (p. 8). Although the scent of love is still fresh when the vandals break through the lines and overrun her base camp, Sephra loses no time springing into action. Sentiment is encapsulated in her final note to Loz: "I am a child of dread, born of veiled face and master number / a sable eye full of Loz and Armageddon . . ." (p. 10). Her message of love is transmitted while she detonates the grenade which breaks the ranks of the enemy and ends her life. Sephra takes her place as a true descendent of Cleopatra and Nzingha.

Here, just as the "bitch" makes her own existence the center of her life, the hero makes survival of the whole an extension of herself, the center of her being, not financial security, not men, not approval, not any of the things that traditionally relegate black women to the uncomfortable balance on the pedestal or to the rearguard vantage point of the kitchen.

Having learned that such women heroes can exist, is it at all important for us to look for or create them in our fiction? It's not an accident that at moments of political upheaval, fantasy or science fiction writing has taken on a greater resonance for the public. George Orwell's *1984* was the fruit of post–World War Two devastation and the bloodcurdling reality of the atom bomb. During the turbulence of the civil rights and antiwar movements of the 1960s, fantasy fiction again regained popularity (*Stranger in a Strange Land*, the *Foundation* series) as those hoping to destroy oppressive traditions looked to the future for utopian visions. The women's movement has spawned a healthy body of fantasy fiction work, replacing the images of passive victims and strident agitators with shrewd warriors and hopeful women activists.

A great many of these have been lesbian characters, rich with the "stereotyped" qualities that Christian described: "fighting spirit, strength, eroticism" (1985, p. 200). All black women hunger for that vision of independent heroics. It has more often been supplied by our poets. Writers like Alexis Deveaux (1985), Colleen J. McElroy (1984), and Cheryl Clarke (1983, 1986) embrace the mythic forms and characters in their poetry. Clarke, like Shange a decade before, has explored the many roads women take away from their ordained paths. In one poem, "Living as a Lesbian Underground: A Futuristic Fantasy," she creates lesbian as hero by casting her as a twenty-first-century resistance fighter. But her revolutionary is admonished not to "get caught sleeping with / your shoes off / while women are forced back to the shelter / of homicidal husbands . . ." and above all to "Leave signs of struggle / Leave signs of triumph" (1986, p. 76). The woman's global struggle is to triumph over the mundane horrors women face every day.

In a more naturalistic poem, "Althea and Flaxie," Clarke reshapes the frequently disparaged butch/fem couple into a heroic vision of black womanhood that stands bowed before no one: "In 1943 Althea was a welder / very dark / very butch / and very proud / loved to cook, sew, and drive a car / and didn't care who knew she kept company with a woman . . ." (1983, p. 15). The poem celebrates thirty years of union between two women whose survival flew directly in the face of social convention. As a lesbian, Clarke begins her writing from a place of rebellion against the established heterosexual order. She then goes an additional step by having the characters in her narrative poems insist upon their independence and disaffection with pretense. They are the stuff myths are made of simply by virtue of their insistence on being.

It is important that our mythic figures exist because ideas do affect experience and theory can affect practice. If we can create a root system, a path to our independent action from our internal and integral sources of power, we can make ourselves the center of our universe, if only in our fantasies. We can then change the way in which we view ourselves in this society.

The heroes and mythology that women create can be different from that which is currently familiar to us. The stories and poems that extol the leap women make from dependent to individual are inevitably grounded in the ordinary things that make up all of our lives. And they are always tied to a sense of community. This is the place where heroic change can begin.

The surrealists believed that in order to change the world you had to first change your dreams. The women writers who develop characters of mythic proportions are doing just that. The vampire character I've created in *The Gilda Stories* dreams of a place where death is a part of the natural order of life but not the prevailing currency with which power is acquired as it is now in our nuclear age.

Gilda dreams of a time when the lovers she takes and the brothers she keeps are bound together by mutual respect and need and an expansive concept of progress. I chose to make my black woman hero a vampire for several reasons: no one would understand the cycles intrinsic to vampire mythology of blood and life (rather than blood and death) more than a woman. It was important to link our survival as a people with the power of our humanity rather than brutal force. Unlike myths in which the "monster" disconnects from others completely, the vampire myth hinges on the interdependence of mortal and immortal. Additionally, I wanted a character who had lived intimately with the horrors of our past and still had the capacity to dream grandly of our triumph.

Critics have often neglected to scrutinize fantasy or science fiction or place it within the context of literary and social constructs. But the genre, like any other popular art form, is very intimately related to the sensibilities of the broad-based populace. Poetry, despite its seeming exclusive academic position in contemporary society, is truly a populist oral art form and has provided a forum for rebellious voices for many social movements. Both genres offer a place for women to leave behind the social strictures that bind them to archaic roles. Where women have dared to create heros in either fiction or poetry, they have provided a barometer of our secret fears and secret dreams. And we, as women, should be acutely aware of just how powerful dreams can be.

# References

Baldwin, James. 1953. *Go Tell It on the Mountain*. New York: Dial Press.

Brooks, Gwendolyn. 1953. *Maude Martha*. New York: Harper and Row.

Burford, Barbara. 1989. *The Threshing Floor*. Ithaca, NY: Firebrand Books.

Butler, Octavia. 1979. *Kindred*. New York: Pocket Books.

Christian, Barbara. 1985. *Black Feminist Criticism*. New York: Pergammon Press.

Clarke, Cheryl. 1983. *Narratives, Poems in the Tradition of Black Women*. Latham, N.Y.: Kitchen Table Press.

_____. 1986. *Living as a Lesbian*. Ithaca, N.Y.: Firebrand Books.

DeVeaux, Alexis. 1985. *Blue Heat*. Brooklyn, N.Y.: Diva Publishing.

Gearheart, Sally Miller. 1979. *Wanderground*. Boston: Alyson Publications.

Gomez, Jewelle. 1991. *The Gilda Stories*. Ithaca, N.Y.: Firebrand Books.

Hernton, Calvin. 1987. *The Sexual Mountain and Black Women Writers*. New York: Doubleday.

Lorde, Audre. 1982. *Zami: A New Spelling of My Name*. Watertown, Mass.: Persephone Press.

McElroy, Colleen J. 1984. *Queen of the Ebony Isles*. Wesleyan, Conn. Wesleyan University Press.

Morrison, Toni. 1977. *Song of Solomon*. New York: Alfred A. Knopf.

Parkerson, Michelle. 1983. *Waiting Rooms*. Washington, D.C.: Common Ground Press.

Piercy, Marge. 1976. *Woman on the Edge of Time*. New York: Alfred A. Knopf.

Shange, Ntozake. 1981. *For Colored Girls Who Have Considered Suicide When the Rainbow Is Enuf*. New York: Bantam Books.

Van Sertima, Ivan. 1935. *Black Women in Antiquity*. New Brunswick, N.J.: Transaction Books.

Walker, Alice. 1973. *In Love and Trouble*. New York: Harcourt, Brace, Jovanovich.

_____. 1982. *The Color Purple*. New York: Harcourt, Brace, Jovanovich.

West, Dorothy. 1948. *The Living Is Easy*. New York: Feminist Press, 1982.

# FORBIDDEN WORDS—ENCHANTING SONG

## THE TREATMENT OF DELILAH IN LITERATURE AND MUSIC

### Elaine Hoffman Baruch

The treatments of Delilah in literature and music are so varied as to make her almost unrecognizable from one work to another. In Judges, she is a variant of the nameless woman from Timnath, who was Samson's first and only wife. The biblical Delilah is a victim of her countrymen and perhaps her own greed (the Philistine lords offer her eleven hundred pieces of silver apiece for Samson's secret). In Milton's *Samson Agonistes* (1671), she is Samson's second wife—we hear nothing from the first—who, despite her betrayal, might just love Samson, as she claims. In Handel's oratorio, *Samson* (1741), whose libretto was based primarily on *Samson Agonistes*, Delila's love is emphasized still more—although it is possible that she is here more a lover of pleasure than of Samson. Disobedient to her husband in Milton and Handel, she can be seen as a hero to her people, a Judith or a Jael—with this difference: she is less deadly.

In Voltaire's *livret*, *Samson* (1732), written for an opera by Rameau now lost to us, she is all for love, a priestess of Venus who knows nothing of political duplicity. Her obedience to the High Priest of Dagon leads to her self-betrayal as well as to the betrayal of Samson. She does not forgive herself for what she has done to him unknowingly. In Saint-Saëns's *Samson et Dalila* (1877), Dalila makes the most passionate claims for love of all Delilahs but professes to hate Samson both before and after doing so. She achieves her expressed desire to enchain him through seduction but in so doing may be acting against her deepest impulses.

"In our culture," writes Mieke Bal, "the story of Samson and Delilah is the paradigmatic case of woman's wickedness. The combination of seduction, unfaithfulness, and treason is an unavoidable and fatal one" (1987, p. 38). But this is not Voltaire's reading of Dalila. Even in the other versions, Delilah's possible innocence or at least ambivalence provides a powerful subtext or theme. On some level, we want to find her not guilty.

In all of these works, it is primarily the speaking or singing voice rather than beauty or sexuality that causes Samson's downfall. Yet, in the literary works, Delilah is more faulted for her lack of silence than in the musical ones. Opera is one genre where the woman cannot be silenced. Granted there are those critics like Catherine Clément (1988) who feel that she is almost always purposely silenced by her death at the end. But where love is primary, even the semblance of it, woman's voice is in the ascendency, and opera is the genre of love par excellence. Since opera has more access to the unconscious than mere literary statement, it is not surprising that a woman's voice, even her lies, should be more accepted there, perhaps because music often obscures the libretto and even works against it.

In the Bible, it is Delilah's words that wear down Samson, that cause him to betray himself as well as God. At first, he eludes her. But when she keeps charging him with not loving her, he weakens. "And it came to pass, when she pressed him daily with her words, and urged him, *so* that his soul was vexed unto death: That he told her all his heart . . ." (Judges 16). Three times before, he told Delilah a lie about the source of his strength, and three times she tried to have him bound. But this "Hercules" never learns. One can only assume that the biblical hero wants to reveal his secret, that he does not want the burden of greatness. Still, is he so different from other men? Polly Eisendrath and Florence L. Wiedemann write, "The voice of female insistence is stereotypically characterized as attacking the freedom of men to be independent and rational . . . . Women's anger, aggression and fear are pejoratively described as engulfing and overwhelming, impossible for men to understand and manage" (1987, p. 44). And impossible for them to resist, we might add. Jung suggests another reason — or rationalization — for male response to women's words: "it should be remarked that emptiness is a great feminine secret. The pitifulness of this vacuous nonentity goes to his heart . . . ." (1982, p. 127, par. 183). Perhaps saying to a man, " you don't love me," as Delilah does, arouses pity for this "emptiness."

In *Samson Agonistes,* Samson marries Dalila although there is no evidence for this conjugal union in the Bible. Marriage makes Dalila's betrayal more heinous and allows Milton to speak about the need for women's subjection within the marriage bond, a subjection that Dalila rejects. Samson's marriage to the woman from Timnath is attributed to God's will in the Bible. In *Samson Agonistes*, Samson claims that God impelled this second marriage also. But Joseph Wittreich, in *Feminist Milton* (1987), believes that Milton wonders whether Samson "is compelled from without or within, by divine command or private nature" (p. 124). Milton's Samson has a mind as well as a body. So does his Dalila. If she did not argue so well, if she were not so persuasive, Samson would perhaps not have succumbed. We know this best from her arguments designed to win him back, since all of the action of *Samson Agonistes* takes place after Samson's fall, and after

Dalila's also, if one considers her to have been duped by the Philistines, which is one way of reading the text.

In *Samson Agonistes*, most of Samson's complaints about Dalila have to do with language, that is, with a woman who did not remain silent. The one battlefield on which Samson is not a conquering hero is the linguistic one. Dalila *vanquished* Samson with a *peal* of words. He gave up his *fort* of silence to a woman (ll. 235–236). Three times he says he resisted her but not the fourth:

> . . .when, mustering all her wiles,
> With blandished parleys, feminine assaults,
> Tongue-batteries, she surceased not day nor night
> To storm me. . . . (ll. 402–405)

Here the traditionally playful imagery of love as a kind of war is transformed into something deadly serious.

Have women in patriarchy been enjoined to be silent because men are so susceptible to their voices? It is through the voice that the mother seduces us into life, claims psychoanalyst Joyce McDougall (1988, p. 78). "On the negative side the mother archetype may connote anything secret, hidden, dark; the abyss, the world of the dead, anything that devours, seduces, and poisons, that is terrifying and inescapable like fate" (Jung 1982, p. 110, par. 158). As Wittreich points out, there is no mother in *Samson Agonistes* (nor is one referred to in Saint-Saëns's *Samson et Dalila*). That is, Samson's father, Manoa, has no wife. But there is a negative mother, Dalila, echo of the mother who betrayed all of us, our own, in that she was more faithful to another. That first betrayal prefigures all later ones.

Milton's chorus equates verbal falsity with sexual infidelity. For them, Dalila is "that fallacious bride, unclean, unchaste" (ll.320–321). The woman who speaks too much, who gives away secrets, is likely to give her body away also. (Samson, too, speaks of the "fair fallacious looks" (l.533) of this "deceitful concubine" (l. 537)). The obedient woman must contain her speech as well as her flesh, for poisonous words are not so far from poisonous sexuality. The mouth and the words it utters are both themselves and something else. They can represent a displacement upwards. In clinical practice, as well as widespread folktales, the vagina is seen as a mouth with teeth in it, capable of destoying a man's most precious organ, divesting him of his strength (Lederer 1968). Dalila disarms Samson through her most potent weapon, words. In fact, all use of language represents disobedience on the part of woman in the phallologocentric order except that which is controlled by the man who is supposed to control her.

The phobic fear of a woman's voice and words echoes through the Bible. Proverbs reads: "For the lips of a strange woman drop as a honeycomb, and her mouth is smoother than oil; But her end is bitter as worm-wood, sharp as a two-edged sword" (Prov. 5:3–4). If sometimes the fear expressed is of the *vagina dentata*, at others it is of being swallowed up, engulfed in the mother's womb. "The mouth of strange women is a deep pit: he that is abhorred of the Lord shall fall therein" (Prov. 22:14).

Although traditionally it is the man who can be more prodigal with both his words and body, in Samson's case he who gave both away too freely is subject to blindness. Like Oedipus, Samson married across pro-scribed boundaries. Furthermore, Samson's flaw was to "talk" too much, like a woman. Samson sees his displaced castration as a feminization. Like Creon, another member of the family of Oedipus, the greatest shame for Samson is to be "effeminately vanquished." It is in his helpless state that Milton's Dalila begs to take him back — to her house. Whether out of love, as she says, or for further revenge, as Samson argues, is ambiguous. (She does not want him in the Bible or in Saint-Saëns.) Samson refuses her offer, accounting it worse than toiling in blind enslavement for the Philistines. As John Guillory points out, "his most terrible punishment would be confine-ment to the 'household' " (1986, p. 109). Guillory sees work in the seven-teenth century as a conflict between public and private labor, Dalila's sexu-ality representing the private sphere. "Seduction by the female means really what seduces the male away from the public vocation, means really seduc-tion by the domestic realm itself" (p. 116).

Samson hates himself most because he betrayed God's secret to that lowliest of creatures, a woman, the creature he has become most like. He does not even grant that Dalila has the power of language but rather calls her a hyena (l. 748), an animal that only imitates human speech.

Although language may have been most important in Samson's vanquishing, Dalila's appearance, too, like words, like the sexual act, played its part. Of course, appearance is a form of language also, the silent but potent language of the body. The chorus describes Dalila, when she appears and Samson can no longer see her, in images of exotic and therefore corrupt artifice, reminiscent of Shakespeare's Cleopatra; further reified, she is less than human, a ship, worse, an *it*. It should be remembered, however, that Old Testament standards of beauty were far different from later Christian ones and condoned the use of heavy makeup, perfume, and ornamentation. Perhaps Milton is purposely drawing on this tradition to increase the ambiguity of his treatment of Dalila.

> But who is this? what *thing* of sea or land —
> Female of sex it seems —
> That so bedecked, ornate, and gay,
> Comes this way sailing,
> Like a stately ship
> of Tarsus (lines 710–715)

It is in this scene, too, that Samson calls her a hyena and a "poisonous bosom-snake" (l. 763). Her connection with water, with serpents, aligns her with sirens that destroy but also entice.

Yet, on the human level, she says, credibly enough, that she came back out of love, that she did what she did out of jealousy, that she wanted to know the secret of Samson's strength the better to keep his love. After all, he had wandered before. She did not know that her revealing his secret would have such dire results. She just wanted him to be *her* prisoner, not that of the Philistines. In this sense, she sounds like the lady in the "Joy of the Court" episode in Chrétien de Troie's medieval romance *Erec et Enide*, who exacted a promise from her lover to stay in an enclosed garden for fear he would leave her otherwise. Guillory's explanation can be used to justify Dalila's behavior for Milton's period. "Just as Samson's failure can be expressed as the failure of his public life, Dalila's self-defense can be expressed as the complaint of the housewife, the complaint of the private world against the public" (1986, p. 110).

Furthermore, this Dalila denies that she betrayed Samson for money. There is no reason for us to doubt her. But she, too, succumbed to the power of words, she says. In this regard, husband and wife are alike. All the civil and legal authorities came, "solicited, commanded, threatened, urged" (l. 852). As William Empson pointed out a long time ago, Milton's Dalila would be a far less interesting character if we did not believe it possible that she is telling the truth. But the problem is that this Dalila has too many arguments. When she gets only a negative response from Samson—he accuses her of lust, not love—she salvages her narcissism by asserting that fame is "double-mouthed" (l. 971). She will be acclaimed in her own country, if not loved by him. Like wise men, she put public over private good, she claims in the climax of her reasons for betraying him. In doing so, she inverted "the gender assignments of the very discourse she is calling to her aid," says Guillory (1986, p. 111). This is not entirely the case, even in biblical times, however. In acting like a man, in speaking for *her* "public good" (l. 867), Dalila ceases to be a woman for Samson but becomes a hero for the Philistines. A woman's speech is an act of disobedience or heroism, depending on which side she is on. The worshippers of Dagon allow Dalila entrance into the symbolic realm of language, the realm marked by the phallus, according to Lacan, perhaps because she did what they wanted her to do. One might also argue that the Philistines gave more equality to women than did the patriarchal Hebrews.

It was Elizabeth Tollet, in the eighteenth century, an "all-but-forgotten poetess who gave Handel the original inspiration for his greatest oratorio" writes Robert Myers (1956, p. 62), in rather antiquated terms for the mid-twentieth century. In her poem addressed "To Mr. Handell," she urged him to tell how though "invincible in Force and Mind," "the *Hebrew* Champion fell" "to the fatal Fraud of Womankind" (p. 63). No defender of free speech she—or of women. Handel obeyed. Still Delilah in some ways has more freedom in song than in speech, more freedom to be human in the oratorio and the later opera than in literature or the Bible, perhaps because, as I have indicated, there is more emphasis on love in librettos than in the literary works they come from—even when that love is deemed to be false. Of course, if we consider love to be a misogynistic institution, constructed by men to keep women in their place—a thesis I contest in my book *Women, Love, and Power* (1991)—we would say that women are even more subordinate in music than elsewhere.

In Handel's oratorio *Samson*, Delila sings a love song to Samson, with references to turtledoves *ad nauseam*. These words come not from *Samson Agonistes* but from Handel's librettist, Newburgh Hamilton; they are salvaged by Handel's magnificent music. We might ask why inane words are often disregarded in opera and other musical genres. One reason is that music invites us to regress; if the music is sufficiently powerful emotionally, we are brought back to the realm of the preoedipal in which language *is* highly repetitive and often nonsensical. It is the function of language as intermediary to the mother's body that is then all-important.

Even if we accept the sincerity of Delila's turtledove song, however, its credibility is undercut by her call to *carpe noctem* afterwards, in an aria which claims that not to seize pleasure is the greatest sin, a philosophy not only against the biblical but also counter to Milton's Protestant creed and the place of the wife within it as inspiration for her husband's good works.

But Handel's Delila gets no further than Milton's in trying to recover love (if indeed that is truly what she wants) from Samson. An anonymous review written in 1763 said of the duet "Traitor/Traitress to love" in Handel's *Samson*: It is "a musical scolding match, but is very unpolite and very unnatural. It is certainly very rude to a lady to interrupt her in almost every note; and *Samson* sings a whole strain, after she has left off; whereas *Delilah*, both as a *woman*, and a *wife*, ought doubtless, in propriety, to have had the last word" (Myers 1956, p. 73). A little dig at women's lack of silence no doubt.

It is not virtue that women want in men, lament the chorus in *Samson Agonistes* and Micha in Handel's oratorio (as if men make wise choices in women, as if Samson did). They accuse women of narcissism: "so much self-love does rule the sex, they nothing can love long" (Handel 1741, p. 148). How much anger, hurt, and sense of rejection is voiced here. Whatever else he is, Milton's and Handel's Samson is a victim of wounded narcissism, like Saint-Saëns's Dalila later.

A very different Dalila from Milton's and Handel's appears in Voltaire's libretto *Samson*, written for Rameau. Girdlestone notes that, at first, Voltaire wanted to realize his dream of writing a tragedy without love, in which Dalila would be a type of Judith. But then he feared that most of the audience—the part that wasn't complaining about the work's impiety—

would be disheartened by seeing love treated only as seduction in the theater, where it is always treated as a virtue (Girdlestone 1972, pp. 274–275). Here we see that the audience figured prominently in Voltaire's conception of Dalila and became, in a sense, her partial creator (similarly, the great singer Pauline Viardot influenced Saint-Saëns's conception of Dalila later). Voltaire wrote Mme du Chatelet that he would make an honest woman of Dalila (Girdlestone 1966, p. 136). He does more than that. He transforms her from a follower of Dagon into the grand priestess of Venus. Like Dido with Aeneas, Dalila falls deeply in love with Samson. Unlike in Milton, there is no ambiguity in Voltaire on this point. Dalila's law is tenderness, her duty is to love. Her reason for uncovering Samson's secret is completely different from that in the other versions: it is the condition under which the high priest will allow her to marry the man she loves. Discover the secret of his invincible force so that we can have a peaceful future, urges her leader. Dalila believes him. Her motives are noble, but Voltaire does not want us to take her too seriously. For him, even a good Dalila is dispensable. Voltaire has her commit suicide after she realizes that she has betrayed Samson and therefore herself. It is Voltaire who betrays her most: like Freud two centuries later, in *Civilization and Its Discontents* (1930, p. 103), he accuses her—or, at least, love—of destroying virtue and culture (1732, p. 543). But mainly, Voltaire gets rid of Dalila so that she will not distract us from what he considers more important: Samson.

Yet, ultimately, it was Voltaire the librettist who played the role of the seduced and abandoned heroine in relation to his *Samson*. Never was he to hear his beloved work at the opera, for Rameau lost interest in it. Although he wrote the music for the *livret*, it was never published, and we are left longing, like Voltaire, for those lost chords, those siren songs.

In Saint-Saëns's *Samson et Dalila* (1877), as in Voltaire, we see why Samson succumbed, for the major part of the action occurs before his fall, and Dalila is central here. This Dalila, like Voltaire's, sings of peace and beauty in an extremely effective libretto (by Ferdinand Lemaire), but she does so to betray, not for money, as in the biblical account, but ostensibly for a higher purpose: her people and religion. She is a fascinating character in that she both represents and goes against the "orientalism" of the worshippers of Dagon. (See Locke (1991) for a brilliant discussion of orientalism in *Samson et Dalila*.) In this way, Saint-Saëns can both eroticize *and* ennoble her.

Opera has recently been faulted for betraying women, not just by killing them off but by strengthening gender stereotypes. In *Samson et Dalila*, the characters reveal an opposition between male and female, which we would expect, but strikingly enough for the nineteenth century, with its pervasive theme of the seduction and betrayal of women, it is Samson who acts like the traditional female and Dalila who exhibits the characteristics of the traditional male. He is passive and vulnerable. She is dominant and controlling. He is the one who is seduced and abandoned, by a woman if not by God.

In the composer's opposition between Eastern paganism and Judaic monotheism, our expectations are also reversed. It is the monotheistic male who is enticed by exotic sensuality, while the philistine Dalila uses the body only for what her people see as a moral purpose: the destruction of their enemy. Perhaps most surprising, her passionate love song ("Mon coeur s'ouvre a ta voix") is not a love song at all but ostensibly a total fabrication of feeling. Yet many operagoers are as ravished as Samson is by her utterances of love. Perhaps they, too, are seduced and betrayed. It is in this way that Saint-Saëns can present a multifaceted Dalila: a sorceress who enchants and a purposeful political figure at the same time.

The "stink" of chromaticism that Clément (1988, pp. 56-58) finds so characteristic of women in opera is more the province of Samson than of Dalila here. Perhaps she is not a victim and is able to retain her power over him precisely because she only simulates loves. Still, there *is* love on Dalila's part, the strongest kind: self-love. She desires to be loved for her own sake, not because she loves Samson. What purer love could there be? An early critic, Emile Baumann, says Dalila's great love song, "Mon coeur s'ouvre a ta voix," becomes a kind of hymn to the flesh in which Dalila deifies herself (1905, p. 415). But Dalila is also keenly aware of Samson's narcissistic longings and plays on them.

In *Feminine Endings,* her study of "music, gender, and sexuality," Susan McClary has written, "Perhaps if erotic impulses were valued as positive—if, in other words, arousal were not a pretext for anti-woman hysteria—the whole repertory would be radically different . . ." (1991, p. 68). Perhaps, too, the characterization—if not the music for Dalila—would have been different in Saint-Saëns. In his famous bacchanale of the third act, with its persistent drum beats recalling the composer's sojourns in Africa, where the stark beauty of nature overwhelmed him, what Saint-Saëns reveals is the despotic power of sex. McClary doesn't recognize this power in any of her analyses. Some feminist theorists try to whitewash sexuality the way they try to "pasteurize" the unconscious (Baruch and Serrano 1988, p. 8). But we cannot get rid of the darker elements of either.

The psychiatrist Eric A. Plaut writes that Samson's need for the forbidden woman "reveals the fragility of his potency, for he is dependent on the seductiveness of the woman" (1989, p. 134). The hero would thus seem to illustrate Freud's (1912) theory of the need to degrade the sexual object. I have argued elsewhere that the splitting of the sexual object into bad/sexual and good/tender is far more prevalent in men than in women (Baruch 1991). Plaut, however, believes that both Saint-Saëns's Samson and his Dalila make a split between sex and love—within the same object, claiming that Dalila expresses her hostile sexuality visually and her loving sexuality auditorally.

Is Plaut right? Does Dalila feel love for Samson? Does the music allow us to hear Dalila's interiority, a passion which belies her words? In speaking of Wagner's *Ring*, Carolyn Abbate writes that musical voices of narration may contradict the text—or seem to affirm its meaning. "But whether thus 'polyphonic' or 'monologic,' do these voices ring true?" (1991, p. 170). The question applies to *Samson et Dalila* also. Dalila denies the truth of both words and music in her love song to Samson. To accept this disclaimer is to reduce her behavior to worse than seduction and abandonment, for unlike the typical male seducer, she does not even have the excuse of believing what she says—or sings—for a moment.

But how do we know that she isn't lying about her lying? I would argue that she does feel love for Samson but that she cannot accept this love, so she transforms it into extreme hatred. I don't think that it is her ideology alone that causes this. Rather, it is narcissism and rage. (In this she is like Milton's Samson.) She cannot tolerate what seemed like a rejection on Samson's part when he disappeared earlier, preferring the joys of arms to the joys of her arms. It is power that Dalila wants, power over men. She is even competitive with the high priest—granted that he urges her on by voicing doubts about Samson's love—boasting that only she can conquer Samson, which indeed is the case.

Dalila in Saint-Saëns's opera is no tool, no victim of either a lover or her people. She is a woman alone like Carmen, and unlike the biblical Delilah, lives on a mountaintop, like Venus, and is dependent on no man. On the level of myth, Saint-Saëns's Dalila (and to some extent Milton's as well) is a siren. She enchants through singing and wants to seduce only in order to destroy, and she does this through the voice. The fact that Dalila is a mezzo like Carmen bodes no good for the hero. Dominique Pavesi (1987) has pointed out the correlation of gender, voice, and intentionality. In opera, only sopranos are pure, innocent.

As psychoanalyst François Duparc has said of the nereids, Dalila represents the narcissistic aspect of feminine seduction (the frustrating mother). Like Amphitrite and Thetis, she does not want to return the love of the male who wants her (Duparc 1986, p. 709), or so she says. But this, I think, is because she denies her love. In this sense, she may betray herself most of all.

Samson is susceptible to her in part because she represents the power of the forbidden idea as well as the power of forbidden sex. Certainly he is in rebellion against the Father. Through her, he is searching for the lost maternal voice and for his own lost femininity. Furthermore, Dalila's voice is invested as an object of the drive and becomes a substitute for the lost imaginary phallus of the mother.

Insofar as Dalila is sexually desiring, she represents the forbidden mother. Since she also possesses language and a voice, she is all that the culture condemns and at the same time is fascinated by in woman. But since she is subject as well as symbol, her disobedience—and ours—in one register becomes freedom in another. It is this complexity of Delilah that has spoken to creators through the centuries.

# References

Abbate, C. 1991. *Unsung Voices: Opera and Musical Narrative in the Nineteenth Century.* Princeton, N.J.: Princeton University Press.

Bal, M. 1987. *Lethal Love: Feminist Literary Readings of Biblical Love Stories.* Bloomington, Ind.: Indiana University Press.

Baruch, E. H. 1991. On splitting the sexual object: Before and after Freud. In *Women, Love, and Power: Literary and Psychoanalytic Perspectives.* New York: New York University Press, pp. 103–121.

Baruch, E. H., and Serrano, L. J. 1988. *Women Analyze Women: In France, England, and the United States.* New York: New York University Press.

Baumann, E. 1905. *Les Grandes Formes de la musique: l'oeuvre de Camille Saint-Saëns.* 2nd ed. Paris: Société d'éditions littéraires et artistiques.

Clément, C. 1988. *Opera, or the Undoing of Women.* Betsy Wing, trans. Minneapolis: The University of Minnesota Press.

Duparc, F. 1986. La Peur des sirènes. *Revue française de psychanalyse* 2:709–725.

Eisendrath, P., and Wiedemann, F. L. 1987. *Female Authority: Empowering Women Through Psychotherapy.* New York: Guilford Press.

Freud, S. 1912. On the universal tendency to debasement in the sphere of love. *S.E.,* vol. 11. London: Hogarth.

_____. 1930. *Civilization and Its Discontents. S.E.,* vol. 21. London: Hogarth.

Girdlestone, C. 1966. Voltaire, Rameau et *Samson.* In *La Vie musicale en France sous les rois Bourbons.* 2. série: Recherches sur la musique française classique, 133–143.

_____. 1972. *Le Tragedie en musique (1673–1750) considerée comme genre littéraire.* Geneve: Librairie Droz.

Guillory, J. 1986. Dalila's house: *Samson Agonistes* and the sexual division of labor. In *Rewriting the Renaissance: The Discourses of Sexual Difference in Early Modern Europe,* M. W. Ferguson and N. J. Vickers, eds. Chicago: University of Chicago Press, pp. 106–122.

Handel, G. F. 1741. *Samson: An Oratorio with German-English Text.* Melville, N.Y.: Belwin Mills Publishing Corp.

Jung, C. G. 1982. *Aspects of the Feminine: From the Collected Works of C. G. Jung.* Princeton, N.J.: Princeton University Press.

Lederer, W. 1968. *The Fear of Women.* Orlando, Fla.: Grune and Stratton.

Locke, R. P. 1991. Constructing the oriental "other": Saint Saëns's *Samson et Dalila. The Cambridge Opera Journal* 3:67–108.

McClary, S. 1991. *Feminine Endings: Music, Gender, and Sexuality.* Minneapolis: University of Minnesota Press.

McDougall, J. 1988. Interview. In *Women Analyze Women: In France, England, and the United States,* Elaine Hoffman Baruch and Lucienne Serrano. New York: New York University Press.

Myers, R. 1956. *Handel, Dryden, and Milton.* London: Bowes and Bowes.

Milton, J. 1671. *Samson Agonistes.* In *The Norton Anthology of English Literature,* M. H. Abrams, et al., eds. New York: Norton, 1979.

Pavesi, Dominique. 1987. La symbolique des voix. *Littérature et opéra: Colloque de Cerisy, 1985,* Textes recueillis par P.H. Berthier et K. Ringger. Grenoble: Presses Universitaires de Grenoble.

Plaut, E. A. 1989. Saint-Saëns's *Samson et Delilah:* 3,000 years of blinding guilt. *Medical Problems of Performing Artists* 4:131–135.

Saint-Saëns, C. 1877 . *Samson et Dalila.* New York: G. Schirmer, 1964.

Voltaire. 1732. Samson, opéra en cinq actes. In *Oeuvres complètes de Voltaire,* vol. 2. Paris: Lefevre, Libraire, rue de l'Eperon, 1817.

Wittreich, J. 1987. *Feminist Milton.* Ithaca, N.Y.: Cornell University Press.

# NOTES ON CONTRIBUTORS

**Lila Abu-Lughod** received her Ph.D. from Harvard University; she is an associate professor in anthropology at New York University. She tries to return to Egypt as often as she can, and two of her books, *Veiled Sentiments: Honor and Sentiment in a Bedouin Society* (1986) and *Writing Women's Worlds: Bedouin Stories* (forthcoming from University of California Press) were based on her experiences with the Bedouin community described in her article. From 1987 to 1988, she was a member of the Institute for Advanced Studies, Princeton, when the seminar theme was gender. Her current studies have taken her away from conventional anthropological concerns, such as oral poetry and narrative, to studies of the role of Egyptian television soap operas in constructing national, class, and gender identities in contemporary Egypt.

**Teresa Anderson** is a poet and freelance writer living in Jersey City, New Jersey. She was born during an April blizzard in Hays, Kansas, and raised in Ohio, Indiana, and Oklahoma. Since 1976, she has worked as a writer-in-residence in Oklahoma, Texas, Minnesota, New Jersey, and New York. Her preference for the conviction, passion, and luminous imagery of Latin American poets led her to translate Pablo Neruda's last book of poetry, *A Call for the Destruction of Nixon* (1980). Other publications include *Speaking in Sign*, a book of her own poetry, and numerous poems and short stories in magazines and anthologies. She is currently at work on a translation of Marta Traba's last novel, *En Cualquier Lugar*.

**Jane Foress Bennett** is an associate professor of women's studies at Barnard College, New York, where she currently teaches courses in feminist theory and history. She grew up in Zimbabwe, which taught her about the way powerful "norms" hide their violence; professionally, she is trained as a linguist and has taught courses in Western literature and the political history of languages at the University of Cape Town and the State University of New York (Old Westbury). Her doctoral work involves the noetics of rape stories, and she has worked for several years as a rape crisis counselor.

**Elaine Hoffman Baruch**, who has a Ph.D. in English and comparative literature from Columbia University, is a professor of English and women's studies at York College of the City University of New York. She is the author of *Women, Love and Power: Literary and Psychoanalytic Perspectives* (1991), the coauthor with Lucienne Serrano of *Women Analyze Women: In France, England, and the United States* (1988), and the coeditor of and a contributor to *Women in Search of Utopia* and *Embryos, Ethics* *and Women's Rights: Exploring the New Reproductive Technologies.* Her current project is on literature, librettos, and music: women in French nineteenth-century opera.

**Fan Pen Chen** was born in Taiwan and raised in Libya from the age of nine through sixteen. She moved to Seattle for high school and then studied at Yale and Columbia, where she received her B.A. and Ph.D., respectively. She teaches East Asian history and studies, as well as the history of women in East Asia, at the University of Calgary in Alberta, Canada.

**Miriam Cooke** teaches Arabic at Duke University, where she is the director of Asian and African languages and literature. Her research focus is in Arab women's writings on war, and she has published *War's Other Voices: Women Writers on the Lebanese Civil War* (1988). Her extensive publications on modern Arabic literature also include *The Anatomy of an Egyptian Intellectual: Yahya Haqqi* (1984) and *Opening the Gates: 100 Years of Arab Feminist Writing* with Margot Badran (1990). She is an American scholar who received her doctorate from Oxford University.

**Marjolijn de Jager** was born in Indonesia, raised in the Netherlands, and came to the United States in 1958. She holds a Ph.D. in romance languages (French) and literatures from the University of North Carolina, Chapel Hill. She has taught French and translated literature ever since she arrived in the United States, first in an attempt to introduce her native Dutch literature to the American reading public (whose interest proved to be minimal). For the past several years, to a more enthusiastic response, she has been concentrating on francophone African literature (e.g., V. Y. Mudimbe, *Before the Birth of the Moon* (1989); Ken Bugul, *The Abandoned Baobab* (1991); Charlotte Arrisoa Rabemananjato, "The Herd" in *Afrique, Book Two*, Ubu Repertory Theatre Publications (1991)).

**Nili Rachel Scharf Gold** was born in Haifa, Israel, in 1948. She studied at Hebrew University in Jerusalem and received her M.A. and Ph.D. from the Jewish Theological Seminary in New York. Presently, she teaches at Columbia University, where she is an assistant professor of Hebrew literature and language in the Department of Middle Eastern Languages and Cultures. Her book on the Israeli poet, Yehuda Amichai, the subject of her doctoral thesis, is forthcoming from Schocken Publishing, and she has published various articles on Israeli poets, coauthoring the entry on Hebrew love poetry for the *Princeton Encyclopedia of Poetry and Poetics*. She has spent most of her American years in New York City but misses the Mediterranean, where she grew up.

**Jewelle Gomez** is the director of literature at the New York State Council on the Arts. She is the author of two collections of poetry, *The Lipstick Papers* and *Flamingoes and Bears*, as well as a novel, *The Gilda Stories* (1991). Her essays and reviews appear in numerous publications, including *The Black Scholar*, *The New York Times*, *The Nation,* and *Belles Lettre*, and in anthologies including *Reading Black, Reading Feminist* (1990) and *Twentieth-Century Afro-American Autobiography* (1990). Long a political activist, she was on the founding board of the Gay and Lesbian Alliance Against Defamation (GLADD) and has participated in numerous fund-raising events, such as Art Against Apartheid. She is the 1990 recipient of the Barbara Deming/Money for Women Fund Award for fiction.

**Judith Grossman** was born in London, England, and holds degrees in literature from Oxford University and Brandeis University, Massachusetts. Her publications include a novel, *Her Own Terms*, as well as short fiction and criticism. Her own current work focuses on the difficulties of both women and men under the pressure of divergent gender roles. In 1990, she was the Fannie Hurst Professor of Creative Writing at Brandeis University and has taught at Smith College, Tufts University, and Harvard University. She now teaches in the M.F.A. Program for Writers at Warren Wilson College, N.C.

**Judith Hubback**, M.A., took her degree in history at Cambridge University. Before becoming an analytical psychologist in 1963, she was a teacher, a journalist, and a sociologist. She wrote *Wives Who Went to College* (1957). She has published poetry, *Islands and People* (1964), and in several "little" magazines. Her collection of papers, *People Who Do Things to Each Other* (1988), was followed by a novel, *The Sea Has Many Voices* (1990), which won the first award of the Sagittarius prize. She is a training analyst, working in London, and former editor of the *Journal of Analytical Psychology*, for whom she is currently English consultative editor.

**Wen-chin Ouyang** received her B.A. in Arabic literature, language, and Islam at University of al-Fatih in Tripoli, Libya, and her M.A. and Ph.D. in Arabic literature from Columbia University. She is an assistant professor at the University of Virginia at Charlottesville, in the Department of Oriental Languages, where she teaches Arabic language, literature, and culture. She was born in Taiwan and raised in Libya from the age of four, coming to the United States at the age of twenty-one.

**Sylvia Brinton Perera** is a Jungian psychoanalyst in private practice. She teaches at the C. G. Jung Institute of New York. She has written *Descent to the Goddess: A Way of Initiation for Women* ; *The Scapegoat Complex: Toward a Mythology of Shadow and Guilt*, coauthored *Dreams, A Portal* *to the Source* (with E. C. Whitmont), and published numerous clinical articles. Currently, she is working on Celtic mythology because she finds its themes so relevant to primitive levels of psychic development.

**Tey Diana Rebolledo**, Ph.D., is associate professor of Spanish at the University of New Mexico in Albuquerque, New Mexico, where she teaches courses on Latin American literature and Latin American women writers. She has published extensively on Chicana writings from the 1880s to the present. Her book, *Infinite Divisions: An Anthology of Chicana Literature*, co-edited with Eliana Rivero, will be published by the University of Arizona Press in 1992.

**Lena B. Ross**, Ph.D., is a Jungian analyst. Trained at the C. G. Jung Institute of New York, she has a private practice in Manhattan, where she is director of studies and a faculty member at the Center for Analytical Perspectives (CAP). Disobedience and its central role in the development of the human psyche are of particular concern to her, as well as issues relevant to the formation of male and female ways of relating. Her current project, *First Voice: Discourses in the Feminine Mode,* explores these topics through ancient and modern texts. From 1976 to 1978, she was the recipient of a grant from the Oklahoma Humanities Committee (funded by NEH) for "A Woman's Place," a documentary film series produced for Oklahoma public television (OETA).

**Manisha Roy** is a psychological anthropologist and a Jungian analyst in private practice in Massachusetts. Born in a border town in eastern India, she came to America for higher education at the age of twenty-one. She has two masters degrees (geography and social anthropology) and a Ph.D. in psychological anthropology from the University of California. Her doctoral dissertation, *Begali Women*, was published by the University of Chicago Press in 1975. She has published extensively in anthropology and analytical psychology and taught as an associate and visiting professor in several universities in America and Europe. She writes fiction, both in English and in her mother tongue, Bengali.

**Carol Savitz**, M.A., M.S.W., C.S.W., is a psychotherapist in private practice in New York City and a candidate at the C. G. Jung Institute of New York. Her background includes extensive graduate work in both literature and psychology. She has written numerous papers on the relationship of Greek mythology to analytic practice, and her papers and reviews have appeared in *The Journal of Analytical Psychology* and *Quadrant*.

**Patricia Clark Smith** is an associate professor of English at the University of New Mexico, Albuquerque, where she teaches Native American literature. She graduated Phi Beta Kappa from Smith College and received her M.A. and Ph.D. from Yale University. She has published many articles, essays (including the forthcoming "Grandma Went to Smith, All Right, But She Went from Nine to Five" in *Laborers in the Knowledge Factory: Working Class/Ethnic Women in the Academy* (1992), reviews, interviews, poetry (including *Talking to the Land* (1979)), and short fiction (including "Flute Song" and "Mother Ditch").

**Jeanie Watson** is dean, College of Liberal Arts, and professor of English at Hamline University in St. Paul, Minnesota. Her numerous publications include *Risking Enchantment: Coleridge's Symbolic World of Faery* (1990) and *Ambiguous Realities: Women in the Middle Ages and Renaissance*, coedited with Carol Levin (1987). She has written extensively on fairy tales, poetry, and related subjects and is currently preparing a book manuscript entitled *Cinderella's Children: Nineteenth-Century Fairy Tales in Verse*.

**Jane White-Lewis**, M.A., is a Jungian analyst in private practice in Guilford, Conn., and New York City. She received her analytic training at the C. G. Jung Institute in New York. Currently vice-president of the Association for the Study of Dreams, she has contributed articles and book reviews to the ASD newsletter, to *Quadrant*, and to *Lucidity Letter*. Her chapter, "In Defense of Nightmares: Literary and Clinical Cases," will appear in the forthcoming book entitled *The Dream and the Text: Essays on Literature and Language*.